Andrew Foote

LIBRARY OF NAVAL BIOGRAPHY

ANDREW FOOTE

CIVIL WAR ADMIRAL
ON WESTERN WATERS

Spencer C. Tucker

NAVAL INSTITUTE PRESS
Annapolis, Maryland

Naval Institute Press
291 Wood Road
Annapolis, MD 21402

Library of Congress Cataloging-in-Publication Data

Tucker, Spencer, 1937–
    Andrew Foote : Civil War admiral on western waters / Spencer C. Tucker.
       p.   cm. — (Library of naval biography)
    Includes bibliographical references (p.) and index.
    ISBN 1-55750-820-8 (acid-free paper)
    1. Foote, Andrew H. (Andrew Hull), 1806–1863. 2. Admirals—United
States—Biography. 3. United States. Navy—Biography. 4. United States—
History—Civil War, 1861–1865—Naval operations. 5. United States. Navy—
History—Civil War, 1861–1865. 6. United States. Navy—History—19th cen-
tury. I. Title. II. Series.
E467.1.F68 T83 2000
973.7'5—dc21   99-045406

Printed in the United States of America on acid-free paper ♾

07 06 05 04 03 02 01 00   9 8 7 6 5 4 3 2
First printing

⁓⤳ *Contents* ⤶⁓

ᗌ Foreword ᗏ

Andrew Hull Foote was one of the most important U.S. Navy officers of the mid-nineteenth century. Self-confident and certain that God was with him, Foote approached every challenge aggressively. A zealous reformer, he sought to ban alcohol and flogging in the Navy. A fervent opponent of slavery, he did more than any previous commander of the African squadron to enforce the abolition of the international slave trade. Sensitive when it came to his nation's honor, Foote personally led forces against Chinese forts that had insulted the American flag. Finally, during the Civil War Foote commanded the naval forces that captured Fort Henry and rendered Island Number 10 indefensible, thereby opening the upper South to Union invasion.

The ironclad vessels Foote commanded on the Mississippi, Cumberland, and Tennessee Rivers during the Civil War differed radically from the wooden ships he sailed in the Caribbean and Mediterranean as a midshipman. Foote's career spanned the transition from wood to iron ships, from sail to steam propulsion, and from solid shot fired from smooth-bore cannon to exploding shells fired from rifled ordnance. Foote, however, played little role in the technological revolution. His focus was on individuals. During a Caribbean cruise in 1827 he felt God's call to serve his fellow man and for the next thirty-five years set a personal example for men in the Navy whether opposing the spirit ration, defending the nation's honor, or fighting its wars.

Both the nation and its navy benefited from Foote's multifaceted personality. Seemingly oblivious to danger, Foote exposed himself to enemy fire while attacking fortifications. He authored two books that roused sentiment against the slave trade, yet was a modest, almost quiet man. David Farragut and David Dixon Porter gained greater fame during the

Civil War, but neither inspired more respect among the men he commanded or the army officers he worked with than did Foote. Disabled by a wound early in the war, Foote died in June 1863, a month before the tide of battle turned in favor of the Union at Vicksburg and Gettysburg and brought greater accolades to Federal leaders on land and sea.

Spencer Tucker has given Foote the scholarly biography he deserves. Tucker's study captures both the spirit of reform that swept the navy in the 1830s and 1840s and the bellicose nationalism that characterized so many of its leaders. The preeminent expert on naval ordnance of the era, Tucker writes riveting battle narratives that demonstrate clearly the devastating effect of naval gunfire on fortifications along the western waters during the Civil War. His is a fascinating study that describes the work of naval squadrons in the Caribbean and Mediterranean, off Africa and China, and on the rivers of the United States. He captures also the character of a seminal figure in the early stages of the American Civil War.

The Library of Naval Biography provides accurate, informative, and interpretive biographies of influential naval figures—men and women who have shaped or reflected the naval affairs of their time. Each volume will explain the forces that acted upon its subjects as well as the significance of that person in history. Some volumes will explore the lives of individuals who have not previously been the subject of a modern, full-scale biography, while others will reexamine the lives of better known individuals adding new information, a differing perspective, or a fresh interpretation. The series is international in scope and includes individuals from several centuries. All volumes are based on solid research and written to be of interest to general readers as well as useful to specialists.

With these goals in mind, the length of each volume has been limited, the notes placed at the end of the text and restricted primarily to direct quotations. A brief essay on further reading assesses previous biographies of the subject and directs the reader to the most important studies of the era and events in which the person lived and participated.

It is the intention that this combination of clear writing, fresh interpretations, and solid historical context will result in highly readable volumes that restore the all-important human dimension to naval history.

James C. Bradford
Series Editor

~❧ Preface ❧~

Andrew Hull Foote was a key figure in the February 1862 Union victories at Forts Henry and Donelson in Tennessee that opened the Confederate heartland to the Union. As flag officer of the Union's western naval forces he helped prepare the Union flotilla for battle and established a smooth command relationship with his army counterparts, especially Brig. Gen. Ulysses S. Grant. Later Foote shared in the Union victory at Island No. 10 that opened the upper Mississippi River for the Union. Despite this success, relatively little has been written on Foote, perhaps because his Civil War career as flag officer of the western naval forces lasted only eight months.

Foote's most lasting contributions to the development of the U.S. Navy came before the Civil War. In "Andrew Foote: Zealous Reformer, Administrator, Warrior" (in Bradford, ed., *Captains of the Old Steam Navy*, 115), historian John Milligan called him "one of the more fascinating personages of the old steam navy." Dedicated, resolute, ambitious, and tireless, Foote was a capable administrator and an able captain. Although very much an officer schooled in the traditions of the Old Navy, he was distinguished from most of his fellow officers by his staunch advocacy for naval reform.

Foote dedicated his life to the navy. He got on well with his fellow officers, gave credit where it was due, and was much respected by his peers. As a young officer, however, he experienced a religious conversion and came to consider himself first and foremost a Christian and an agent of Divine will. His faith led him to believe that he could change the world around him, and that meant the navy. Foote became an ardent social reformer as well, which also set him apart from most of his brother officers in the pre–Civil War navy.

Foote crusaded zealously for abolition of the daily grog ration. The *Cumberland* became the first temperance ship in the navy while Foote was its executive officer. His continuing crusade against alcohol aboard ships finally reached fruition in 1862. Foote also supported Christian missionary activity, Catholic as well as Protestant.

His determination to see the slave trade eradicated led Foote to become a leading advocate of more forceful measures on the part of the United States, even to cooperating with the Royal Navy. To call public attention to the continuing African slave trade he wrote about his experiences on patrol off western Africa in a book, *Africa and the American Flag*.

A dedicated patriot, Foote believed that American trade had to be protected and insults to the flag avenged. In 1856, while commanding the sloop *Portsmouth* on China station, Foote personally led a shore force of sailors and marines to capture and reduce the four Chinese barrier forts guarding access to Canton after the Chinese fired on vessels flying the American flag.

Foote was also a capable administrator, as he demonstrated while stationed at the Philadelphia Naval Asylum and the Brooklyn Navy Yard, and while in command of the western flotilla. He was interested in furthering education in the navy and probably would have made a mark as superintendent of the Naval Academy at Annapolis had the Civil War not intervened and denied him the opportunity. Fair and sympathetic to the shortcomings of sailors, he was much sought after for naval courts-martial. He opposed civilian and political appointees in the administration of the navy, and he was active in helping to reform the seniority system and weed out deadwood. In short, Andrew Hull Foote was far more than a Civil War naval hero. He was one of the principal social reformers of the U.S. Navy.

I am delighted that Naval Biography Series editor James Bradford of Texas A & M University and the Naval Institute Press concurred when I suggested that Foote deserves an up-to-date biography. I am grateful to the staffs of the Library of Congress, the National Archives, the Huntington Library, the New York Historical Society, and the New Haven Colony History Society. Many of the illustrations are from the collection of the Naval Historical Foundation, and I am grateful for their assistance with these and for the right to reproduce them. Donald S. Frazier provided the maps in these pages for which I am also thankful. The Virginia Military Institute generously provided research funding. I have followed the general rules of this series for endnotes but would be happy to share the complete references with those who are interested. I would also like to take this opportunity to point out that an article in *The American Neptune* on Foote's African service is drawn from chapters five and six.

A number of individuals read the manuscript and made helpful suggestions. These include former colleagues at Texas Christian University Don Worcester, Steven Woodworth, Bruce Elleman, and Gene Smith; and distinguished retired Virginia Military Institute professors John G. Barrett and George M. Brooke. William D. Hager was also of much assistance. I am especially grateful to James Bradford for his keen editing skills in helping to prune back the manuscript to the requisite length. And as usual my wife, Beverly, read my work and made many helpful comments and editing suggestions. I take full responsibility for any errors, however.

Andrew Hull Foote is in many ways emblematic of a period of great change in the navy. He is an immensely fascinating and important figure in U.S. Navy history. I hope this biography does him justice.

~Chronology~

12 Sept. 1806	Born in New Haven, Connecticut
June 1822	Enters U.S. Military Academy at West Point
4 Dec. 1822	Receives warrant as midshipman, U.S. Navy
Jan.–Nov. 1823	Service on schooner *Grampus* in Caribbean
Dec. 1823–Apr. 1827	Service on sloop *Peacock* and frigate *United States* in Pacific Squadron
22 June 1828	Marries Caroline Flagg
27 May 1830	Promoted to lieutenant
May 1833–Feb. 1836	Flag lieutenant onboard ship of the line *Delaware* in the Mediterranean
Aug.–Nov. 1837	Service on steam battery *Fulton* at New York
Nov. 1837–June 1840	Second lieutenant on sloop *John Adams* in the Pacific
4 Nov. 1838	Caroline Flagg Foote dies
Nov. 1841–Aug. 1843	Executive officer of the Naval Asylum at Philadelphia
27 Jan. 1842	Marries Caroline Mary Street
Aug. 1843–Nov. 1845	First lieutenant on the frigate *Cumberland* in the Mediterranean
June 1846–June 1848	Assigned to Charlestown Navy Yard in Boston
Sept. 1849–Dec. 1851	Captain of the sloop *Perry* on Africa station
19 Dec. 1852	Promoted to commander
1854	Publishes *Africa and the American Flag*
Mar. 1854–June 1855	Executive officer of the Naval Asylum at Philadelphia
June–July 1855	Member of Naval Efficiency Board

Apr. 1856–June 1858	Captain of the sloop *Portsmouth* in the Pacific
16–22 Nov. 1856	Shells, then captures, Canton barrier forts
Oct. 1858	Appointed executive officer of Brooklyn Navy Yard
29 June 1861	Promoted to captain
30 Aug. 1861	Appointed commander of Union naval operations on western waters
11 Nov. 1861	Promoted to flag officer
6 Feb. 1862	Captures Fort Henry on Tennessee River
14 Feb. 1862	Repulsed in attack on Fort Donelson on the Cumberland River; wounded
15 Mar.–8 Apr. 1862	Participates in siege and capture of Island No. 10
14 Apr.–9 May 1862	Participates in siege of Fort Pillow
9 May 1862	Relieved in failing health by Capt. Charles Davis
9 May–Aug. 1862	On extended leave for health reasons (formally detached from the Mississippi Squadron command on 17 June)
30 July 1862	Promoted to admiral with date of rank 16 July 1862
Aug. 1862	Head of Bureau of Equipment and Recruiting
3 June 1863	Named to replace Adm. Samuel Du Pont as commander of South Atlantic Blockading Squadron
17 June 1863	Falls ill with Bright's disease in New York City on his way to take up his new command
26 June 1863	Dies in Astor House Hotel, New York City

Andrew Foote

❧ I ❧

FAMILY AND
EARLY BACKGROUND

*A*ndrew Hull Foote was born in New Haven, Connecticut, on 12 September 1806, the second of six sons of Samuel Augustus Foot and Eudocia Hull Foot.[1] The Foots were a prominent Connecticut family descended from the Puritan Nathaniel Foote, who was born in England in 1593, emigrated to Watertown, Massachusetts, in 1630, and then moved to Wethersfield, Connecticut, in 1635. Most of Nathaniel Foote's descendants were farmers, who nonetheless filled responsible civil positions. Andrew's paternal grandfather, John Foot, graduated from Yale College in 1765 and succeeded his father as pastor of the Congregational church at Cheshire, Connecticut, until his death in 1813. Father and then son served as pastors of the same church for nearly one hundred years.

Andrew's father, Samuel Augustus Foot, was born in 1780. He entered Yale at age thirteen and was graduated in 1797. A man of "delicate" health, he studied law with a judge and was admitted to the bar. He then entered the shipping business in New Haven, and by 1803 he had his own business in the West India trade. That same year he married Eudocia Hull, daughter of Connecticut militia general Andrew Hull of Cheshire.[2]

The New England shipping business suffered during the Embargo of 1807, but the War of 1812 and the consequent British blockade ruined it.

In 1813, when Andrew was only six, Samuel Foot gave up his business and moved his family to the ancestral farm in the village of Cheshire, a dozen miles from New Haven. After a brief stint as a gentleman farmer, Foot was elected to the General Assembly in 1817. He aligned himself with reformers who sought a written constitution to replace the old colonial charter, and he also advocated universal male suffrage and a revised system of taxation, all of which went into effect at a constitutional convention at Hartford in the summer of 1818.[3] That same year, Foot, running as a Republican, was elected to the U.S. House of Representatives, where he immediately became involved in a dispute over slavery in the Missouri Territory. Although he was no supporter of slavery, he worked with southern representatives to secure a compromise, angering his Connecticut constituents in the process. He defended his position as being necessary on constitutional grounds and to prevent possible civil war, but his stand cost Foot his seat in Congress when his party leadership refused to place his name on the ballot for the next election. Foot remained popular locally, however, and in 1820 was reelected to the Connecticut General Assembly.

Foot returned to Congress during the years 1823–25. In 1825 he again served in the General Assembly, where he was elected speaker. In 1827 he was elected to the U.S. Senate, where he is principally remembered for his "Foot Resolution" of 29 December 1829, which called on the Senate Committee on Public Lands to consider both temporarily limiting the sale of public land and abolishing the office of surveyor general. Daniel Webster of Massachusetts and Robert Hayne of South Carolina later debated this resolution in the Senate, and it was during this debate that Webster uttered the famous phrase, "Liberty and Union, one and inseparable, now and forever."

Religion was of central importance in the Foot household. The Foots were staunch Congregationalists, and Andrew's elder brother, John, later recalled that the boys were brought up "upon purely patriarchal and Puritan principles."[4] The Sabbath was strictly observed from Saturday night until Sunday evening. The family attended church each Sunday, and any reading that day was to be in the Bible or some other religious book. Although Samuel Foot had charge of the family, Eudocia ran the household and supervised their children. A devoted mother loved by her children, she nonetheless did not hesitate to employ corporal punishment when she thought it necessary.

The Foot family seems to have been close-knit and happy, and the boys were free on Saturdays to play, fish, or hunt. Andrew was apparently well adjusted and popular with his peers, but strong willed. John recalled that their father once told him, "I think I have been able to control my family pretty well, all except Andrew—I have never tried to do more than guide him." At any rate, John believed that Andrew's strong will was behind his naval success. Certainly it enabled him to overcome two childhood obstacles: stuttering, which he conquered when his parents required him to speak slowly and beat time with his right hand; and lefthandedness, which was considered abnormal and unacceptable in those days.

Education was also important in the Foot household. Andrew first attended school in New Haven. After the family moved to Cheshire, he attended the district common school for three years, and then, at age nine, followed his brother John to the Episcopal Academy of Connecticut. Located in Cheshire, it had the reputation of one of the best preparatory schools in the country. The academy admitted children without reference to age or religion as long as they could read and write, but it did have an Episcopalian bent in instruction and many of its graduates went on to become Episcopal clergymen. It says something of the rigidly Congregationalist Foots that they were willing to send their children to an Episcopal school to get the best possible education for them, although location and inexpensive tuition were probably other factors.

Academy education began with the basics of reading, writing, spelling, grammar, geography, arithmetic, bookkeeping, and catechism. Once he had mastered these subjects, a student would go on to the Classical Department, a combination prep school and junior college. New England colleges recognized its excellence by awarding third-year standing to Classical Department graduates.[5]

Andrew attended the academy for six years. A capable but not brilliant student, he apparently made friends easily among the seventy students there. John Foote remembered his brother as "very genial and good-natured, and as a subaltern implicitly obedient. . . . There was never any cant about him and he seemed to enjoy life and to get much out of it."[6] Future U.S. secretary of the navy Gideon Welles was one of Andrew's schoolmates at the academy, and although he was three or four years older than Foote, the two were in some of the same classes. Welles noted in his diary after Foote's death that "there sprang up an attachment between us that never was broken. His profession interrupted our intimacy, but at long intervals we occasionally met, and the recollection of youthful friendship made those meetings pleasant."[7]

Andrew completed his studies at the academy in 1821 at age fifteen. His family expected him to go on to college, but he had his heart set on becoming a naval officer. When the Foots had lived in New Haven, Samuel Foot's offices were on the "Long Wharf," and young Andrew must have seen his father off when he occasionally sailed to the West Indies in one of his vessels. Andrew wanted to "visit foreign nations," but another influence must have been the new prestige that came to the navy in the aftermath of its individual ship victories early in the War of 1812. Isaac Hull, captain of the frigate *Constitution* during its victory over the British frigate *Guerrière,* was a distant relative of Eudocia Foot.[8]

Foote's family tried to dissuade him from making the navy his career; his mother was particularly concerned about the dissolute reputation of young naval officers of that day. But Andrew was adamant. He informed his parents that if necessary he would wait until he reached the age of twenty-one, when he could enlist without their consent. The most his parents could do was to delay his plans. They were aided in this by the overabundance of naval officers, which made it virtually impossible for young men to secure midshipman appointments.[9]

The navy's role in the War of 1812 and the excitement of fighting against the Barbary States had led Congress in 1816 to enact the country's first real peacetime naval building program, but public enthusiasm ebbed as the economic boom that followed the War of 1812 became economic recession. Naval building appropriations were slashed, and between 1816 and 1822 the navy decreased the number of its ships almost by half, and its personnel from fifty-five hundred men to four thousand. A navy that was being reduced in size did not need new officers. With an immediate navy career unlikely, Andrew decided instead to attend the U.S. Military Academy at West Point. His grades at the academy were good enough to admit him to West Point, and the elder Foots agreed that he could go there until a naval appointment became available.[10]

Andrew left for West Point in June 1822. The Military Academy was then run by the army engineers, and the curriculum placed a heavy emphasis on mathematics, something that was bound to be useful to a naval officer. As it happened, Foote's time at West Point was brief. On 4 December 1822, Secretary of the Navy Smith Thompson appointed sixteen-year-old Andrew Foote an acting midshipman. He was to serve a six-month probationary period at sea. If his commanding officer reported favorably on him at the end of that period he would receive a warrant backdated to the time of the provisional appointment. Samuel Foot's influence undoubtedly played a part in securing the warrant, as it had in Andrew's appointment to West Point, for the president and the secretary of the navy appointed midshipmen on the recommendation of members of Congress and influential citizens.

Regardless of the circumstances of his appointment, Andrew immediately resigned from West Point and joined the navy. He was ordered to report immediately to the schooner *Grampus,* then preparing to sail for the West Indies, at a monthly salary of nineteen dollars.[11]

·❦2❦·

MIDSHIPMAN FOOTE
Learning the Profession

*A*t the time Foote secured an appointment as an acting midshipman, the U.S. Navy was increasing its presence in the Caribbean in an effort to suppress the rampant piracy there. Spain's Latin American empire was in collapse, and the emerging Central and South American states were fighting both Spain and each other. As part of their struggle for independence these states issued a great many letters of marque authorizing private ships to wage war. By 1818 and 1819, commerce raiding in the Gulf of Mexico, the Caribbean Sea, and the West Indies had become endemic; there was even pirate activity along the south Atlantic coast of the United States. Historian Gardner Allen estimated that from 1815 to 1823 there were some three thousand acts of piracy in the region.[1]

The United States had initially been slow to react, but by the end of 1821 the navy had established convoys and had a little squadron in the Caribbean. In 1822 the navy officially created the West India Squadron, and that March the Committee on Naval Affairs recommended that the navy send additional vessels to the Caribbean. The piracy problem gained in importance when U.S. Navy lieutenant William Howard Allen, captain of the schooner *Alligator,* was shot and killed on 9 November 1822 while leading an attack against pirates. His death led to a public outcry in the United States. On 20 December, Congress appropriated $160,000 to enable the navy to purchase a number of smaller vessels specifically for operation in shoal waters for the suppression of piracy.[2]

In February 1823 Secretary Smith Thompson appointed Capt. David Porter to succeed James Biddle as commander of the West India Squadron, and that same month Porter sailed from Norfolk in the sloop *Peacock* along with eight small schooners, a transport, and the steamship *Sea Gull*. The latter, a converted two-hundred-ton New York ferryboat, was the first steamer to engage in wartime operations in the U.S. Navy, possibly in any navy.

After establishing his headquarters at Key West, Porter set to work ferreting out pirates. He had more success than his predecessor, partly because he had better vessels to work with, but also because of his own natural aggressiveness, a trait that eventually led to his court-martial and resignation from the navy. The *Grampus* was ordered to join Porter's squadron on 7 December 1822, and sailed from New York three weeks later, on 1 January 1823, under the command of Lt. Francis Gregory with Acting Midn. Andrew Foote among the crew.[3]

Samuel Foot accompanied his son to New York to present him personally to Lieutenant Gregory, who was also from Connecticut and a friend of several years' standing. Foot reportedly told Gregory that he was placing his son in his care and hoped that he would watch over him as carefully and kindly as if he were a brother or son. When father and son said goodbye on the deck of the schooner, Samuel Foot told Andrew to be faithful to his training at home, to do nothing that would cause his parents embarrassment, and to remember his duty to his country and to God.[4]

The midshipmen were quartered in "steerage" on the berth deck, just above the waterline and forward of the lieutenants' mess and staterooms. The damp, cramped quarters had almost no ventilation and offered no privacy. Midshipmen were apprentices, but they were also serving officers with responsible shipboard duties. They assisted the lieutenants, under whose guidance they learned their trade at sea. Midshipmen had to master the names and locations of twenty-six different sails, the many parts of the ship, and the functions of different yards, braces, and halyards. They also had to learn seamanship, navigation, and gunnery, as well as how to splice rope and how to make sails. Most of these skills were acquired through practice and repetition, and midshipmen could often be found in the tops and yards or attending to sheets, backstays, and braces. Midshipmen had to learn their stations in various situations; they relayed messages and saw to it that orders were carried out. They also assisted lieutenants commanding the gun divisions. Each had to keep a journal, which was presented several times each month to the captain for inspection. Midshipmen were also required to keep accurate records of the watch, quarter, and station bills, and to keep track of the seamen and see that they were in their proper stations. They had to maintain records of clothing belonging to the seamen under their supervision, which they were to inspect on a regular basis. In port they had to be available for boat duty, for no boat could leave the ship without a midshipman in charge.

Midshipmen served smaller amounts of deck time than seamen did because they were also expected to spend time in study. But this schedule could vary dramatically, depending on the captain. Classes were taught either by a schoolmaster onboard just to instruct the midshipmen or by the ship's chaplain, who was also expected to interest himself in the midshipmen's spiritual well-being and attempt to offset the more worldly education imparted by the seamen. Schoolmasters and chaplains were found only on the largest ships, however; Congress did not authorize mathematics teachers to replace chaplains as the primary instructors of midshipmen until 1831, although it was 1835 before they were considered important enough to be included in the Navy Register.[5]

Lieutenant Gregory was a capable commander with prior command experience in the West Indies. His schooner, with a crew of less than seventy men, was an excellent introduction to the navy for a new midshipman. At age sixteen Foote was actually somewhat older than most midshipmen; some entered the navy at thirteen. Probably his schooling at the Episcopal Academy gave him an advantage educationally over his colleagues on the *Grampus*. Foote worked hard to learn his profession. In his spare time he studied Nathaniel Bowditch's *New American Practical Navigator*, the standard work on navigation. He also followed Gregory around to soak up specialist knowledge. In his first service afloat Foote acquired the work habits that would stand him in good stead in his later career.[6]

Over the year it was stationed in the Gulf of Mexico the *Grampus* performed such duties as escorting convoys and searching for pirate vessels; the ship also visited Matanzas, Havana, Tampico, and New Orleans. On his first cruise Foote also learned some of the perils of naval service. In a letter to his friend William Browne of Cheshire, he described a storm the schooner had weathered at sea:

> I hope you will excuse my negligence in not writing before this time, for I assure you it did not proceed from want of affection, but on account of the inconvenience in writing while at sea on board a vessel of this tonnage. . . . When we left Havana for Tampico, and had made the land, the wind commenced blowing a heavy gale from the northeast, so that it carried away our topmast studding-sail boom, and sprung our mainmast. She took in hogsheads of water in the wardroom and steerage; life ropes were rove on the windward side of the vessel, and one of the officers observed that "we were going to — with studding sails set." . . . I am very pleased with the service. I had a desire to visit foreign nations. The duty of the officers is nearly as hard as that of the men, as we have to be on watch one third of the time day and night, four hours on and eight off.[7]

Beginning in April 1823 the *Grampus* spent several months off the coast of Yucatán chasing pirates. A number of the men spent time on detached service away from the schooner in barges or cutters and even ashore. Foote is said to have distinguished himself in this disagreeable duty. The boats were quite small and lacked suitable accommodations, in some cases even cover. Weather conditions were often difficult, and sickness and disease were constant threats. Indeed, in August yellow fever broke out in the squadron, and Porter ordered his ships back to Key West. Despite the best efforts of doctors, twenty-three of the twenty-five officers in the squadron who became ill died. Lieutenant Gregory succeeded in keeping a healthy ship, a valuable lesson for young Midshipman Foote.

As a consequence of the yellow fever and normal ship repair schedules, the U.S. Navy presence in the region was much reduced in the fall of 1823. In September, Porter ordered the *Grampus* to make one last cruise in the gulf off the Mexican coast and then return home. The sloop arrived at Norfolk on 27 November 1823.[8]

After the *Grampus* was secured for the winter and its officers given leave, Foote returned to Cheshire to visit his family. Having successfully completed six months of sea duty, he was now eligible to become a permanent midshipman. Ahead lay the more daunting challenge of acquiring the skills and knowledge necessary to pass the examination for promotion to lieutenant. That meant a regular sea tour, and Foote immediately applied to the Navy Department for such an assignment.[9] His request was promptly granted. On 6 December 1823, he was ordered to the sloop *Peacock,* then fitting out at the Gosport (Norfolk) Navy Yard for Commo. Isaac Hull's Pacific Squadron under the command of Master Comman-dant William Carter. (That rank was equivalent to today's lieutenant commander. At that time the U.S. Navy had only three officer ranks: lieutenant, master commandant, and captain.) It took three more months to fit out the *Peacock* and gather a crew for the long cruise ahead. Dur-ing much of this time Foote stayed in Washington with his father, who was again representing Connecticut in Congress. On 11 December 1823, Foote was warranted a permanent midshipman, backdated to his enlist-ment the year before.[10]

The ambitious young Foote expressed his aspirations for the cruise in a letter:

> We are ready for sea, and only waiting for sailing orders from the Department; but we hear little from Washington except the next Presidential election, the Greek cause, and the Holy Alliance, which I sincerely hope may produce a war. Then the prospect of the naval officer would brighten, and in the space of a few years would elevate us who are now in service to the highest rank, which will take some time if the country remains at peace with all nations much longer.[11]

The *Peacock* finally sailed on 29 March 1824 to join Hull's Pacific Squadron off Peru. Carter commanded a crew of 145 officers and men; Foote was one of six midshipmen. Soon after leaving Norfolk the sloop ran into trouble when a bolt of lightning from a violent, swift thunder-storm struck the ship, instantly killing four seamen and seriously injur-ing several others. The *Peacock* reached Rio de Janeiro without further incident, however, and there the crew received a brief liberty.

After ten days in Rio the *Peacock* again set sail. Again the ship's luck turned bad. Smallpox broke out aboard, felling twelve men and depriv-ing the crew of much-needed hands. The passage from Rio to Valparaiso, Chile, took fifty-six days. The *Peacock* did not tarry in Valparaiso, how-ever, and soon sailed again, this time escorting a convoy of merchantmen to Callao, Peru, arriving on August 15 and joining the other two ships in Hull's squadron, the frigate *United States* and the brig *Dolphin.*[12]

Peru at that time was engulfed in war, part of the general turmoil that had broken out in South America in 1807 as the former colonies sought to secure their independence from Spain. The war for Peru had begun in earnest in September 1820 when British sailor-of-fortune Lord Thomas Cochrane led a squadron escorting sixteen transports carrying an invasion force under General José de San Martín. Cochrane also blockaded Callao, where the Spanish squadron lay at anchor. The following November he personally led 250 men in a cutting-out operation there; one of the most daring feats of the age of fighting sail, it netted the Spanish frigate *Esmeralda*.

In July 1821 San Martín captured Lima, and the port of Callao then capitulated. A year later San Martín and Simón Bolívar joined forces, although San Martín soon retired from revolutionary activity. Bolívar then organized the Republic of Peru with its capital at Lima. Just nine days before the arrival of the *Peacock* at Callao, Bolívar's forces won a great victory at Junín north of the capital.

When the *Peacock* reached Callao, the city was again under Spanish control. The United States was endeavoring to maintain a neutral position. Commodore Hull's task was to preserve American rights, and that meant protecting U.S. merchantmen from seizure by both sides. Although U.S. sympathies were with the revolutionaries, the federal government in Washington refused to recognize the validity of the largely paper blockade of Callao by the revolutionary navy until such time as it could be actually maintained. This meant that the revolutionaries had no right to seize U.S. ships for violating their blockade. Commodore Hull, who was a distant relative of Foote's, proved to be the right man to carry out this difficult policy. Although always firm and correct to both sides, he nonetheless courted Bolívar, whom he received onboard the *United States* with a twenty-one-gun salute. Bolívar promised Hull that he would maintain a legal blockade.[13]

Shortly after the *Peacock* arrived at Callao, the Americans and Spanish came close to exchanging blows. A Peruvian admiral entered the harbor with a frigate and two brigs and began a blockade. The Spanish naval force inside the harbor consisted of one frigate, two brigs, and ten gunboats. On 12 September two large Spanish vessels arrived at Callao as reinforcements: the seventy-four-gun ship *Asia* and the twenty-two-gun brig *Constantia*. The revolutionaries had only a thirty-six-gun frigate and one ten-gun brig. Hull ordered the *United States* to weigh anchor to avoid getting caught in a possible crossfire, and as an added precaution he called the crew to quarters. The Spanish commander chose to interpret these actions as a sign of belligerence and sailed his ships under the protection of the harbor fort rather than engaging the revolutionaries. Foote wrote to a friend at home that when one of the Spanish warships sailed past the *United States* the situation was so tense that "it would have taken little provocation for her to have been complimented with a broadside from Uncle Isaac."[14]

On 8 September 1824 Foote transferred from the *Peacock* to the *United States*. Within weeks of his sloop's arrival at Callao, Master Commandant Carter had been involved in a dispute that caused Hull to return him to the United States to stand trial. In the resulting reshuffling of squadron officers, Foote requested and secured a transfer to the flagship. The *United States* was larger and had better accommodations; no doubt Foote also believed that serving in a large warship would be to his advantage in preparing for the lieutenant's examination.[15]

Foote apparently thrived aboard the flagship. During that time he also spent four days in Lima, only nine miles from Callao. Once one of the richest cities in the world, it had been ravaged by the recent fighting and had changed hands frequently. Foote visited Lima's historic sites, including the palace where Pizarro had lived, and also noted other sights:

> I forgot to mention the walking-dress of the ladies, which is admirably calculated to carry on an intrigue. The part from the waist down contains thirty yards of silk, plated in such a manner as to set perfectly smooth, in order to show a fine shape. The robe covering the head is also silk, and large enough to conceal the face, excepting one eye. Equipped in this manner, I have seen ladies watch the movements of their husbands by following them through the city, the virtuous not being distinguished from the vicious.[16]

When the flagship's three-year tour ended, Hull ordered the *United States* to New York. The ship sailed on 24 January 1827 and made the passage around Cape Horn without incident. After stopping at Bahia, Barbados, and St. Thomas en route, the *United States* arrived at New York on 24 April.[17]

On learning that the flagship was to sail for home, Foote focused his attention on preparing for the lieutenant's examination. The 1818 Navy Rules and Regulations called on midshipmen to acquire a thorough knowledge of all the duties on a warship as well as naval tactics, and no midshipman could be promoted to lieutenant without first passing an examination on these subjects. Regulations called for this to occur when the midshipman had reached the age of eighteen and had served at least two years at sea. The examinations, which were given each fall and spring, usually lasted one to two hours and were conducted before the entire examining board. Successful candidates showed a thorough knowledge of rigging, stowage, and the handling of ordnance. They had to demonstrate skills in arithmetic, geometry, trigonometry, and navigation, including astronomical observations. But the most important part of the examination, and the one that usually determined whether a candidate passed, was knowledge of seamanship, the ability to handle a vessel under sail.[18]

Throughout his life Foote made a habit of thoroughly preparing himself for future tasks. This was now manifest in his work for the lieutenancy exam. To improve his chances Foote joined forces with a fellow midshipman aboard the *United States*, Charles Henry Davis. The scion of a prominent Boston family, Davis had joined the navy in the summer of 1823 and was on his first cruise. The two spent long hours together in their quarters writing down everything they could remember about the working of the ship; ultimately they had a notebook full of material. Later in their lives the two men liked to recall that they had produced the first book of seamanship in the service. In any case, this shared experience forged a close friendship between the two men that lasted their entire lives.[19]

After returning to New York on 24 April, the *United States* was towed to the navy yard, and the crew was paid off. Foote rushed off to Baltimore to stand for the examination. Only twenty-two of the midshipmen who had joined the navy in 1822 passed. Foote was among these, but his friend Davis was not allowed to take the exam. In order to reduce the number of midshipmen standing for the exam, the navy had extended the time to qualify to five years' total naval service, including three years at sea. When he was finally allowed to take the examination, in 1828, Davis also passed.[20]

Foote's joy at passing the examination must have been brief, for, although eligible, he was not promoted. The nation was at peace, and the War of 1812 and the Barbary Wars, combined with the lack of a mandatory retirement age, had created a surplus of naval officers. Promotion in the U.S. Navy was on the basis of time in grade, and there simply were no lieutenancies available. Foote would have to continue as a midshipman until a slot opened up and he could be appointed to it on the basis of seniority.

The problem Foote faced is evident in the Navy Register for 1828, which reflects the state of the navy at the end of 1827. The U.S. Navy had only twenty vessels in commission then; nineteen others were laid up in ordinary (in mothballs, as it is known today). The navy had thirty-three captains and twenty-nine master commandants. Even counting shore duties such as staffing the various navy yards, there were too many officers for the slots available. The surplus was especially pronounced at the junior levels, where there were 228 lieutenants and 392 midshipmen. To Foote, the prospects for promotion must have seemed bleak indeed.[21]

But Foote was not allowed time to brood. After his examination he returned home to Cheshire, where he learned that his father had been elected to the U.S. Senate. Then, after a little more than the three months of shore leave allowed those returning from a cruise, Foote was again at sea. It was not the station he wanted. Foote had applied for the Mediterranean Squadron, the largest and most popular in the navy. Instead, on 26 August 1827, he sailed in the new sloop *Natchez* for another tour in the West Indies.

Master Commandant George Budd, who as a second lieutenant had been the highest-ranking officer on the frigate *Chesapeake* to survive the ill-fated 1813 duel with the *Shannon,* commanded the *Natchez.* The West India Squadron comprised an assortment of smaller sloops and brigs charged with maintaining a naval presence in the unstable Caribbean. Midn. Charles Davis, Foote's study companion, served onboard the squadron's flagship, the sloop *Erie.* Despite Foote's unhappiness at not being promoted and failing to secure the assignment he sought, he was still determined to make the navy his career. He was proud of his service record and hopeful of eventual promotion.[22]

This brief tour in the Caribbean proved momentous, for during it Foote underwent a life-changing event. Although he had been raised in a staunch Congregationalist family and his forbears had been ministers at the church in Cheshire, Foote had followed his father's more secular approach to life. In any case, navy life was not an environment in which religion would be expected to flourish. Yet in 1827, while the *Natchez* was on West Indian station, the twenty-one-year-old Foote experienced an epiphany. He was standing night watch with the sloop at anchor when he was approached by one of the lieutenants, evidently a strong Christian who had tried to talk to Foote earlier about religious subjects. Foote had rebuffed the lieutenant then, telling him that he intended to be honest and honorable in all things and that was all the religion he needed. But evidently what had been said affected him. On this second occasion the two fell into an extended conversation on a beautiful moonlit night. As soon as his watch was over and he could be alone, Foote fell to his knees in prayer. Over the next several weeks he spent most of his free time reading his Bible. At some point during this time, while climbing the ladder to the deck, he experienced a sense of feeling and purpose that caused him to resolve that in the future "henceforth, in all circumstances," he would "act for God."

Foote wrote his mother to tell her the news, probably in part because her deep Christian faith had prevented her from approving a naval career for her son. He began the letter to her with the words, "Dear Mother, you may discharge your mind from anxiety about your wayward son." He then told her what had happened and assured her that she need not worry about his possible corruption in a naval career.[23]

Although Foote remained a Congregationalist for the rest of his life, his extensive travels helped to give him a more Catholic outlook; he did not favor one denomination over another but rather sought whenever he could to promote Christianity in general. His strong sense of Christian conviction is everywhere evident in his letters and journals. Foote's brother John later related a discussion between Foote and their father after this cruise during which Foote tried to reconcile service to the Almighty with a career in a service dedicated to using force to achieve national goals. Foote's father asked him whether he thought a navy was necessary. Foote replied: "Certainly, the seas must be policed." Foote's father then asked, "Should the navy be in [the] charge of good or bad men?" "Of Good men," Foote replied, and also declared that his doubts were gone. After this Foote seemed convinced that he was to act as God's agent in a profession that should be God's instrument.[24]

Foote's Christian convictions came to be manifest in three ways: support for missionary activities, opposition to the African slave trade, and a crusade for temperance in the navy. No one in his day was a stronger advocate of making the navy a better place for its officers and men. With his newfound faith also came a belief in absolute certainties and an unshakable will to see a cause through to its completion once he believed he was in the right.[25]

On 8 October 1827, Foote transferred from the *Natchez* to another sloop in the squadron, the *Hornet,* commanded by Master Commandant Alexander Claxton. His short time in the *Hornet* was apparently uneventful, and Foote was home again on 4 December 1827. After the men were discharged, Foote traveled to Cheshire to spend Christmas with his family. Orders dated 1 January 1828 formally detached him from the West India Squadron. Foote would now experience an extended period of fourteen months onshore. At this point promotion to lieutenant must have seemed remote indeed. In 1828 the navy had 682 officers for only twenty ships. The Navy Department did create a new rank, passed midshipman, and Foote received a new warrant, dated 24 May 1828, making him one of the first ten men to hold that rank.[26]

Time ashore did have some good points. It allowed Foote a chance for reflection and the opportunity to be with his family as well as a female friend, Caroline Flagg, also of Cheshire. On 22 June 1828, the two were married. The marriage was a relatively short one. Caroline died ten years later, in 1838. The Footes had two daughters; the first, Josephine, died in 1836 at age four; the second, of the same name and born in 1837, survived both her parents.

Although he was quite happy in his new married life, Foote longed to return to sea and advance his career. Perhaps his father's position as U.S. senator helped him secure a billet. In any case, on 5 October 1828 Foote was appointed to the sloop *St. Louis* as sailing master under Master Commandant John D. Sloat. The *St. Louis* was ordered to join Commo. Charles C. B. Thompson's Pacific Squadron, whose mission was to show the flag off the west coasts of North and South America and in the islands of the South Pacific, an area of growing importance to U.S. whaling and commercial interests. It took some months to ready the *St. Louis* for sea, but finally, on 14 February 1829, the sloop sailed from Norfolk. Foote would be away almost three years.[27]

In a sloop such as the *St. Louis*, the post of sailing master invariably went to the senior of the midshipmen posted aboard; the sailing master was second in importance only to the first lieutenant, who had overall charge of the vessel. The sailing master was responsible for all day-to-day ship operations. He had to account for all stores and supplies; he kept all records; and he reported daily to the captain. He also had to maintain the ship's log and had to be a skilled navigator, as he regularly plotted the vessel's location.[28]

By summer the *St. Louis* was on Pacific station with Thompson's three other vessels: the frigate *Guerrière,* the commodore's flagship; the sloop *Vincennes;* and the schooner *Dolphin.* Most of the time during that first year on station the *St. Louis* patrolled the coasts of Chile and Peru, still a volatile area thanks to unrest fueled by competing territorial claims by the region's newly independent nations. Bolívar, the president of Greater Colombia—which he claimed included Ecuador and Venezuela—was having trouble with Peru, which in turn was encroaching on Colombia and Bolivia.

In July 1829 the *St. Louis* visited Guayaquil. Bolívar's forces had just recaptured the city from Peru, and the Americans on the sloop hosted a lavish party for Bolívar and other leaders of the Colombian army. The only other incident of note during this cruise came on 16 April 1831. That night, as the *St. Louis* was at anchor off Callao, an attempt was made to assassinate the Peruvian vice president, General La Fuente. He escaped and sought refuge on the sloop, where he was soon joined by a supporter, Gen. William Miller. Since the Peruvian government did not demand their return, and indeed seemed glad to be rid of them, the two generals remained onboard for some time.

By now the commodore's flagship was in very poor repair. The *Guerrière*'s condition became so precarious that the Navy Department ordered it home early in 1831 before its replacement could sail. As Commodore Thompson also departed in the frigate, Sloat commanded the squadron for the next five months, until Master Commandant Gregory, Foote's first commanding officer, arrived in the *Falmouth*.[29]

During this cruise Foote put his religious convictions into practice. The *St. Louis* was a small vessel, and there was no chaplain onboard. In such circumstances it was the captain's responsibility to conduct religious services once a week. Foote wanted to do more and approached Sloat about conducting Sunday school for the ship's boys and any crewmen who wished to participate. With Sloat's approval, Foote, assisted by the captain's clerk, read a chapter of the Bible to the twenty or more members of the crew in attendance and then led a discussion. Word of this activity reached the United States and received the enthusiastic endorsement of the American Seamen's Friend Society, an organization formed in 1826 to further morality and improve conditions for seamen. The society printed a letter from a sailor on the *St. Louis* in its new publication, the *Sailor's Magazine* (founded in 1828). In the letter the sailor noted that twelve to fifteen members of the sloop's crew had been converted and were avidly reading the Bible and other religious books.[30]

Foote's father became involved and wrote a letter to the American Seamen's Friend Society in which he extolled the positive activities of an unnamed officer aboard the *St. Louis*. The elder Foote offered to pay the costs of postage if the society would send copies of its publications to the sloop for the crew to read. The society accepted the offer, and Midshipman Foote reported to his father that the pamphlets were widely appreciated by the crew. Samuel Foot then shared this letter with the society.[31]

Both Foote and his father expected much from the Seamen's Friend Society in terms of reform. Samuel Foot wrote to the society to encourage its efforts, and Andrew Foote also wrote, from Callao, and sent twenty dollars for a lifetime membership, as did his wife, Caroline. This was a considerable commitment, representing as it did nearly a month's pay. It also represented the beginning of Foote's lifelong association with the society. As the editor of the *Sailor's Magazine* later wrote, "Our cause has no better friend than Andrew H. Foote."[32]

Sometime in the summer of 1830 Foote received word of his promotion to lieutenant with the commission date of 27 May 1830; his pay increased to forty dollars a month, along with extra rations. He ranked 9th of only 11 lieutenants commissioned in 1830, and ranked 253rd among the 255 lieutenants in the navy.

With the arrival of Gregory and the *Falmouth*, the *St. Louis* sailed for home, arriving at New York on 9 December 1831. Lieutenant Foote obtained leave and hurried off to Cheshire to be with his family.[33]

~3~

LIEUTENANT FOOTE
Around the World

*I*n order to advance professionally Foote needed time at sea. He believed he had earned assignment to the Mediterranean Squadron, the most prestigious sea duty in the U.S. Navy. The Mediterranean Squadron had the best ships and also offered the most interesting ports of call, but it was a difficult posting to obtain as officers lobbied intensely for it. Heeding the navy maxim that "a cruise around Washington is worth two around Cape Horn," Foote paid a visit to his father in Washington, D.C., where Samuel Foot still represented Connecticut in the Senate. Undoubtedly Foot introduced or reintroduced his son to individuals who might be able to help in his quest.

Foote then returned to Cheshire to wait. Having received no word from the navy, on 1 October 1832, just four days after the birth of his daughter Josephine, he applied for a six-month leave of absence. Evidently he was enjoying the time in Cheshire with his family, including long horseback rides and helping to instruct Sunday school at the church where his grandfather and great-grandfather had been ministers.

On 1 May 1833, Foote at last received orders assigning him to the coveted Mediterranean posting. He must have been pleased to receive orders to the flagship, the seventy-four-gun *Delaware,* and especially pleased that Commo. Daniel Patterson had appointed him flag lieutenant, in effect his aide. This was a plum assignment for a lieutenant who stood near the bottom of the navy list, and Patterson probably made the appointment at least in part because of Foote's father. Foote's orders sent him to Norfolk to await the return of the flagship from the Mediterranean. The *Delaware* arrived on 17 June and that same day became the first vessel to use the navy's first dry dock, a steam-operated facility at the Gosport Navy Yard.[1]

Workmen at the Gosport Yard immediately began preparing the *Delaware* for its return to the Mediterranean. In addition to the normal crew complement the *Delaware* was to bring back two hundred replacements for the squadron along with the new U.S. minister to France, Edward Livingston. On 29 July President Andrew Jackson traveled to Norfolk to inspect the *Delaware*, which sailed the next day for New York to pick up Livingston and his family. While the ship was in New York Vice President Martin Van Buren paid a visit, along with Secretary of the Navy Levi Woodbury and the three members of the Board of Navy Commissioners. The *Delaware* then departed for France, arriving at Cherbourg on 12 September after an easy Atlantic passage.

Before and during the passage Foote got to know the other officers. The stern and rigid Henry E. Ballard was the *Delaware*'s captain. Ballard's ship had the reputation as the best-disciplined and neatest vessel in the navy. Franklin Buchanan was the second lieutenant. Foote became fast friends with three other lieutenants aboard: George Magruder, Thomas Turner, and Thomas Selfridge, all of whom shared his interest in naval reform.[2]

Chaplain Charles S. Stewart of the *Delaware* made a deep impression on Foote. He wrote to a friend in Cheshire that Stewart was an "accomplished scholar" and "polite gentleman" who had "proposed and carried out a plan of evening prayers on board, which except with him in the frigate *Guerrière*, stands without a precedent in our service." Stewart had his work cut out for him; Foote also noted that aboard the ship "but three or four out of nearly one thousand souls are professing Christians." Despite Stewart's efforts, evening prayers were rarely held and sometimes there was no Sunday service.[3]

The lack of religious conviction aboard the *Delaware* seems to have stimulated Foote's own religious views and practices. If the challenge were greater, so would he be in his faith and witness. He would show others that it was possible to be both an effective naval officer and a sincere

Christian. He would proclaim his beliefs in public where he could and lead by example where he could not. One of Foote's close friends, the Reverend George B. Bacon, firmly believed that it was religious fervor that motivated Foote to widen his scope of knowledge beyond what was necessary simply to be a technically proficient naval officer, and that his religious interests led Foote into such areas as politics, writing, and science. Certainly Foote's strong religious convictions underlay his reforming zeal to improve conditions for naval personnel.[4]

The *Delaware* spent several weeks at Cherbourg. During this time a party of the ship's officers accompanied Ambassador Livingston to Paris, where they were received by King Louis Philippe. After leaving Cherbourg the liner sailed for the Mediterranean, weathered a bad storm in the Bay of Biscay without incident, and then sailed along the Portuguese coast before turning east and anchoring at Gibraltar. After three days at that British base the *Delaware* sailed again, and on 3 November anchored at the Mediterranean Squadron's winter port of Mahon on Minorca in the Balearic Islands. There the crew passed the winter months preparing the ship for an extended Mediterranean cruise. In the course of these preparations Patterson transferred his flag from the frigate *United States* to the *Delaware*. A number of officers switched ships at this point, Chaplain Stewart and Captain Ballard transferred to the *United States*, and Capt. John B. Nicholson came to the *Delaware*. Foote remained on the flagship, where he was given charge of the ship's signals as well as being Patterson's aide.

While the *Delaware* was laid up at Mahon, Foote had ample opportunity both to go ashore and to write letters home. Port Mahon was a large and well-protected harbor with a city of some fifteen thousand people, about half the island's population. The city was built largely of whitewashed buildings with distinctive red-tiled roofs. There were numerous bars and gambling houses to provide diversion for the crew and a significant source of revenue for the Mahonese. Foote had no interest in these, but he was impressed with the cathedral organ, said to be the second largest in the world. Foote enjoyed horseback riding and hiking among the ancient ruins in the countryside. He also loved social occasions and must have enjoyed the Carnival season with its many balls and festivities.[5]

In April 1834 the *Delaware* departed Mahon on an extended cruise to show the American flag in the eastern Mediterranean. The ports of call included Naples, Alexandria, Jaffa, and Constantinople. During the stop at Alexandria, Patterson welcomed onboard the Egyptian ruler, Mohammed Ali. Foote joined a large shore party from the *Delaware* that included Patterson's three daughters for an extended trip up the Nile. He also visited the Holy Land. His group landed on the coast, traveled inland to Jerusalem, and visited the Jordan River valley and the Dead Sea. Foote and the others even climbed Mount Lebanon. It must have been a fantastic experience for a man who had given over his life to Christianity.[6]

The *Delaware* spent two years in the Mediterranean visiting all the major ports of call and sailing as far east as Syria. In September 1835, during a stop at Naples, Patterson entertained the king of Naples onboard the flagship; the king reciprocated with a reception for the officers ashore.[7]

On 15 November 1835, with the crew's enlistments about to expire, the *Delaware* sailed for home. En route the ship experienced a difficult winter crossing of the Atlantic and severe storms off the American coast. There was a sad ending to the successful cruise. Two days before the *Delaware* arrived at Hampton Roads, on 16 February 1836, one of Patterson's three daughters died at the age of twenty-three. Sick for some time, she had been much moved by her trip to the Holy Land and had resolved to lead a more Christian life. As Patterson's aide, Foote must have had opportunities to talk with her about her decision.[8]

Foote returned home to a changed situation. For one thing, his father was no longer a U.S. senator. In 1833 Democrats controlled the Connecticut legislature and blocked Samuel Foot, a member of the National Republicans now known as the Whig Party, in his bid for reelection. But Foot was not out of office for long. That same year he won election to the House of Representatives. In the 1834 Connecticut elections the Whigs successfully blamed a statewide business depression on the Democrats and won a narrow margin of seats in the state legislature, which elected Samuel Foot governor. Unfortunately, Foot's tenure in that office was not successful. The state's economic slump continued, and this time it was the Whigs who took the blame. In the 1835 elections the Democrats once again won control of the state legislature and the governorship. After that, Foot retired to his farm and left politics altogether, save for a single appearance in 1844 as a presidential elector for Henry Clay.[9]

Andrew Foote must have viewed the decline in his father's political fortunes with some trepidation. He was now on leave on reduced pay, and to make matters worse, with the nation in an extended period of peace the navy was in decline. The country was also in the midst of an economic crisis, the Panic of 1837. The Jacksonian Democrats concentrated on reducing expenditures and the national debt, and this meant fewer funds for the navy. There were far too many officers for the navy's eighteen ships. To help remedy this situation, the Navy Department created the designation of "waiting orders" or "furlough" in 1835 and placed 219 of its 786 officers in this category. Lieutenants, the rank with the largest officer surplus, made up half this number; on his return to the United States Foote ranked 199th among the navy's 259 lieutenants.[10]

Despite the bleak prospects of a prolonged period before he could win promotion to master commandant and the likelihood of long periods ashore at reduced pay and allowances, Foote was determined to pursue his naval career. One way he might achieve notice was as an advocate for naval reform. The navy's system of promotion by seniority and retirement by death largely protected him from retaliation by conservative senior officers. There was then a great divide in the navy between the senior officers, many of whom had fought in the War of 1812, and younger lieutenants, who advocated change. Foote might hope to follow naval reformers such as Franklin Buchanan, Samuel F. Du Pont, Uriah P. Levy, Matthew F. Maury, Matthew C. Perry, and Robert F. Stockton.

Foote also worked to maintain the Washington political connections he had developed while his father was in the capital. In the summer of 1836 he traveled there to meet with some of Samuel Foot's former colleagues. When Martin Van Buren succeeded Andrew Jackson as president in 1837 he retained Mahlon Dickerson as secretary of the navy. This was probably a plus for Foote, because Dickinson was known for rewarding officers with political connections.[11]

At home, Foote and his wife went through a difficult period with the death in December 1836 of their four-year-old daughter, Josephine. Caroline had just become pregnant with their second child, another daughter, who was born in June 1837 and named for her late sister.[12]

It is unlikely that Foote spent all his time at Cheshire. Officers on furlough were periodically called to short terms of duty, either to sit on courts-martial or to perform duties at the various navy yards. And Foote must have been confident that the right assignment would come along, for he actually turned down two that were offered during this time. The first was an assignment as recruiting officer for the Brazil Squadron; he

won release from this on the argument of lameness contracted while
serving on the *Delaware*. The second, offered in June 1837, was on the
Lexington, then fitting out at Boston and bound for the Pacific Squadron.
Foote rejected this posting because of the imminent birth of his second
child and his two previous tours with that squadron.[13]

In August 1837 a much more appealing post became available: Foote
was offered an assignment to the steam battery *Fulton* at the Brooklyn
Navy Yard. One attraction of this situation was its closeness to his home.
Another was that the *Fulton* marked the real beginning of a steam navy
for the United States. Yet another reason was the *Fulton*'s captain:
Matthew C. Perry, "the father of the steam navy" and probably the leading advocate of reform in the U.S. Navy.

Secretary Dickerson had promoted the building of the steamer and
had selected his friend Perry first to oversee the construction and then
to command it. Perry was the obvious choice for the job. In January 1837
he had published an outspoken article in the *Naval Magazine* in which
he pointed out that the U.S. Navy had fallen to eighth place in the
world, behind Egypt; that its ships were woefully behind the times; and
that while the Royal Navy had twenty-one steamers and France twenty-
three, the United States had none. Perry argued for steam, iron ships, and
guns designed to project shells (the so-called Paixhans guns that were
carried aboard all French capital ships).

The second experimental steamer in the U.S. Navy to bear that name,
the *Fulton* was a seven-hundred-ton side-wheeler, 180 feet in length and
armed with four 32-pounders. Like all the early steamers, the *Fulton* was a
hybrid that carried both sail rig and steam stacks. The two steam engines
produced a combined 625 horsepower. The *Fulton* was intended to provide
harbor protection, with the assumption that it would be able to break up
any blockade. Thus, like its namesake predecessor, the *Fulton* was little
more than a coastal defense battery. Although Perry did manage to sail the
Fulton to Washington in May 1838, where President Van Buren inspected
it, and although it served as an instrument for reform, the steamer was
hardly seaworthy. Yet, Perry reported to the Navy Department in February
1838 "that seagoing war steamers of 1400 or 1500 tons could be built to
cruise at sea even for twenty days, and yet be as efficient and as safe from
disaster as the finest frigates afloat, while the expense would be considerably less." In 1839 Perry used the *Fulton* as a gunnery platform at Sandy
Hook to test-fire new shell guns and projectiles, proving their worth.[14]

It says something for Foote's reformist approach that he wanted to be a part of the new steam navy. But Perry was attractive to Foote for yet another reason, for he was also an advocate of naval education. Congress had earlier passed legislation to lessen the nation's dependency on foreigners in the service. This move allowed the navy to enlist boys aged thirteen to eighteen as apprentices, and Perry established a successful training program for them.

Foote's service on the *Fulton* lasted only three months. On 4 November 1837, Secretary Dickerson ordered him to the second-class sloop of war *John Adams* as first lieutenant to Cdr. Thomas W. Wyman. The *John Adams* and the frigate *Columbia,* which served as the flagship, constituted Commo. George C. Read's East India Squadron. Dickerson's sailing orders called for Read to visit various ports in Africa and China, then return to the United States by way of the Sandwich Islands (Hawaii) in a two-year circumnavigation of the globe. Read was ordered to protect American commerce and pay particular attention to showing the flag in the East Indies, where American trade was growing rapidly.[15]

Executive officer on a cruise of this type was a plum assignment. It says much for Foote that Commander Wyman, who had entered the navy in 1810 and had been Foote's first lieutenant aboard the *Delaware,* specifically requested his posting to the *John Adams.*[16] As the executive officer, Foote in effect ran the ship under the captain's supervision. Among his many responsibilities was properly preparing the ship for the long voyage.

It took fully six months to prepare the two ships for the cruise. Perhaps the most difficult problem was obtaining seamen. Because the ships would be on distant station for such a long time, the men would have to enlist for a full two-year tour. Although Foote had the *John Adams* ready to sail by the end of December 1837, the ship still lacked a full crew, and the Navy Department made matters worse by diverting some of the men to Philadelphia to help sail the *Philadelphia* to Norfolk.[17]

While awaiting the sloop's sailing, Foote found time to travel to Washington to make the rounds there. He also kept up his association with prominent naval reformers, including Cdr. John C. Long. A member of the Naval Lyceum and a director of the American Seamen's Friend Society, Long opposed the grog ration aboard ships and the use of flogging. He had known Foote since the start of his naval career. Long had been a lieutenant aboard the *Peacock* when Foote was a midshipman; later they had served together on the *St. Louis.* Long wrote Foote that he expected to secure command of a large ship soon, and should Foote not sail with Wyman, there was no one else he would rather have as his first lieutenant: "Your known habits of temperance and principles of religion would give me great confidence in such a supporter and with such an officer I think I should not fail."[18]

The *Columbia* and the *John Adams* finally departed Hampton Roads on 6 May 1838, bound for the island of Madeira. Because of their different sailing qualities, the two ships were often separated at sea for weeks at a time, although they were usually in port together. For Foote, who was much interested in different cultures, the sloop's landfalls brought welcome excursions ashore if his shipboard duties allowed. Often these were in the company of George Magruder and Thomas Turner, two lieutenants from the *Columbia* whom Foote had served with on the *Delaware*. The three men took their Christian religion seriously, and they and Chaplain Fitch Taylor of the flagship all became fast friends.[19]

After a brief stopover at Madeira the squadron sailed on to Rio de Janeiro, where it then prepared for the long passage across the South Atlantic. After several weeks at Rio, the two ships sailed separately, the *John Adams* departing on 25 July. Each had an easy passage across the Atlantic. The *John Adams* stopped at the East African port of Zanzibar, where Wyman and his officers visited the sultan in his palace before the sloop sailed on to Bombay.[20]

The *John Adams* reached Bombay eight days before the *Columbia*, and during the wait Foote had the opportunity to explore the city. His visits ashore brought him for the first time into contact with American Protestant missionaries. The Bombay mission was then some twenty-five years old, making it the oldest such enterprise abroad. His meetings with the missionaries made a profound impression, causing Foote to reflect on how much his own work coincided with theirs. For the remainder of his life, when he was abroad Foote sought out Protestant missionaries and tried to support their work.[21] Wyman authorized Foote to continue his practice of conducting religious instruction for the men. On Sundays Foote usually read to the crew of the *John Adams* from the Episcopal Book of Common Prayer or from printed sermons he had brought with him. He especially enjoyed informal voluntary prayer meetings on the berth deck. And for the ship's boys he organized a Sunday school.[22]

The British authorities at Bombay entertained the squadron's officers ashore, and Read reciprocated aboard the flagship. On leaving Bombay, the two ships sailed to Portuguese Goa, the first American warships to call there. Then they sailed around the southern tip of India to Colombo, Ceylon, where they anchored on 25 November. Tropical diseases were now taking a toll on the men. On the voyage from Bombay to Goa, three men in the crew of the *John Adams* died of cholera.

Four days after arriving at Colombo, the Americans learned that on 26 August 1838, off the west coast of Sumatra, pirates had attacked and looted an American ship, the *Eclipse*. The captain and a crewman had been killed and several others wounded. Read immediately ordered his ships to prepare for sea, and the squadron departed Colombo on 1 December.[23]

As American trade with the Dutch East Indies had increased, so too had pirate depredations against American ships. In 1830 Sumatran pirates had attacked and plundered another American ship, the *Friendship*, in the process killing the captain and a number of other crew members. President Andrew Jackson had on that occasion ordered Capt. John Downes and the frigate *Potomac* to Sumatra to demand both an indemnity and punishment for the guilty. Downes was not able to determine the names of the guilty, but he bombarded several towns in the area, an action subsequently endorsed by the American public.

Read planned a similar response. On 19 December his squadron arrived off the town of Quallah Battoo (Kuala Batu). Here Read was able to confirm the report concerning the *Eclipse* and also learned that the pirates had distributed some of their plunder to local rajahs in order to ensure the rulers' protection. After several discussions with the rajah at Quallah Battoo failed to produce the pirates, Read set a deadline of sunset on 24 December. When this expired without the desired result, Read was convinced that the rajah was merely stalling for time. He brought his ships near to shore and ordered them to open fire on the forts protecting Quallah Battoo. According to Rev. Taylor, an eyewitness, most of the American shot fell without effect in the nearby jungle, but the forts were destroyed and four people were killed. There were only three answering cannon shots during the half-hour-long American bombardment. Two of the forts then raised white flags. Read reported: "After a few shot well directed at the Rajah's fort, I directed the firing to cease."[24]

Read then moved against the port town of Muckie (Mukkee) thirty miles to the south, where some of the pirates were reported to be living. The American ships arrived there on the evening of 30 December, and the same pattern repeated itself. The Americans demanded that the rajahs give up the pirates, only to be met by delaying tactics. On the morning of 1 January 1839, Read ordered the two ships towed and warped in to about two hundred yards from the town, from which point they opened fire. Wyman then went ashore with 320 sailors and marines from the two ships to burn Muckie and its five forts. The thousand residents of the town had already fled, and the Americans accomplished the destruction without incident or casualties. After two and a half hours ashore, during which they spiked twenty-two guns from the forts and threw them into a ditch, the landing party returned to the ships. While Wyman was ashore, Foote commanded the *John Adams* and directed the covering fire.[25]

From Muckie the squadron sailed to Soo-Soo, arriving there on 4 January. Read was preparing to move against that town for harboring some of the pirates when the rajah of Quallah Battoo sued for peace, offering both an indemnity of two thousand dollars to the owners of the *Eclipse* and a pledge to keep the peace and protect vessels flying the American flag. The other rajahs also made peace. Read accepted this arrangement, and a few days later the squadron returned to sea.[26]

On 5 February 1839, the two warships arrived at Singapore. By now many of the crewmen were sick from dysentery, scurvy, smallpox, and cholera. Although Read sent a number of them ashore to be cared for, six men from the *Columbia* and three from the *John Adams* died. At this time there was little knowledge of communicable diseases, and Foote attributed the sickness to the noxious night air and climate.[27]

The Americans remained in Singapore for two months. Foote soon established contact with American missionaries there, a half dozen of whom were awaiting Dutch approval to establish the first American missions in Borneo. Foote, Magruder, Taylor, and Turner regularly met and dined with them, and on Sundays the missionaries came aboard the American ships to conduct services. Foote established a particularly close friendship with the Reverend Alfred North, who with his wife ran a school for boys. The two men agreed to correspond for the rest of their lives, no matter what the distance that might separate them. Before he left Singapore Foote gave North a substantial cash gift, which was used to purchase a twenty-volume encyclopedia.[28]

Although the fresh fruit available at Singapore ended the scurvy aboard the American ships, the other sicknesses continued. As a result, Read called off his plan to send the *John Adams* to Bangkok, Manila, and

Canton. Read believed that the best way to end the health problems was to get his ships to sea. When the monsoons at last lifted, on 28 March, the American squadron sailed from Singapore for Macao. During the voyage the two ships separated, with the *John Adams* detouring to Manila en route. The *Columbia* had a particularly difficult passage to Macao as illness continued to ravage the crew. In the year since leaving the United States the *Columbia* had lost twenty-nine crewmen, and the *John Adams* nearly the same.[29]

The *Columbia* arrived at Portuguese Macao on 28 April, followed by the *John Adams* a month later, but the sea voyage had done nothing to alleviate the health problems plaguing the squadron. Foote was fortunate not to be among the sick.[30] When the American squadron reached Macao, tensions were running high between the Chinese and the Western governments, especially the British, who had been importing huge quantities of opium to sell in China. The imperial government was determined to stamp out the opium trade, which had become a plague for the Chinese people. The opium trade had been initiated by the British to alleviate a trade imbalance. The British had been importing considerable quantities of Chinese products, especially tea, for which the Chinese demanded payment in silver. Searching for a product the Chinese especially desired, the British hit on opium. Large quantities of the drug were grown in India and shipped in fast British and American ships to China, where the smuggled opium brought vast profits.

The opium problem came to a head at Canton when the Manchu government, which had been steadily declining in influence, decided to adopt a tough line. The Manchus appointed the incorruptible Lin Zexu (Lin Tse-hsu) as high commissioner with full authority to halt the importation and sale of the drug. He arrived in Canton in early March 1839 and immediately ordered the several hundred foreign merchants there to surrender all their opium for destruction. He also ordered the confiscation of all ships found carrying the drug. When the foreign merchants refused to comply with Lin's instructions, he suspended all foreign trade out of Canton on 22 March and ordered Chinese servants to foreigners to leave their jobs. Lin next ordered troops to seal off the foreign compounds in Canton and blockaded river access to the sea.

The *Columbia* and then the *John Adams* arrived at Macao in the midst of this controversy, and the American merchants, fearing violence, urged Read to stay. The Portuguese authorities were also pleased to have potential American naval support riding at anchor in the harbor. But Read was determined not to get involved in internal Chinese matters and to limit any actions on his part to protecting American lives and property. In any case the situation soon temporarily resolved itself. Aware of their difficult position inside a city of more than a million Chinese, the foreign merchants at length agreed to hand over to Lin 22,291 chests of opium. The British merchants then left the city, but most of the Americans stayed on to continue legal trade with the Chinese. This temporarily delayed the start of the so-called Opium Wars.[31]

Over the next several months the American squadron prepared for the voyage across the Pacific to the Sandwich Islands. Foote met a number of American missionaries in Macao who were learning the Chinese language and customs while awaiting permission to enter China. The relaxed situation in Canton during this time allowed many of the men to visit that city. Foote probably joined Rev. Taylor on trips there and may have met the renowned American Dr. Peter Parker, who had established a hospital at Canton.[32]

At some point during the squadron's three-month stay at Macao Foote was shocked to learn in letters from his family that his wife, Caroline, had unexpectedly died more than six months earlier, on 4 November 1838. Foote was a widower at age thirty-two. If anything, this tragedy strengthened his Christian convictions and determination to rededicate his life to God and act as his agent on earth. Apparently Foote also gave serious thought to leaving the navy and entering foreign missionary work. These thoughts, however seriously he entertained them at the time, were fleeting; he soon resolved to continue God's work within the U.S. Navy.[33]

On 6 August 1839 the East India Squadron departed Macao for the Sandwich Islands. The very first night at sea the ships ran into a typhoon that lasted several days and damaged both vessels; the *Columbia* suffered extensive damage to its sails and masts. The rest of the two-month trip across the Pacific Ocean was uneventful as far as weather went, but not disease. Twenty-six men aboard the *Columbia* died, and 120 were on the sick list when the ship arrived in Honolulu harbor on 10 October.[34]

Lieutenant Foote and his close friends were soon involved in a dispute ashore that involved Protestant missionaries. In 1839 the Sandwich (Hawaiian) Islands were ruled by a native monarch, King Kamehameha III. Americans, British, and French merchants were all active in the islands, and small foreign communities had been established there.

American missionaries, many of them from New England, sought to win converts but also tried to improve the lot of the Hawaiian people, who had been decimated by imported diseases—for which they had no immunity— and alcohol. The missionaries were soon advising the king on a variety of matters, and this led to a series of laws, including one that banned native women from visiting foreign ships for the purposes of prostitution. During his visit to the islands in 1830 as chaplain on the *Vincennes,* the Reverend Charles Stewart had proudly reported considerable strides in education and the quality of life for the Hawaiian people, noting that missionaries had become the most important advisers to the king.[35]

The influence of the missionaries continued to grow, and in 1838, in the course of a great religious revival, some ten thousand converts joined the Protestant churches. American planters and French Catholics in the islands were upset by the missionaries' reform program, and especially by their growing influence over King Kamehameha. The French were also angry that the king had twice forbidden French Roman Catholic priests to establish a mission. The king's decision to ban the importation of alcohol in 1838 had also led to considerable anger against the missionaries.[36]

This unrest brought the sixty-gun French frigate *l'Artemise* to Honolulu in early July. The ship's captain, Cyrille Pierre Theodore Laplace, made it clear to the king that the government of France regarded the missionaries as the chief villains in what were regarded as anti-French policies. Laplace told King Kamehameha that he had been ordered to demand a treaty guaranteeing Catholics the same privileges extended to the Protestants. He also demanded a site in Honolulu for the French priests to construct a Catholic church as well as a new commercial treaty that would allow the French to import wine and brandy nearly duty free. The king was also ordered to give Laplace twenty thousand dollars as a guarantee of his good faith. Laplace threatened to declare war if the king did not agree to these conditions within three days. Laplace then informed the British and American consuls that in the event of hostilities he would guarantee protection aboard his ship for all foreigners except missionaries, who, he said, were "a part of the native population, and must undergo the unhappy consequences of a war which they shall have brought on this country."[37] King Kamehameha, caught unawares by the appearance of the French frigate and with no means of resisting, had to sign the treaty. On 20 July Captain Laplace, having undone much of the missionaries' reform efforts, sailed away in *l'Artemise*.[38]

This was the general situation in the islands when Read's squadron arrived at Honolulu. Foote and his friends from the *Columbia*—Magruder, Turner, and Rev. Taylor—soon went ashore to visit with the missionaries. Magruder already knew many of them from a previous stay when he was a lieutenant in the *Vincennes*. The Reverend William Richards, who had recently resigned as chief interpreter and adviser to the king, treated the visitors to a large luau.[39] Undoubtedly the missionaries hoped to solicit the help of the lieutenants and Rev. Taylor in reversing the effects of Captain Laplace's visit. But Foote noted that few in the squadron believed that Laplace had done anything wrong; most seem to have thought that the missionaries had overstepped their place and were getting their just deserts.

Foote did not believe this was true, and within a week of his arrival, aided chiefly by Lieutenant Turner, he completed his own investigation of the situation, which left "no doubt" as to the innocence of the missionaries. Twelve years before, he had promised to act for the Lord, and here were the Lord's agents under attack. Here, too, was an opportunity to teach the "enemies of a religion" a lesson. All the missionaries he talked with assured him that the king's decisions to ban French Catholic priests and prohibit importation of liquor had been at his own instigation, not theirs. Foote kept a careful record of his meetings—in part so that there could be no doubt of what transpired but also, apparently, so that his own name would be closely associated with the matter when it became public in the United States.[40]

Foote advised the missionaries to present their case to Commodore Read, who was the highest American authority available, asking him to convene a court of inquiry in which officers of the squadron would hear and decide the validity of the charges against the missionaries. At the very least the facts would then be a part of the public record. The missionaries followed Foote's suggestion and contacted Commodore Read. When Read failed to respond within a week after receiving their request, Foote told the missionary leaders that this was probably from his reluctance to be drawn into a matter so far removed from his normal authority and that could create diplomatic difficulties with France. Foote suggested that the missionaries address another request to Read, this time pointing out that the American public would expect him to act in this matter and also that they were prepared to forward a copy of their appeal to the Board of Commissioners for Foreign Missions for publication.[41]

Running the risk of pitting himself against his senior commander was a dangerous course for a junior lieutenant, and it certainly could have cost Foote his naval career. A further complication was that Read had been born in Ireland and might be expected to show sympathy toward the Catholic position.[42] Foote persisted despite these considerations, and also despite the fact that the squadron had been in Honolulu for three weeks and was preparing to sail. He himself drafted the third appeal to Read. Sent on 29 October, it asked for a response to the missionaries' earlier appeals to appear before a court of inquiry and reminded Read that the missionaries planned to send a copy of all proceedings to the U.S. government and the American Board of Commissioners for Foreign Missions. The missionaries asked Read to delay the squadron's sailing for a few days and pointed out the dangerous precedent that would be set by a failure to investigate allegations that the rights of Americans abroad had been threatened.[43] Foote also visited with the American consul, who, like Read, had declined to get involved. Foote told him that the American public would expect action. And he said that the junior officers of the squadron were prepared to "enter upon the investigation, with, or without the Commodore's association, if he would only give his assent."[44]

The third request produced a response from Read. While he declined to hold an inquiry on the grounds that there would be no time for it before the squadron sailed, he did provide some support for the missionaries' position by stating that he had discovered no evidence to substantiate Captain Laplace's charges. Read's response did not satisfy either the missionaries or Foote and Turner. The former decided to proceed with their position pamphlet, which would include all correspondence on the matter.

Samuel Castle, one of the missionaries' leaders, drew up the pamphlet. In it he stated that the missionaries had never advocated persecution of the Catholics. It was their advocacy of reform that had attracted so many natives to the Protestant faith, and Catholic jealousy alone had prompted the French to intervene. Foote and Turner suggested that the pamphlet be accompanied by a covering letter signed by naval officers attesting to the character and goodwill of the missionaries. Foote drafted this, but as he and Turner were both busy with a court-martial on the *John Adams,* they did not help put together the pamphlet itself. This had unfortunate results.[45]

Foote's covering letter stressed that the missionaries were U.S. citizens and hence entitled to their government's protection. He stated that so far as he could determine the missionaries had had a salutary effect on the native population, and further said that they should be commended rather than condemned for their actions. Foote passed his letter around the two ships for the officers to sign. A majority—at least thirteen—signed, including surgeons and mathematics teachers. Foote's name was at the head of the list.[46]

Probably Foote was so convinced of the correctness of his case and the importance of his Christian witness that he did not care that he had gone outside normal protocol in not informing Read of his actions. The surprising thing is that so many of the other officers signed the letter. Those on the *John Adams* may have trusted Foote's judgment, but they were also probably influenced by the fact that Foote was the ship's second in command. Those who signed the letter, however, did so only on the understanding that it would not be published without Read's express consent.[47]

The controversy was not long in coming to a head. Fifty copies of the pamphlet were printed, and one soon fell into the hands of the French consul. He also learned of Foote's covering letter, which was falsely represented as being quite critical of the French government. The consul went to Read to demand a copy of Foote's letter in order to send it along with the pamphlet to Paris. He also made it clear that he regarded Foote as the major source of the friction. A furious Read called Foote to the flagship.

In their meeting Read reminded Foote that he could not become involved in the dispute and expressed his surprise that his officers had taken this action without consulting him. Foote asked the commodore to read his letter, but he refused. Foote left the meeting determined of the rightness of his cause and unwilling to back down, even if it cost him his commission. He was adamant that the truth should come out and that he must follow the dictates of his conscience. Foote wanted the letter to be published, but he did not want to offend Read gratuitously. Convinced that Read would find the letter acceptable, he asked Rev. Turner to prevail on the commodore to read it, which Turner did. Read then discovered that Foote's letter was circumspect and moderate in tone and did not attack the French; as a result, although he made it clear to Foote that he was displeased with all the excitement the letter had generated, he withdrew his objection to its publication. A meeting was also arranged in which the letter was read to both the French and British consuls, who also found it inoffensive.[48]

With the affair resolved to the general satisfaction of all concerned, the American squadron could now sail. Foote's letter was published on 3 November. The day before, Foote had sent a letter to the missionaries warning them to be less secular in their approach and more circumspect in their remarks, to be judicious in their relations with non-Christians, and to be certain they made no disparaging remarks about other Christians. He also advised that they would be more successful in their endeavors if they shortened the length of their sermons. Shipboard services did not last more than forty minutes, and officers and men agreed that this was the proper length. Foote closed by saying that he hoped his remarks did not offend and that he was only trying to help their cause.[49]

Although the squadron's stay in Honolulu was longer than Read had intended, it had a salutary effect on the health of his men. With fresh fruit and a better climate, the health of the crews on the two ships dramatically improved and the scurvy quickly disappeared. The dysentery also tapered off, although before ending it claimed more than a dozen additional lives.[50]

On 4 November the American squadron left Honolulu for Tahiti. Once at sea Foote began organizing his correspondence and records of the time spent in Honolulu in case he was called on to explain his conduct after his return to the United States. He penned a lengthy account of events and a number of letters to prominent naval figures such as his former commander Daniel Patterson and the Reverend Charles Stewart. Clearly Foote was seeking to mobilize public opinion should the navy move against him. In his letters Foote laid out events as he saw them and made clear his responsibility as sole instigator of the controversial letter supporting the missionaries. He concluded that he would have followed the same course even knowing that it would have cost him his commission. He called on his friends to see to it that copies of both the pamphlet and his covering letter were sent to leading politicians and members of the Board of Commissioners for Foreign Missions.[51]

In early December, after a cruise of thirty days and twenty-five hundred miles, the *John Adams* joined its faster consort at Tahiti, a beautiful island rich in tropical vegetation and with an abundant food supply. Foote noted that "the men [of Tahiti] are larger and better proportioned than in the Sandwich Islands, and the women are beautiful." Foote sensed the island's siren call, noting in his journal, "So seductive are these islands that one almost ceases to wonder at the mutiny of the *Bounty.*" But Foote also found the natives less civilized than the Hawaiians and quite licentious.[52]

The Americans learned that Captain Laplace and the French frigate *l'Artemise* had preceded them. Tahiti also had its tensions between Catholics and Protestants, and Laplace had imposed on the Tahitian queen a similar obligation to protect Catholic missionaries and to allow them to build Catholic churches where Protestant churches already existed. But here the parallel with Hawaii ended; there were no New England Congregationalist missionaries for Foote to defend, only English ones.

Commodore Read had stopped at Tahiti to investigate a report that the American consul there had been injured while defending two Roman Catholic priests whom the Tahitian government had ordered expelled. He came to the same conclusion Commo. Charles Wilkes had reached when his exploring expedition had stopped at the island some months before: the priests were not Americans, and the consul had overstepped his authority. Foote agreed, noting in his journal that the reason for the consul's behavior was that he was not only a Belgian but also a Roman Catholic.[53]

In Tahiti, Foote continued to organize his papers and prepare for a possible defense of his actions in Honolulu. He talked with Rev. Taylor about the latter's plan to write a book about the cruise. Taylor told Foote that he planned to give a prominent place to the controversy involving the Hawaiian missionaries and, because their views of the incident were so similar, asked Foote to write down his recollections to be included in the book. These were to be in the guise of a letter written to a friend in the United States. As in his other letters on the subject, Foote asked that its recipient try to secure its publication, and it was actually reprinted later in the *New York Observer.*[54]

The squadron soon departed Tahiti for South America. During the passage Foote underwent considerable soul searching. He spent long hours alone in his cabin in prayer and reflection concerning his experiences during the cruise. In retrospect, he believed his response to the missionaries had been inadequate and that he was not doing enough to demonstrate his religious beliefs and "Christian consistency." On 7 January he noted in his journal his own lust for fame, "the secret whisperings of pride." To counter these Foote renewed his dedication to his faith and his determination always to act for God. On 7 February he wrote:

> In the name & merits of Christ, with the acceptance of the Holy Spirit & the mercy of God the Father I do here in this holy presence resolve to take the scriptures as the guide of my actions & my feelings. I resolve to use all those helps which religion works, & christian conversation so amply furnish, to incite a spirit of love and obedience. I resolve to watch and pray, to bear in mind that the Christian life is a warfare, that one must be uncompromising in his principles and conduct, and never shrink from avowing my profession and hope in Christ, whether such around be in unison with the sentiments of those associated with me or not. I resolve to guard my tongue from speaking injuriously of others, to avoid levity of manner, on the one hand, and moroseness on the other, to perform the executive duties of the ship with impartiality and justice, feeling at all times that my official acts will be closely criticized in consideration of my profession of Christian principles. I resolve statedly to devote night and morning suitable time to meditation and prayer, letting no day pass without one hour being wholly spent in religious reading and other exercises.
>
> I resolve to look alone to Christ as our mediator and atoner. To the Holy Spirit for its moorings, and to God in his mercy for grace and assistance, to help me in that holy and lively exercise of faith which will enable me to keep these resolutions made in His presence, and grow in grace to become meet for an inheritance among the Saints in glory. Amen.[55]

The squadron was at Valparaiso in early February and also stopped at Callao before sailing around Cape Horn. The weather was now cold with squalls of snow and hail. The ships also received mail from home for the first time in almost a year. In his journal Foote dwelt on family matters, particularly the plight of his young daughter, Josephine, and reflected on whether there was life after death. These concerns, bad weather, and unspecified difficulties with another officer all kept Foote in a deep depression, which in turn pushed him more into fasting, prayer, and meditation, especially as he eschewed assistance from fellow officers.[56] The squadron arrived at Rio de Janeiro on 23 April 1840. Still depressed, Foote noted his shame at "the pride and vanity" he felt when visitors to the ship complimented him on its excellent appearance.[57]

By June the squadron was in the North Atlantic, and as the ships neared Boston and home Foote's spirits at last began to lift. Soon he would see his family again. Days from his destination he wrote his last journal entry of the cruise. In it he again reflected on the centrality of Christianity in his life: "Christ is all in all." His highest goal must always be to confirm to God's will.[58]

On 16 June 1840, the *John Adams* and *Columbia* tied up at the wharf at Charlestown Navy Yard in Boston. In its circumnavigation of the globe the squadron had traveled more than fifty-five thousand miles and visited more than twenty major ports. The cruise had cost the lives of more than seventy men onboard the *Columbia* and nearly that number on the *John Adams*. The survivors were simply glad to be home. They had been away more than twenty-five months.[59]

❧4❧

THE CAMPAIGN FOR TEMPERANCE

On 24 June 1840, after more than two years away from home, Foote left the *John Adams* and hurried home to his family in Cheshire. His daughter, Josephine, was about to celebrate her third birthday, and the two were virtual strangers. Despite the pain he felt over his wife's death, the time at home allowed Foote to recover his spirits. His journal entry on his thirty-fourth birthday, 12 September 1840, shows that he was no longer in spiritual turmoil and that he was reconciled to his worldly self:

> Oh how mingled are the emotions of my mind. It seems as if love, joy, gratitude, on the one hand, with sorrow and contrition of soul on the other, were all at work within me. The Christian is told in the Word of God that Christ is an all-sufficient Saviour, and he is able and ready in all circumstances to sustain us in a life of *perfect obedience,* if we exercise faith in him. May this year be so passed as to meet thy acceptance; and if I am to leave this world before its expiration, enable me cheerfully to acquiesce.[1]

Although Foote was glad to have time ashore with his family, his stay there would be much longer than he anticipated or wanted, again the consequence of the overabundance of naval officers. He was much in demand as a guest lecturer because of widespread public interest in the

East India Squadron's around-the-world cruise and from his active promotion of American Protestant missions overseas and growing reputation as a spokesman for the spiritual needs of sailors. He also traveled to Cleveland, Ohio, to visit his brother John, who had recently moved there, and he maintained an active correspondence with naval reformers and missionaries he had met overseas.[2]

While he was awaiting orders Foote wooed Caroline Augusta Street, his twenty-four-year-old second cousin and the eldest daughter of Augustus Russel and Caroline Mary Street, a socially prominent New Haven family. On 27 January 1842, the two were married in New Haven; from all accounts their marriage was a happy one. They had three sons, two of whom survived their father, and two daughters.[3]

On 22 November 1841, after nearly eighteen months ashore, Foote finally secured a naval billet when the Navy Department appointed him executive officer to Commo. James Biddle at the Naval Asylum. Located at the Philadelphia Navy Yard, the Asylum was both a hospital and convalescent home for disabled and infirm sailors and a naval school for midshipmen. It was here that Foote began the naval reform work that he pursued the rest of his career.[4]

Since 1799 the Treasury Department had deducted twenty cents a month from the salaries of naval personnel to go toward establishing a "home" for convalescing and disabled sailors, although it was some time before the Navy Department decided to build such a home on the grounds of the Philadelphia Navy Yard. Located on some twenty acres of land, the three-story granite-and-marble structure was completed in 1833. It had rooms for 180 residents and apartments for officers and staff. Unfortunately, the Asylum was on swampy ground next to the Schuykill River and thus a breeding ground for malaria.[5]

The staff of the Asylum had a strange mix of missions, for into this setting replete with habitual drunkards were introduced in 1839 the young and impressionable navy midshipmen. Commodore Biddle was largely responsible for this move; he had become governor of the board of the Asylum in August 1838, and he was also president of the Board of Examiners, the navy captains who met to test eligible midshipmen for promotion to lieutenant.[6] Improving the education of its midshipmen was part of the growing movement toward professionalism within the U.S. Navy in this period. Before the school was established their training had been at best haphazard and was largely left to individual ship captains. Few ships had regular teachers, and the midshipmen aboard such ships could expect no more than a few hours of instruction each day. Most midshipmen learned largely through observation and practice. This was neither an efficient nor an effective system, and the obvious solution was to establish a naval academy; yet Congress had repeatedly rejected calls for such an institution, not only because of the expense but also from the belief that it would help to create a naval aristocracy.[7]

Commodore Biddle strongly believed that the system of educating midshipmen had to change, and in 1839 he convinced the Board of Examiners to shift the next year's annual examinations from Baltimore to Philadelphia and to assign midshipmen not at sea to the Asylum to prepare for the exam. On 15 November 1839, Secretary of the Navy James Paulding approved the plan, assigning to the Asylum fifteen midshipmen awaiting duty.[8]

In 1840 more midshipmen arrived at the Asylum. From 9:00 A.M. until 2:00 P.M. they attended classes in algebra, geography, physics, and moral philosophy. After that they had free time until lights-out at 9:00 P.M. They were housed in twenty-four basement rooms, which were described as "cold, damp, cheerless and unhealthy." Certainly many of them, especially the older ones who had already spent several years at sea, were unhappy with the arrangement, which they referred to as "Biddle's nursery." Morale was low and discipline lax; duels were not unknown, and there were fights with civilians when midshipmen went into Philadelphia.[9]

When Foote arrived as the Asylum's executive officer at the end of 1841, the facility housed some one hundred pensioners and thirty-four midshipmen with one professor of mathematics. This was an ideal assignment for the reform-minded Foote, although during his first few months there he was somewhat distracted by his upcoming wedding. He was also concerned that he was becoming too worldly and sought God's help in making the marriage successful and an example for others. During these months the Asylum's professor died of pneumonia and an outbreak of smallpox caused classes to be suspended for six weeks; and Commodore Biddle left the Asylum, to be replaced in April by Commo. James Barron. Foote played an important role in this transition. Foote's first biographer, James M. Hoppin, asserted that Foote had been ordered there expressly to oversee the "care and education" of the midshipmen because he understood the importance of experience at sea combined with formal instruction on land, especially as the navy changed from sail to steam.[10]

In addition to problems associated with expanding the school, the Asylum was the site of many turf battles between the hospital, which was under the control of the Bureau of Medicine and Surgery, and the school and pensioner parts of the facility. In November 1842 Barron asked to be relieved of his assignment, and on the thirtieth of that month Foote became the Asylum's temporary commanding officer.[11]

Foote did his best to improve the situation for the midshipmen, who had continued to complain about the unhealthful nature of their basement rooms. He got a surgeon from the naval hospital to inspect these facilities and then secured Secretary of the Navy Abel Upshur's permission to relocate the midshipmen in quarters on the Asylum's ground floor.[12] Foote's chief accomplishments at the Asylum came with the pensioners, however. He tried to improve the quality of their lives by securing them single rooms where possible, and he established a library and sought additional funds for the men's use from Upshur.[13]

Foote also continued his practice of conducting worship services in the form of weekly Bible study and Sunday school. Once, when his brother John visited and asked for him there, a sentinel told him that Foote was in "his church." Because the Bureau of Medicine and Surgery had taken over the Asylum's chapel, Foote utilized the midshipmen's recreation room as "his" church; there John Foote overheard his brother's "earnest entreaties to his hearers to become good men."[14]

Particularly disturbing to Foote was the fact that most of the elderly pensioners were habitual drunkards. Indeed, it was his service at the Asylum that led Foote into his lifelong crusade for temperance. Previously he had not been particularly concerned with the issue. At Philadelphia he told his brother John:

> I made up my mind that as a naval officer I could not be a temperance man. I met with persons of all nations. I was obliged to conform to their customs. But when I came here I found these old sailors dreadful drunkards. Whenever I gave them any privilege, they invariably got drunk. I could do nothing with them. At last I signed the pledge myself, and they followed me.[15]

At the Asylum Foote saw fully the ravages alcohol could exact and concluded that it was a moral and social evil. As was usual with the outspoken Foote, once he had made up his mind he was unshakable.[16]

The daily grog ration was traditional in the naval service, and this applied to the pensioners as well, and even to ships' boys and midshipmen.

The grog ration grew out of the Royal Navy practice of serving a mixture of half rum, half water twice a day. Naval regulations required that every person in the service be allowed to receive a half pint (eight ounces) of distilled spirits—in the U.S. Navy that usually meant rye whiskey—every day. U.S. Navy practice was to serve four ounces of whiskey and four of water at dinner and at supper. At the time, liquor was both cheap and plentiful, and water fit to drink was often hard to come by. Also many, perhaps most, Americans believed that alcohol was beneficial to health. The navy issued grog on the assumption that it helped prevent disease, but its only positive benefit was probably in warding off depression. As historian Christopher McKee noted in writing about grog in the early U.S. Navy, "More often than not, it was the best part of the meal and made the rest bearable."[17]

When Foote arrived at the Asylum the temperance movement was increasing its influence throughout the country. In the summer of 1842, Congress passed a bill proposed by Secretary Upshur that cut the navy grog ration in half—to a gill (four fluid ounces)—substituted an ounce of tea, coffee, or cocoa, and added two ounces of sugar to the daily ration. Congress also provided pay supplements to those who gave up their grog ration altogether. Finally, no man in the navy under the age of twenty-one, either officer or enlisted man, was allowed a grog ration.

Among the officers who took the lead for temperance in the navy were Lt. Charles Wilkes and Capts. Foxhall A. Parker, John C. Long, and Joseph Smith. But it was Foote, at the Asylum and later aboard the frigate *Cumberland*, who became the foremost advocate of the effort to end the grog ration and bring sobriety to the U.S. Navy.[18] At the Asylum, Foote's crusade took the form of an appeal to the pensioners to forgo their daily grog ration and take a pledge of abstinence. He was the first to sign such a pledge, and he preached God's damnation if the men failed to repent and follow his example. Foote was surprisingly successful. Most pensioners did indeed forsake their grog ration; the few incorrigible troublemakers were expelled from the Asylum. In place of the grog ration those signing the pledge received fourteen cents a week, which allowed them to purchase necessities such as straw hats, towels, needles, and thread.[19]

Foote saw alcoholism as a social evil attributable to moral weakness rather than disease, and he now added abstinence to his own evangelical exhortations. By reason and example he would help right men's evil ways. Protestants believed that in the process of evangelism one might help to save his or her own soul; bringing others to God helped atone for one's own past sins.[20] Foote also believed that abolishing the grog ration would substantially improve efficiency in the navy, which was itself to blame for the problem because it in effect encouraged drunkenness. Foote's solution was to abolish the grog ration altogether and replace it with tea, coffee, or cocoa. The navy could then pay the men an extra dollar a month in lieu of the ration, and everyone would benefit.[21]

The Asylum pensioners appreciated Foote's efforts on their behalf. On 4 February 1843, forty-three out of forty-eight men present at the facility sent a petition to Secretary Upshur and Representative John Quincy Adams calling for improvement in their conditions. They added high praise for Foote and his efforts on their behalf: "He has done us a great deal of good in making us all sober men. We once thought that old sailors could not do without grog. Now there is not a man in the house that draws his grog, and we feel like human beings, and hate the sin of getting drunk."[22]

In February 1843 Secretary Upshur detailed Cdr. William W. McKeon as the new director of the Asylum and Foote reverted to the post of executive officer. At the same time Upshur authorized midshipmen to live off the facility if they so desired; this freed up more rooms for the pensioners, who now had their own rooms. The chapel was also restored.[23]

After being in command at the Asylum for four months, Foote no doubt found it hard to return to a subordinate role. He now wrote to Secretary Upshur requesting assignment to a recruiting post at the New York Navy Yard. This posting would have the advantage of being close to his home near New Haven and would also allow Foote to help determine the type of men who joined the service. He told Upshur that he was willing to go on "leave of absence" status until such a post became available. Upshur concurred and informed Foote that he could depart as soon as McKeon reported that it "could be done with convenience." Evidently McKeon found Foote too valuable to let go right away; Foote remained at the Asylum another six months.[24]

During his remaining time at the Asylum Foote continued to work with the midshipmen, but he also busied himself with petitions to the Navy Department for captain's pay during the period he had served as the commanding officer. Naval regulations entitled junior officers to receive the pay of a senior position when they were actually holding it. Upshur rejected two appeals from Foote, first for captain's pay and then for that of commander. Foote asked Upshur to reconsider, but Upshur told him that the Philadelphia Asylum had not been designated as either a captain's or a commander's position and thus Foote was not entitled to supplementary pay. Foote continued to press his case until an exasperated Upshur bluntly told him to desist. Foote's interest in this was likely not the pay as much as it was personal pride and the recognition to which he believed he was entitled. As one of his biographers has noted, ego was "something most naval officers of the time had in excess, but which Foote, at least in the privacy of his journals, battled against as unchristian behavior."[25]

Upshur's rejection did not keep Foote from presenting the Navy Department with a bill for the $450 that he had spent in refurbishing the captain's quarters at the Asylum. When his appeals went unanswered he even enlisted his father to write on his behalf. In the midst of this, in July 1843, Upshur resigned to become the secretary of state, and Foote was forced to recommence the process with his successor, David Henshaw. Finally, in August 1843, Foote received word that he would be reimbursed.[26]

Foote went to Washington to thank Henshaw in person and lobby for a new assignment. Their meeting went well; the secretary praised Foote for his work at the Asylum and offered him the post of first lieutenant on the forty-four-gun frigate *Cumberland*, which was then fitting out at Boston and slated to become the flagship of the Mediterranean Squadron. This was a choice assignment indeed, and Foote accepted it immediately.[27]

The *Cumberland* posting was perhaps most important to Foote's career in the friendships he made there. When he arrived at Boston Foote met the *Cumberland*'s captain, Samuel Breese, and the commander of the squadron, Commo. Joseph Smith, who flew his pennant in the frigate. Both Breese and Smith had distinguished themselves in the War of 1812, especially on Lake Champlain, and Smith became a lifelong friend and mentor to Foote. After the Mediterranean cruise was over, Smith became chief of the Bureau of Yards and Docks, which put him in position to further the younger officer's career. Foote also got to know Smith's flag lieutenant, John A. Dahlgren, who later became the navy's most noted ordnance expert and inventor of a family of guns that bore his name. Dahlgren and Foote became fast friends and remained so the rest of their lives. Often during the cruise they took shore leave together, although Dahlgren noted that Foote was not much interested in art and seemed always in a hurry, "as all first lieutenants will be," to see as much as possible and them move on to the next site. Dahlgren wrote his wife, Mary, "Foot is a warm friend to me and never suffers any chance to pass of manifesting his feelings. His high standards as an officer & a man make this very valuable to me."[28]

While the *Cumberland* was taking on stores in Boston, some of the crew tapped into a barrel of whiskey and became drunk, insulting and attacking one of the ship's officers. For this offense the men were flogged. Foote was determined to continue the temperance work he had begun at the Asylum, and he used this incident to start a total abstinence society on the ship, beginning with the officers. On 20 November 1843, the frigate sailed from Boston for the Mediterranean. During the passage across the Atlantic Foote worked on the officers, usually accosting them at meals, when he would produce engravings depicting the effects of alcohol on the stomach. Dahlgren, who did not drink, backed him. More important, Foote had the full support of Commodore Smith, who earlier that same year had established a temperance society aboard his receiving ship at Boston. With Smith behind the effort it was difficult for the officers to resist.

Securing the support of the seamen was much more difficult, but once Foote set his mind on a course there was no dissuading him. He used Sunday services to advantage; with no chaplain onboard, Foote conducted the prayer services, which he closed with powerful sermons that usually treated abstinence. He used a positive approach, stressing the advantages that would accrue to those who took the temperance pledge. Dahlgren noted that the men were "always very attentive" and that Foote did much to keep order on the ship.[29]

By the time the *Cumberland* reached Port Mahon there was a marked difference in the crew's behavior. Dahlgren wrote to his wife that this was no doubt the result of "abstinence from liquor," and he credited the ship's officers, especially Foote, for their example. Dahlgren was amazed that fewer than ten men returned drunk from their liberty at Port Mahon, and that there was no evidence of liquor being smuggled aboard the ship. The *Sailor's Magazine* reported that "cocoa water" took the place of grog aboard ship.[30]

The officers were not so easy to persuade. Despite their quite moderate habits of drink, Foote could not get them to sign his temperance pledge or attend his religious services. It was also clear that Captain Breese was less than enthusiastic about Foote's reforming efforts, and relations between the two men steadily deteriorated. Dahlgren also developed a strong dislike of Breese; he informed his wife in confidence that the captain was a poor seaman who knew "nothing of his profession and [was] unwilling to follow any counsel."[31] Breese was in poor health, and much of the time he kept to his cabin or stayed ashore, leaving the frigate's management to Foote and even to Dahlgren. Undoubtedly a measure of the friction that developed between the *Cumberland*'s captain and first lieutenant resulted from Breese's poor seamanship and the fact that Foote was noted for his excellent ship handling. This tension did not go unnoticed, however, and adversely affected order aboard the ship.[32]

Foote's relations with other officers on the *Cumberland* also deteriorated, with the notable exception of Dahlgren. The degree to which Foote's temperance activities conditioned this is impossible to say, but the quality of food in the officers' mess figured prominently in the dissension. Foote had charge of buying the officers' food and drink and supervising its preparation, and apparently some of the men were not pleased with his efforts. By early August the officers were split into two factions, with neither side talking to the other. Breese belatedly tried to rectify the situation by transferring one of the frigate's lieutenants, but this had little effect. Finally Foote resigned as caterer and was succeeded by Dahlgren. Undoubtedly Dahlgren was a compromise; he supported Foote's abstinence activities and he disliked Breese. In any case, the situation in the wardroom soon improved. Foote's correspondence makes no mention of this tension, and there is no indication that it affected him.[33]

Much of the squadron's time at sea was spent showing the flag in various Mediterranean ports. The *Cumberland* sailed to Toulon and visited ports in Italy as well as Athens, Smyrna, Syria, Alexandria, and Malta. During the winter months the squadron was at anchor at Mahon and the officers found it easy to secure leave. With many officers traveling or simply living ashore during those months, there was extra space on the ship, and some wives were able to live aboard with their husbands. Foote's wife, Caroline, and her parents were then on an extended tour of Europe, and Foote traveled to see Caroline in Paris, Spain, and Italy. She in turn spent some weeks during the Christmas season of 1844–45 occupying the captain's cabin aboard the *Cumberland*.[34]

Foote continued his abstinence efforts among the crew, and in the fall of 1844 he secured the signatures of every man aboard save one. In return for yielding their daily grog ration, each man received a pay supplement. Finally, the effort was complete when on 3 November forty members of the *Cumberland*'s crew were sent home in the frigate *Columbia*. Dahlgren described them as the crew's "refuse." Among them was the one seaman who had refused to take the pledge. Dahlgren was thus able to write that there was "not a man in the ship who draws his spirit ration." Most of the ship's liquor was sent ashore, and the *Cumberland* became the first temperance ship in the U.S. Navy.[35] Later, in his 1 November 1845 farewell address to the crew of the *Cumberland*, remarks that were subsequently printed and distributed in pamphlet form, Foote noted:

> Look around, and we see ourselves in a ship where that great enemy of man— the enemy to his hopes and happiness—ardent spirits, is abolished. Who would have believed a man, thirty years ago, had he predicted that a ship, a frigate—a flag-ship, too, of the squadron—would cruise a year without the grog-tub? But it has been done, and I have strong hopes that in thirty years hence every man-of-war will cruise without a grog-tub, and that liberty in almost every port, and money every month, as has been the case in this ship, with many other changes, will also take place, rendering life in a man-of-war comparatively respectable and happy.[36]

Foote was realistic enough to know that temperance was not the solution to all the ills aboard the ship. He knew that some of the men had violated their pledge and that others would do so in the future. He did ask that the men reflect on the benefits from temperance and seek to apply it when they returned to civilian life.[37]

Foote was determined to expand his temperance crusade to include the entire navy, and toward that end he decided to submit a petition to Congress. Two hundred and fifty men signed his petition calling for abolition of the grog ration, including Commodore Smith, Captain Breese, and the other officers. In January 1845 Congressman George P. Marsh, a Whig from Vermont, presented the petition to the House Committee on Naval Affairs. With the movement to abolish the grog ration gathering strength in the country, the House gave increasing time to this issue and to the abolition of flogging as well. Although the committee did recommend abolishing the spirit ration, Foote's petition and the effort to abolish flogging failed to gain sufficient support to become law. In 1849 John Rockwell, a Whig representative from Connecticut, attached an amendment to abolish the spirit ration to a naval appropriations bill, but the bill was voted down, 71 to 63.[38]

The *Cumberland* remained at Mahon until mid-April 1845 undergoing general repairs and reprovisioning, and then again visited ports along the Mediterranean, including Palermo, Malta, Trieste, Tripoli, Minorca, and Toulon.[39] The *Cumberland*'s cruise was now coming to an end. In two years the frigate had shown the American flag throughout the Mediterranean. But the nation's eyes now turned toward Mexico, where war was looming. Efforts by President James K. Polk (1845–49) to secure the Rio Grande border for Texas and purchase New Mexico and California steadily increased tensions between the two countries. The *Cumberland*'s officers and crew expected to be sent to the Gulf of Mexico when they left the Mediterranean. But when the orders arrived at Toulon on 23 September, the *Cumberland* was told to return to Boston. The *Plymouth*, the only other U.S. warship in the Mediterranean, was to go to the gulf. The *Cumberland* returned to Mahon to ready for the crossing, and on 1 October sailed for home. The ship made a fast crossing of the Atlantic and arrived at Boston on 8 November 1845.[40]

Detached from the *Cumberland* on 12 November, Foote received the customary three months of shore leave and traveled to Cheshire. At the end of the three months he wrote to the commander of the Charlestown (Boston) Navy Yard, Commo. Foxhall Parker, to ask for an assignment there. It must have been difficult for him to request a shore billet when war with Mexico seemed imminent, but Foote was suffering from a severe case of ophthalmia, an eye disease contracted from the dazzling waters of the Mediterranean, and was not fit for sea duty. Foote's friend Dahlgren suffered from the same affliction and had been forced to take a six months' leave of absence before his eyesight improved.

Because he had yet to recover fully his eyesight, and also because his father was in poor health, in February 1846 Foote requested a three months' extension in his assignment to Boston. Secretary of the Navy George Bancroft granted the request and subsequently ordered Foote to report as executive officer to the Charlestown Yard on 1 June 1846. Foote noted later that the ophthalmia "confined me to my bed for five months." His eye problems persisted at least until 1848.[41]

In May 1846, as Foote was receiving his orders to Boston, war began between the United States and Mexico. For the next two years, as the war raged, Foote remained at the Charlestown Yard. Much of those in the northeastern United States saw the war as a piece of southern villainy to expand the slaveholding territory, but Foote's lack of involvement in the fighting was not for ideological reasons but simply because his continuing eye problems made him unfit to serve at sea.

Foote's services were, however, in demand ashore. Commo. Joseph Smith, now chief of the new Bureau of Yards and Docks, wanted Foote to take an assignment at the Gosport Navy Yard. Although Foote declined the post, the two men continued to correspond, with Smith advising Foote on efforts in Congress to bring about temperance in the navy. The two remained very close, and because Smith continued in this post at the Bureau of Yards and Docks in Washington for the next twenty years he was well placed to help Foote in his subsequent naval career.[42]

Reportedly Foote did a fine job at the Charlestown Yard and won praise from Commodore Smith for his work there. He brought order to the yard, reorganized its fire department, oversaw a temperance society and Sunday school, and sat as a member on various courts-martial.[43] Never one to waste time, Foote also began to conduct naval experiments at the yard and came up with a bow propeller for steam warships. He believed that such a propulsion device would create a partial vacuum and throw aside much of the water offering resistance to the bow of the ship, thus yielding greater velocity than a stern-mounted propeller. Foote sent memoranda on his invention not only to Smith but also to the chief of the Bureau of Construction and Repair, Commo. Charles Morris. Although Smith offered encouragement, both he and Morris were unconvinced of the propeller's utility, and Foote ultimately abandoned the experiment.[44]

In September 1846 Samuel Foot, who had been in failing health, died at age sixty-five. John, Andrew's elder brother, now lived in Ohio, and many family responsibilities thus fell to Andrew. Strangely, it was in the days following his father's death that Andrew Foote decided to add the letter *e* to his spelling of the family name. Earlier ancestors had used the extra *e*, but not Foote's father or grandfather. Just what prompted this is unclear, but the *e* appears at the end of his last name in a letter written to Commo. Charles Morris on 20 October 1846. Foote's children continued the practice.[45]

Foote remained at the Charlestown Navy Yard post for two years until he was granted a leave of absence on 1 June 1848.[46] At the end of 1848, his family now included three children: In addition to his eleven-year-old daughter, Josephine, a son, Augustus, was born at the navy yard in April 1847. A second son, William, followed in December 1848.[47]

When his service at the navy yard ended, Foote actively sought a sea command. He had been in the navy for twenty-seven years, nineteen of them as a lieutenant. Few U.S. Navy lieutenants had his experience at sea or his reputation for excellent seamanship. In addition to these two essentials, Foote had powerful friends in Washington. But for four years he had not been at sea and he desperately wanted his own command, even though his eyesight was not completely recovered. Now, on 28 September 1849, Secretary of the Navy William Ballard Preston ordered Lieutenant Foote to report to the Gosport Navy Yard, there to take command of the brig *Perry*, which was being fitted out for service off the coast of Africa. Foote was hesitant, for this was not the service he desired, but he would look back on this assignment as one of the most rewarding of his entire naval career.[48]

❧ 5 ❧

AFRICA SERVICE

*T*he deployment of the *Perry* was part of an international effort to suppress the slave trade. The role of the United States in such efforts had been minimal up to that point; most of the effort to stop slaving had been carried on by the Royal Navy. There was strong antislavery sentiment in Britain, and in 1807 that government had abolished the British slave trade. Following the Napoleonic Wars, Britain stationed warships off the west coast of Africa to stop and inspect all vessels suspected of being slavers. When the British captured such vessels they returned the slaves to Africa and brought the crews to trial.

Initially the United States had supported the British enterprise. Although slavery was legal in the United States and the country was one of the world's principal slave-owning nations, the U.S. government had outlawed the importation of slaves after 1 January 1808. The law provided for forfeiture of slave-carrying vessels and their cargoes, with disposal of seized slaves left up to the state in which the ships were condemned. Congress strengthened this law with an act passed in March 1819 that offered a fifty-dollar bounty to informers for every illegally imported slave seized on land or at sea. A year later, in May 1820, Congress empowered President James Monroe to return illegal slaves to Africa and at the same time declared the foreign slave trade a form of piracy and provided the death penalty for Americans caught engaging in it.[1]

Secretary of the Navy Smith Thompson (1819–23) established a U.S. squadron to join the Royal Navy on African patrol and to capture slavers when and where they could be found, but few U.S. warships visited the African coast to enforce the ban. Thompson had first directed the ships of the Mediterranean Squadron to return to the United States via the West African coast and the West Indies, but this accomplished little. In 1821 he ordered Lt. Robert F. Stockton to cruise against the African slave trade in the new schooner *Alligator* and do what he could to assist efforts by the American Colonization Society to resettle freed slaves in Liberia. Thompson also ordered Lt. Matthew C. Perry to take the schooner *Shark* to cruise near the Madeiras and the Cape Verde Islands. But these efforts, too, were ineffectual; neither Stockton nor Perry had a notable effect on the slave trade.[2]

The Royal Navy's enforcement of antislaving measures was hindered not only by the failure of the U.S. Navy to provide significant assistance off Africa but also by the steadfast refusal of the United States to permit the British to search vessels flying the American flag, although most other nations had granted such permission. This was the natural consequence of the long and painful history of British searches of U.S. ships and impressment of American seamen, one of the major causes of the War of 1812.

Even as staunch an abolitionist as Secretary of State John Quincy Adams (1817–25) opposed granting the Royal Navy the right to search American ships. When British foreign secretary George Canning asked if there was anything more evil than the slave trade, Adams said, "Yes, admitting the right of search by foreign officers of our vessels upon the seas in time of peace, for that would be making slaves of ourselves." Strong southern political pressure also worked against enforcement of the ban on slaving, manifesting itself in declining congressional appropriations.[3] In 1819 Congress authorized $100,000 for suppression of the slave trade, but this shrank to $50,000 in 1823 and to $7,433.37 in 1839.[4]

As a consequence, most of the African slave trade was carried on in American-built vessels flying the Stars and Stripes. Swift American clippers immune from British search crowded the slave ports of Rio de Janeiro and Havana. Spanish, Portuguese, and Brazilian ships would often sail from Cuba or Brazil with false papers and an American onboard. If the ship were stopped by a Royal Navy vessel, the American would identify himself as the captain and present his fraudulent papers. By the early 1840s the situation was so bad that Governor of Liberia Thomas Buchanan claimed that the American flag was the chief obstacle to ending the slave trade.[5] In 1844 the American minister to Brazil reported:

> I regret to say this, but it is a fact not to be disguised or denied that the slave-trade is almost entirely carried on under our flag in American-built vessels, sold to slavers here, chartered for the coast of Africa, and these sold, or sold here—delivered on the coast. And, indeed, the scandalous traffic could not be carried on to any great extent were it not for the use made of our flag, and the facilities given for the chartering of American vessels to carry to the coast of Africa the outfit for the trade and the material for purchasing slaves.[6]

The slave trade could be very lucrative. On its very first voyage, the fast, 460-ton, Baltimore-built *Venus,* which had cost thirty thousand dollars, transported eight hundred slaves, which were then sold at a net profit of some three hundred dollars apiece, netting eight times the purchase price of the ship. Such profits seemed to justify the risks involved, even to the loss of the vessel.[7]

Mounting public pressure over the slave trade led President Martin Van Buren in 1838 to order the U.S. Navy again to patrol the West African coast. Although Secretary of the Navy James K. Paulding sent a number of small, fast vessels there, little was accomplished in actually halting the traffic in slaves.[8] In 1841, tension over the stopping of American ships by Royal Navy cruisers led President John Tyler to declare in a speech to Congress that he recognized no difference between the rights of visit and search. If the British detained ships that turned out to be bona fide American, Tyler said, they would be liable for damages. London, however, continued to press the United States either to permit Royal Navy searches or to send a sufficient number of vessels to the African coast to investigate suspected slavers flying the American flag. Finally, in 1842, the Webster-Ashburton Treaty, which settled the long-running boundary dispute between the United States and Canada, provided for the maintenance of joint British-American squadrons to suppress the slave trade along the African coast. Each power committed itself to maintaining an African squadron mounting at least eighty guns.

While the two squadrons would operate independently, they were to coordinate their actions to secure maximum effectiveness.[9]

In 1843, as a result of the treaty, Congress provided funds for a much larger Africa Squadron. Commanded by Commo. Matthew C. Perry, the squadron comprised four ships mounting a total of ninety-three guns. Perry's orders were to protect American commerce and suppress the slave trade as carried out by Americans or under the U.S. flag. But the orders also reminded Perry that Washington did not recognize the right of any other nation (i.e., Britain) to visit or detain vessels belonging to American citizens.[10]

Thus, in 1849, Foote found himself part Commo. Francis H. Gregory's five-ship African Squadron, which mounted a total of seventy-eight guns. Although not an abolitionist at this point, Foote was nevertheless determined to enforce the agreement on the slave trade. The squadron had an immense area to patrol, from westernmost Africa at Cape Verde in Senegal to Cape Frio in southern Angola. Slave ships might be loading their cargoes from any creek or estuary along five thousand miles of coastline. The West African coast was wild and inhospitable. Long known as the "white man's grave," the area had fewer than one thousand white inhabitants, the vast majority of whom were traders restricted to the few coastal settlements.

Given the paucity of its resources on station and the vast distances involved, it is hardly surprising that the U.S. African Squadron captured few slavers. From 1842 to 1850 it took only ten suspected American slavers, none of these during 1846–50. Despite Britain's willingness to risk America's anger by stopping all suspected slave ships, by 1847 as many as 100,000 slaves were being shipped to the New World each year.[11]

African service was immensely difficult. Most slavers were fast and difficult to catch, and conditions along the African coast were appalling. Searing heat alternated with torrential rains, ports of call were few, and ship crews ran the risk of contracting exotic diseases while in open boats on patrol. As one naval historian put it, "Hard work, yellow fever, frustration and adverse criticism were the usual rewards for African service."[12]

Although he was pleased to have his first command afloat and to be reunited with Gregory, his friend and first commanding officer, Foote was not excited about the prospects of African service. He actually wrote to influential Whig friends in Washington in an effort to get his orders changed to the Mediterranean Squadron. As it turned out, however, Africa was an ideal assignment for the highly principled Foote. He would have ample opportunity there to witness the horrors of the slave trade and help to prevent that traffic while protecting vessels flying the U.S. flag.[13]

The *Perry,* rated at ten guns, had been built at the Norfolk Navy Yard: launched in May 1843 and commissioned that October. The ship was 105 feet between perpendiculars and had a molded beam of 25 feet and a depth in hold of 11 feet, 6 inches. At 280 tons, the *Perry* was one of the faster ships in the U.S. Navy. Because the ship was judged "tender," in 1845 its rig was slightly modified and its armament reduced below its rate, a rarity in the navy. In and out of service throughout its life as a U.S. warship, the *Perry* had already cruised off Africa. Its armament consisted of two 32-pounder long guns and six 32-pounder carronades, and the crew numbered half a dozen officers and eighty seamen and marines.[14]

Foote busied himself preparing the *Perry* for sea, but he also found time to write to his close friends Commodore Smith and Lieutenants Dahlgren and Magruder for advice concerning his first command. All provided encouragement. Smith and Magruder exhorted Foote to continue his temperance activities, and Smith urged him to continue his regular Sunday services. Dahlgren made suggestions regarding the *Perry*'s ordnance. All three officers urged Foote to make the health of his men his top priority and to maintain firm discipline. To Dahlgren, Foote wrote in a pessimistic tone regarding his eyesight. Dahlgren replied that after five years with the same disease he had now recovered sufficiently to do away with glasses after having had to wear them for ten years. He urged Foote to be "cheery and hopeful," never an easy task for Foote.[15]

Recommissioned on 17 November 1849, the *Perry* underwent sea trials and then sailed from Hampton Roads for Africa on the twenty-seventh. Foote was pleased that he had been able to get all his crew members to sign the temperance pledge before sailing. The *Perry* made a fast twenty-three-day crossing of the Atlantic without incident, although most onboard were seasick because of stormy weather. The sloop joined the rest of the squadron at Porto Praya in the Cape Verde Islands on 21 December. Foote noted in his journal that the passage took half the time of some other Atlantic crossings.

After reporting to Gregory in the *Portsmouth* Foote prepared his ship for the adverse conditions that lay ahead. The continued stormy weather affected Foote's mood. He had stayed up late on deck at nights during

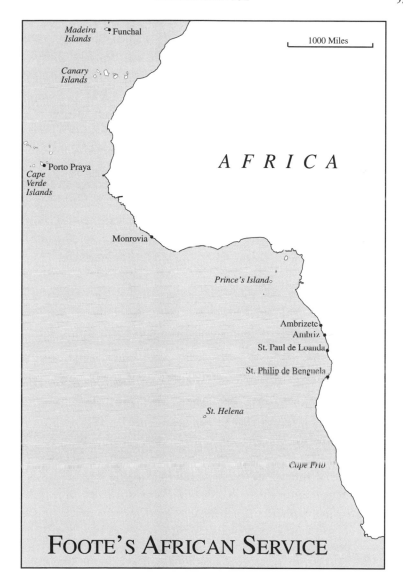

FOOTE'S AFRICAN SERVICE

the crossing and as a consequence had had little sleep, and he worried about his eyesight and health in general. Increasingly Foote turned inward and spent much time in prayer seeking forgiveness and guidance. On the first of January he wrote in his journal: "May God forgive, for His Son's sake, all my sins, and grant me his continual presence during the year upon which we are entering."[16]

In early January 1850 British authorities informed Gregory that American slavers were active along the African coast south of the equator. This area was south of the usual American cruising zone; indeed, no U.S. warship had been there for three years. Foote and Gregory conferred and agreed that the *Perry* should undertake a cruise of at least five months off the African coast as far south as thirteen degrees south latitude. Gregory called on Foote to carry out Secretary of the Navy Preston's instructions: to intercept American slavers while protecting lawful U.S. vessels from search by other nations, to examine principal slave-trading points below the equator, to cooperate with the Royal Navy where possible, to exercise his own judgment in other matters, and to look to the health of his crew.[17]

Foote was not optimistic about the latter, given his own poor health, and he judged his ship poorly equipped for the upcoming cruise. He had also discovered that his master and passed midshipmen were poor navigators; this forced him to take his own reckonings, which severely taxed his eyes. Despite these problems, Foote confided in his journal that he hoped the cruise would give him an opportunity to do humanity's work and that in the process he might "obtain a name" for himself, for "with the exception of doing good to our fellow man of how little value is everything else in this life."[18]

The *Perry* departed the Cape Verde Islands on 9 January 1850 and arrived at Monrovia, Liberia, ten days later to take on provisions for the long trip south. Foote was also able to secure fifteen days' additional provisions from the sloop *Yorktown* at Monrovia.[19] Founded in 1821 by the American Colonization Society with the aim of resettling blacks in Africa, the Republic of Liberia in 1850 was led by capable President Joseph J. Roberts, a Virginian of African descent. Foote arranged an exchange of visits, and when Roberts came aboard the *Perry* welcomed him with a twenty-one-gun salute. Monrovia's population was then two thousand people, and Foote was much impressed by what he saw there. He urged U.S. diplomatic recognition of Liberia and became an energetic supporter of the American Colonization Society. Convinced of the superiority of Western civilization and also of the duty of the whites to guide and uplift blacks, Foote saw a great future for America's freed slaves in Liberia. American Christian missions could play a key role by spreading the gospel and introducing a system of public education.[20]

Certainly Foote's visit to Monrovia was influential in shaping his attitude toward blacks. He believed that former slaves, despite having begun their lives in bondage, had "capacity beyond what we are inclined to admit."[21] In his 1854 book, *Africa and the American Flag*, Foote would state that while blacks had yet to add anything of beauty or importance to the world, Christianity would help them realize their promise. So, rather than sensing that the problem might lie with the attitudes of whites in the United States and working to change these, Foote argued that blacks could realize their potential by settling in Liberia.[22]

After a brief stop at Monrovia the *Perry* sailed south, reaching St. Philip de Benguela, the southernmost point of the ship's sailing station, forty-one days later, on 7 March. During the passage the *Perry* stopped and boarded three vessels; all were found to be legal traders.

Foote's health had worsened. In addition to problems with his eyesight, he developed headaches and lumbago and often was unable to leave his bed. The ship's doctor administered quinine and blisters. Foote wrote in his journal that his illness and disappointments had helped him spiritually: "I hope to trust in God, to recognize if it be his will that I die in this foreign land [or] in sea. I commend all my friends to his helping. I have tried to act well my part in life, but fear that as a follower of the Lord I have been sadly remiss; still I cling to Him."[23]

Foote was also having problems with several of his officers, including Acting Master Maurice Simons, but most notably with 1st Lt. William B. Renshaw. Although Foote was not opposed to corporal punishment, he preferred to influence the crew through example and religious instruction and use flogging as a last resort, but Renshaw and others did not agree with such an approach. Although this strife left him depressed, Foote wrote in his journal on 29 January: "I am determined however to carry out my own system wherever I do command."[24]

Foote was also handicapped in his operations because St. Philip de Benguela was so hopelessly removed from Porto Praya. It took the *Perry* two months to reach its southernmost station, leaving little cruising time before the brig would run short of water and provisions and have to return to Porto Praya. In his report to the Navy Department Foote argued unsuccessfully for a base closer to the center of slave-trading activities.[25]

On arriving off the Portuguese settlement of St. Paul de Loanda (Luanda), Foote learned that his duties extended far beyond an effort to intercept slavers. American merchants were conducting a growing trade in the region in dyestuffs, gums, and palm oil. In fact, the American financial stake was actually greater than that of the British, French, or Portuguese, all of whom had squadrons along the southern African coast and consuls to protect their interests.[26]

In a report to the Navy Department Foote recommended that the United States establish a permanent African coastal presence in "one or two men of war" and diplomatic personnel as well. He also detailed how slave running was conducted by ships carrying two sets of papers, one American and the other Brazilian. An American ship would be sold in Latin America but retain its original papers. It would sail to Africa with an American captain and crew and legitimate cargo. There its identity would change. Usually a Portuguese or Brazilian captain and crew would come onboard along with the cargo of slaves. It would then sail with the American papers, which the captain would present if the ship was stopped and boarded by the Royal Navy. In the unlikely event that it was stopped by a U.S. warship, the captain would present the ship's legitimate foreign registration.[27]

Although Foote publicly expressed his approval of the U.S. stance on refusing British captains the right to search ships flying the American flag, privately he was troubled by it, especially when he learned how slavers were using the American flag to avoid capture. The barque *Navarre*, for instance, was boarded by HMS *Firefly* on 19 March "when under American colors, and captured under Brazilian colors." The ship had six Americans in the crew but was clearly Brazilian. Foote believed that the U.S. government's approach had put the United States "on the side of the slave traders."[28]

The British captains patrolling off southwest Africa were glad to have a U.S. warship in the area and approached Foote about cruising with them. He quickly agreed, and the *Perry* soon headed for the area around Ambriz, a notorious slave port, to patrol with several British warships. Most of the time the *Perry* operated with HMS *Cyclops*, a steam frigate commanded by Capt. George F. Hastings. Foote stopped and checked all ships flying the U.S. flag and used the brig's boats to search close to shore for slavers and slave collection points. The boats were sometimes away for a week or more, often lost from sight in squalls and fog.[29]

The work was difficult, and it took a toll on Foote's health. Forced to spend much of the time in bed in his cabin, Foote became convinced that he was near death. The duty also affected his crew. Several applied for reinstatement of their grog ration, but Foote managed to talk them out of it. Foote continued to have problems with Renshaw, who had by now alienated much of the crew and the other officers.[30]

Foote must have been greatly cheered by the arrival in early April of the sloop *John Adams* to join the *Perry* on patrol. The association did not last long, however; the *Perry* was low on supplies and water and soon had to depart for Prince's Island in the Gulf of Guinea, there to rendezvous with Commodore Gregory and the *Portsmouth*. The *Perry* arrived at Prince's Island on 27 April, and Foote immediately reported to Gregory. The *Perry*'s cruise had lasted 107 days: 80 at sea and the remainder at anchor at various points along the coast.[31]

Gregory acknowledged receipt of Foote's letters and recommendations, which he believed the secretary of the navy would consider "most favorably." He also commended Foote for the "zeal, ability, and energy" with which he had discharged his duties. But as the *John Adams* was running short of provisions and would soon have to leave its patrol, Gregory ordered Foote to secure needed stores from the flagship and return to Ambriz.[32]

The brief stay on Prince's Island had done wonders for Foote's health. He enjoyed several restful days ashore, eating fresh food and being able to bathe. Not unrelated to the improvement in his health was his success in persuading Gregory to take on Lieutenant Renshaw as his flag lieutenant. Renshaw's transfer had an immediate calming effect aboard the *Perry*, and the crew again appeared happy.[33]

Gregory's new instructions to Foote were the same as before, with one notable exception. Gregory was unhappy with reports that the British were detaining suspect American-flag vessels and then threatening to hand them over to American warships for search. Gregory wanted Foote to assert U.S. authority if necessary. If a British captain decided to detain a suspected American ship, he must do so on his own authority and not think he could rely on U.S. Navy connivance.[34] Foote disagreed. He had come to realize that the American flag was not "conclusive proof" of nationality. While it would be wrong for the crew of a British warship to stop an American vessel and search it, no matter what its cargo, this did not apply to a ship that was falsely flying the American flag.[35]

Foote's boarding instructions, however, followed Gregory's orders:

If a vessel hoists the American flag—is of American build, has the name and place of ownership in the United States registered on her stern, or has but a part of these indications of her nationality—you will on boarding ask for her papers, which papers you will examine and retain, if she exacts suspicion of being a slaver, until you have searched sufficiently to satisfy yourself of her real character. If the vessel be American and doubts exist as to her character you will detain and bring her to this vessel, or if it can be done more expediently, you will dispatch one of your boats, communicating such information as will enable me to give specific directions, or to visit the vessel in person.

If the vessel be a foreigner, you will on the moment of ascertaining the fact, leave her, declining even the request of the captain to search, or to endorse her character as it must always be borne in mind that our government does not permit the search and detention of American vessels by foreign cruisers, and is consequently particular to observe towards the vessels of other nations the same line of conduct, which she exacts from foreign cruisers toward her own vessels. You will also remember that our squadron is on this coast solely for the protection of American commerce, and for the suppression of the slave trade as far as it may be carried on by American citizens, or under the American flag.[36]

The *Perry* now returned to its station off Ambriz. After boarding several vessels, all of which turned out to be legal traders, on 6 June Foote got lucky, probably because no U.S. Navy vessels were expected in the area for some time. At 3:00 P.M. a lookout on the *Perry* spotted a large ship standing in for Ambriz. An hour later the *Perry,* which had no colors flying, overhauled the ship, which had "Martha, New York" painted on its stern. The *Martha*'s captain, believing the brig to be a Royal Navy vessel, shortened sail and promptly hoisted the American flag. Foote then sent 2d Lt. (Acting 1st Lt.) Madison Rush to board the suspicious ship. Foote had known Rush as a midshipman at the Philadelphia Asylum and had great confidence in his judgment.

But as Rush's boat rounded the stern of the *Martha,* the captain, Henry M. Merrill, recognized the U.S. Navy uniform. He promptly ordered the U.S. flag hauled down and the Brazilian flag raised in its stead. When Rush demanded the ship's papers, Merrill said he had none. At the same time a lookout on the *Perry* saw men aboard the *Martha* throw something overboard and Foote sent another boat to retrieve it. It turned out to be the captain's writing desk containing the ship's log and papers identifying Merrill as an American citizen and stating that the majority owner of the vessel was another American, living in Rio de Janeiro. Although no slaves were aboard, all the equipment for the dreaded "middle passage" from Africa to the West Indies or the United States was in place, including a fully laid slave deck, 176 water casks filled with 100–150 gallons each, 150 barrels of farina and several sacks of beans to keep the human cargo alive during the passage, four hundred spoons, four boilers for cooking, and thirty to forty muskets.

Foote had ordered Rush to hold the ship to the first flag it raised. Captain Merrill, whom Rush had brought to the *Perry*, protested to Foote that his vessel could not be searched or seized while it was under the Brazilian flag. When Foote replied that he would seize the ship as a pirate vessel for sailing without papers, Merrill confessed that the *Martha* was indeed a slaver and that he had expected that same night to take onboard eighteen hundred slaves and would have been at sea before daybreak.

Although Merrill begged him not to do it, Foote ordered the *Martha's* thirty-five-man crew placed in irons and sent the ship to New York under Rush's command, along with Simons and a prize crew of twenty-five men, there to be condemned and sold. In New York, Merrill jumped bond and escaped punishment; his first lieutenant was convicted but sentenced to only two years in prison. The rest of the crew, being foreigners, were released. The capture of the *Martha* earned Foote congratulations from Captain Hastings, who told him that he had given the slave trade "the heaviest blow" it had received since he had been on the African station.[37]

The rest of the *Perry's* cruise was uneventful, although the men had to work harder than before because their numbers had been reduced by about one-third. Foote himself was buoyed by his triumph; short of officers, he busied himself with the daily operations of the ship. He was pleased that the crew retained a positive attitude despite the difficult conditions and added work. More than ever Foote believed that his approach to shipboard discipline, rather than the corporal punishment Renshaw favored, was correct. He wrote in his journal: "I shall in future insist upon my own system being rigidly followed."[38]

When at their next meeting Gregory praised Foote for the efficiency and hard work of his reduced crew, Foote saw an opening and attributed his success to his methods of discipline and especially to a grog-free environment. Foote's system of discipline was not quite perfect, however, as evidenced by the fact that the same week he ordered two of his crewmen flogged, one for drunkenness and the other for smuggling alcohol aboard ship.[39]

In early August the *Perry* returned to St. Paul de Loanda for a prearranged meeting between Foote, Gregory, and British squadron commander Arthur Fanshawe. On 15 August Commodore Fanshawe arrived in the *Cyclops* and the three men met to see if they might resolve their differences regarding searches of possible slavers. Fanshawe claimed that all of the vessels that had been taken by the Royal Navy were at least partially Brazilian. Had any of them clearly been U.S. vessels, he said, the British would not have interfered with them. Gregory argued that the British had indeed interfered with bona fide U.S. merchant ships, and that even if they were involved in illegal trade these ships were off-limits to British interference. Gregory said the U.S. Navy would be responsible for U.S. ships involved in the slave trade. As he put it, "We choose to punish our own rascals in our own way."[40]

Foote took no part in the discussions. It would have been inappropriate for him as a junior officer to question his commander, especially in such a delicate diplomatic matter, but Foote was clearly unhappy with the official U.S. position regarding searches. As he put it in his journal, "I had little or no sympathy for them & rather than had them escape was gratified that the English had captured them." Foote would have preferred that U.S. warships had taken them, but until the *Perry*, no U.S. warship had been off the southern African coast in at least two years and the United States had only rarely met its obligation to maintain an eighty-gun squadron on antislavery patrol.[41]

The meeting between the British and American commanders was interrupted on 18 August with the arrival of a British ship bearing news of a suspected slaver in Ambriz, less than a day's sail away. The Royal Navy had boarded it in the belief that it was Brazilian; on learning that the ship was American, they requested a U.S. Navy warship to conduct the search. Gregory immediately dispatched Foote to investigate. As the *Perry* was not quite ready to sail, Foote went on ahead in the brig's launch, which was commanded by Renshaw, now temporarily reassigned to the *Perry*. Unable to get along aboard the *Portsmouth*, too, Renshaw was about to return to the United States with dispatches but had volunteered for this duty.

Five hours later the *Perry* set out after its launch, and Foote was able to intercept the suspected slaver, the brigantine *Chatsworth* of Baltimore. The ship's papers seemed to be in order, but the crew was entirely foreign with the exception of the young American captain. Foote was certain the *Chatsworth* was a slaver and instructed Renshaw to sail it to Loanda for disposition. There he explained to Gregory his reasons for seizing the ship: the cargo included one hundred bags of farina, jerked beef, and casks and barrels sufficient to carry water for a large slave cargo;

and the *Chatsworth* also carried a quantity of plank sufficient to build a slave deck. A letter from the reputed owner of the ship, written in Portuguese, instructed the American captain to leave the ship whenever he was directed to do so by an Italian supercargo by the name of Francisco Serralunga, who seemed to be the final authority on the ship. Furthermore, the *Chatsworth* was known to have shipped a cargo of slaves on its last voyage and had been apprehended at a location notorious for slaving. Although Gregory agreed with Foote that the *Chatsworth* was probably a slaver, he nonetheless ordered the ship released, concluding there was insufficient evidence to gain a judgment in a U.S. court.[42]

At the end of August Gregory returned to Porto Praya; before departing he told Foote that, much as he regretted it, no other ships were available and the *Perry* would have to continue its patrol duties along the southern African coast. On 24 August 1850, the brig began another three-month cruise in the area. Foote had not forgotten about the *Chatsworth*, and he attempted a ruse in hopes of catching it in the act of slaving. The *Perry* originally sailed south from Loanda, but once out of sight of land Foote ordered a new course to the north for Ambriz. Again he caught the *Chatsworth* off Ambriz and conducted a thorough search, and again he could find no evidence of slave running. When Foote departed Ambriz on 5 September, he left behind some men in the brig's cutter to keep the *Chatsworth* under surveillance.[43]

Foote then sailed the *Perry* north to the Angolan port of Ambrizete. Believing it would be to the benefit of an American-owned factory there, Foote went ashore to meet with the queen. He reported to Gregory that he had tried to impress on her the advantages that would accrue from "trading with our people with gum, copper, bronze, instead of permitting her own people to be sold as slaves for the purchase of goods." The queen complained about boats from warships chasing her fishing boats and taking their catch, "the principal support of her people." Foote assured her that the U.S. Navy was forbidden to do this and that "we were her friends and the friends of her people." Foote concluded that occasional visits with native authorities would help increase U.S. trade.[44]

When the *Perry* again returned to Ambriz, Foote learned that four thousand slaves had been gathered at the port and were awaiting shipment. Determined to prevent this, on 11 September Foote ordered the *Chatsworth* seized. To ensure that this time the charges would stick, Foote secured statements from legitimate traders in the area that the ship had earlier been engaged in slaving activities and that its owner in Rio had admitted ordering it on another slaving voyage.

Foote informed Gregory that he could prove the *Chatsworth* carried both U.S. and Brazilian papers. He also managed to secure a confession from the ship's master of its true mission. The Italian supercargo, "Serralunga," who was ashore inspecting the slaves to be loaded when the vessel was seized, protested what he described as an illegal seizure and asserted that no U.S. court would ever condemn the vessel for slave running. He also threatened to sue Foote for at least fifteen thousand dollars in damages; Foote said he was willing to run that risk. Almost certainly Serralunga was Theodore Canot, a prominent figure in the African slave trade known as "Mr. Gunpowder" for his violent rages. Foote believed he was the real owner of the *Chatsworth*. Ignoring Serralunga's threats, Foote sent the *Chatsworth* to Baltimore under Acting Sailing Master Edmund Shepherd and Midn. Oliver P. Allen, where after a prolonged trial in district court the ship was indeed condemned as a slaver. Foote believed it to be a greater loss to the African slave trade than the loss of the *Martha*.[45]

In defying his commanding officer's earlier judgment and possibly embarrassing him, Foote once again risked his naval career; he also laid himself open to possible personal financial ruin. Just as he had done in Honolulu back in 1839 when he defended the American missionaries who were trying to improve the lot of the native Hawaiians, Foote pursued the course he believed to be morally correct, regardless of possible personal consequences.

The rest of the *Perry's* cruise was without incident, and on 19 September Foote ordered the ship to sail for the small island of St. Helena in the South Atlantic. During the passage there the *Perry* chased one vessel, which turned out to be a Portuguese brig. On 10 October the *Perry* arrived at Jamestown, St. Helena, for a ten-day stay and a well-earned rest for the crew. Foote promptly gave the men forty-eight hours' liberty.

Foote used his time on the island to visit sites of interest, including the residence where Napoleon died. He met many of the locals and welcomed a number of them aboard the brig. One of these was Caroline Jamish, a most attractive young woman of about nineteen. The forty-four-year-old Foote was immediately smitten. The two became close friends, and Foote described her as "a model lady. The ideal of woman." He confided in his journal that save for the fact that he already had an "encumbrance," Caroline would have been "in imminent danger" of being taken to the United States in his cabin. In a rather astonishing statement for one who always struggled to put the world and his ego aside, Foote wrote: "I have always had the vanity to suppose that any young lady to whom I might lay siege would ultimately yield."[46] There is no reason to assume that Foote's relationship with the young woman was anything but correct; Foote was happily married and told Miss Jamish to look on him as a father. Nonetheless the relationship was quite flattering to Foote and certainly enhanced the pleasure of his stay at St. Helena.

Foote also established a very cordial relationship with the British authorities on the island, although he did press his case in the matter of several vessels the British had captured. Foote held that because these ships carried false U.S. papers they should be considered as under U.S. Navy jurisdiction. The British may have thought this a matter of ego or cash incentive for Foote, but it was instead a purely legal issue. Privately he acknowledged that much of American African trade was indirectly bound up in the slave trade, and he never doubted the motives of the British: "I really believe . . . that the British officers generally mean to do right & act liberally in the suppression of the slave trade. Our flag has been much abused & I do wish that an arrangement might be made by which all slavers might be taken by any nation."[47]

After a passage of ten days from St. Helena the *Perry* arrived back at Loanda, where it remained for two days before cruising off Ambriz in the company of the *Cyclops*. Foote was able to report to Secretary of the Navy William Graham that after the capture of the *Chatsworth* there were "no suspicious American vessels on the Coast."[48]

At the end of December, his ship's food and stores almost depleted and his crew reduced to half by the need to man the captures, Foote ordered the *Perry* to return to Porto Praya. By then Foote and two young acting lieutenants were the only remaining officers. The *Perry* had been almost constantly on station for an entire year, during which time it had sailed some twenty-one thousand miles and had seriously damaged the southern African slave trade. In reflecting about the cruise in his journal, Foote expressed pride in his accomplishments. Without doubt it had been the most taxing year of his life, but "with God's blessing" he had handled a difficult and responsible diplomatic and naval assignment well and had accomplished much for himself, for the navy, and for his country.[49] In a private letter to him, British commissioner Jackson commended Foote, noting that Foote's captures had "at once changed the face of things. . . . And from the date of those very opportune captures not a vessel illicitly assuming American colors had been seen on the coast.[50]

On 8 January 1851, the *Perry* dropped anchor at Porto Praya. Foote hoped and fully expected that Commodore Gregory would order the *Perry* home. He and his men were worn out, and the *Perry* was now in serious need of repairs. Foote's concerns about his ship were real. Before leaving the United States he had pointed out that the brig had been rushed back into service without the overhaul it should have received after its previous cruise. But the chief of the Bureau of Construction Equipment and Repair, Commo. Charles Skinner, had informed Foote that repairs were unnecessary because the *Perry* would be gone no more than a year. Within a month after sailing, on 22 December 1849, Foote had written a long letter to Skinner enumerating his complaints: the *Perry* was leaking badly, the copper was worn out, and much of the rigging needed to be replaced. Now, more than a year later, he could add to that list the need for a new suit of sails and new wood and iron fittings.[51]

Instead of sending the *Perry* home, however, Gregory, who had few ships and a vast area of responsibility, ordered Foote to take his brig back on another Angolan cruise. Foote believed this could be a death sentence for him, and it led him to an explosion of anger and an indiscretion that almost caused Gregory to order him home without his ship.[52] The unstated and real causes of the feud that developed between the two men were Foote's anger at seeing his ship the only active member of the squadron and Gregory's refusal to allow the brig and its crew to go home. In order to relieve the serious shortage of officers on the *Perry*, Foote had requested that officers on the flagship be transferred to him. He especially wanted Lt. William C. Porter as his executive officer. Protocol and common sense dictated that he first informally ask Porter and then Gregory before making a formal request. A misunderstanding occurred, however, leading to a series of sharp notes between Foote and Gregory. Foote even asked to be relieved of his command to plead his case personally before the secretary of the navy. To his credit Gregory worked to defuse the situation by assuring Foote of his full confidence, support, and friendship based on their years of service together. Foote accepted Gregory's remarks as proof of vindication and made little subsequent mention of the affair in his journal.[53]

Assisted by two additional officers—one of them newly promoted First Lieutenant Porter—and some men to replace those sent home in the two prize crews, Foote now busied himself preparing the *Perry* for yet another cruise below the equator. The preparations included installing a new suit of sails provided by the sailmaker on the *Portsmouth*.

Foote also sought to make his points about his grievances by corresponding with weightier individuals. As usual, he turned to the sympathetic Commodore Smith, in the guise of informing him about the progress of the antislavery efforts. Foote pointed out that suppression of the slave trade would require more vessels and greater naval cooperation with the British. At the same time he told Smith about his own deteriorating health as well as the poor condition of his ship. Foote also wrote Connecticut senators Truman Smith and Roger Baldwin, telling them of his accomplishments and urging them to use their influence to return the *Perry* before it and its captain's health were irretrievably lost.[54]

The *Perry* departed Porto Praya on 20 February and arrived off Ambriz twenty-two days later. This third cruise off the coast of southern Africa was uneventful. British officials at Loanda informed Foote that there was now little slavery activity in the area, with only one slaver being taken since January. Foote then sailed his brig north to the vicinity of the mouth of the Congo River, another active point for the slave trade, where he again actively cooperated with the British squadron. The new British commodore told him that joint British-American efforts had virtually ended the slave trade on the southern coast. As the *Perry* represented almost the entire American effort in that regard, Foote must have been pleased.[55]

The more relaxed nature of the third cruise was reflected in a second visit to St. Helena in late May. There Foote again saw Caroline Jamish, and at the island's Baptist mission chapel he gave a lecture on the Christian missions of India. Later, after returning on station, Foote allowed his crew liberty in Elephants' Bay along the African coast south of the Congo River, where the men fished and hunted. Foote hoped to obtain a few rare tropical birds as specimens for the Philadelphia Academy of Science, but apparently the men were not sufficiently good shots.[56]

After a stop at Monrovia the *Perry* returned to Porto Praya on 30 June. Foote was disappointed that no U.S. warships were in port, as he had hoped to find the squadron there and receive orders to return home. The *Perry* was now leaking badly and its rigging and ironwork had further deteriorated. Foote was particularly anxious to sail the Atlantic in the summer; a winter crossing might prove disastrous for the brig in its weakened state. Morale was low and discipline had sharply deteriorated. There was a corresponding increase in punishments, and a number of members of the crew now petitioned Foote for restoration of the grog ration. Foote noted in his journal that even the officers were affected and "in a great state of excitement and indignation at Commodore Gregory."[57]

The new squadron commander, Commo. Elie La Vallette, had sailed a few days earlier but left word that Foote was either to wait at Porto Praya or to proceed to Funchal, Madeira. Foote elected to do the latter. The *Perry* arrived at Funchal on 8 August and spent six weeks there, and the shore liberty led to a prompt improvement in the crew's morale. Foote was furious, however, when he learned that Gregory, without personally inspecting the brig, had informed his successor that it was fit for additional service. Although the nimble *Perry* was the only one of Gregory's ships suitable for extended coastal work against slavers, Foote was certainly justified in his conclusion that the ship and its crew had earned a trip home. For the past two years the *Perry* had been the only vessel in the squadron actively employed while the other warships had remained largely in port. Foote now came to view Gregory as jealous of his accomplishments and determined to punish him, especially over the *Chatsworth,* which one British official claimed Gregory had "let slip through his fingers."[58] Foote also professed to be appalled by reports of lax discipline on the *Portsmouth,* and chose to believe stories that the crew of the flagship had talked Gregory out of patrolling the coast and had persuaded him to sail instead to Funchal, where the men passed the time drinking, gambling, and whoring onshore.[59]

The crew of the *Perry* behaved well at Funchal, considering the temptations available there. Foote had a good time ashore participating in the island's lively social life. He even visited a local winery to watch Madeira wine being made, although he declined to taste it. Foote became close with a number of wealthy Englishmen who wintered on the island, especially Lord Newborough and his wife, who had arrived on their steam yacht, the *Vesta.* Foote was clearly infatuated with Lady Newborough and noted in his journal that she had been called the most beautiful woman in England. Every day during the week the Newboroughs were at Funchal, Foote either dined with them or went on some excursion with Lady Newborough. For years thereafter he corresponded with the

Newboroughs. Although Foote was certainly lonely for his wife and family, he was also not above flattering his ego. He saw nothing untoward in his flirtations, and even praised himself in his journal for his conduct at Funchal in the face of the temptations he encountered there.[60]

After leaving Madeira on 20 September, the *Perry* arrived at Porto Praya on 1 October. Foote kept the brig near the port so he could react quickly in the event of orders to sail for home. Finally, on 12 November, Commodore La Vallette arrived at Porto Praya, came aboard the *Perry*, and informed Foote that he had just received orders dated 17 June to send the ship home. Foote could not understand why it had taken five months for the orders to reach him and blamed Gregory, who, he believed, should have acted on his own initiative.[61]

Foote and his crew worked quickly to prepare the *Perry* for what would now be a hazardous winter Atlantic crossing. On 15 November the crew hoisted anchor and the *Perry* sailed out into the Atlantic, accompanied by cheers from seamen on the other ships of the squadron: the *Porpoise*, *John Adams*, and *Germantown*. Foote wrote above the date of his journal entry for 17 November: "Home Sweet Home." Below that, he wrote: "Thus adieu to the coast of Africa. I hope from my heart to realize the goodness of our heavenly Father in directing me thus far in my course of duty. I shall never perhaps in life be called upon to act again so responsible a part on my own judgment."[62]

The Atlantic crossing, although cold, was without incident and was accomplished in twenty-six days. The only stormy weather encountered was off the U.S. coast on the approach to New York harbor. Believing the brig might be driven out to sea again if he waited for a pilot, Foote brought his ship into port himself. On 23 December 1851, the *Perry* tied up at the Brooklyn Navy Yard and was soon placed in ordinary, having been gone twenty-five months and traveled 40,500 miles.[63]

~6~

NAVAL REFORM ASHORE

*A*lthough he was glad to be home, Foote was to spend the next four years ashore, the longest such period since he had joined the navy. Tired and spent, he was no doubt pleased by his initial reception. He received an official letter of thanks from Commodore Gregory extending his "fullest commendation" for the way in which Foote had carried out his duties, and Secretary of the Navy William A. Graham (August 1850–June 1852) wrote to congratulate Foote on his safe return and to assure him of the complete satisfaction of the Navy Department. Secretary of State Daniel Webster also expressed approval. And Foote's confidante in Washington, Commodore Smith, reported that his talents were well appreciated and that he had "won honor and glory enough to rest upon your laurels for some time."[1]

Indeed, Foote's achievements had been remarkable. His crew had stopped and boarded seventy vessels. They had seized only two of these, but they were among the most important slavers taken in this period and both actions had been upheld by U.S. courts. Put in perspective, during the period 1843–57 the U.S. African Squadron took only nineteen vessels, of which only six were condemned. Foote's tally was a third of the total.[2] Foote also had worked hard to prevent disease and sickness in his ship. It is remarkable that not one crewman died during the *Perry*'s two years in African service; the death rate for the British squadron during the same period was 5 percent. Foote attributed the excellent health of his crew to not allowing the men to stay onshore at night and their lack of a grog ration.[3] Although Foote and his men were disappointed that they received no prize money for the two African captures, Foote at least had the satisfaction of having established his reputation as an energetic naval commander and an accomplished seaman. Later he claimed this was worth more to him than any financial gain.[4]

During the years Foote had been away on Africa duty, slavery had become an even more divisive issue in the United States. While still in Africa Foote had learned of the Compromise of 1850, and he had written in his journal that he considered the new fugitive slave legislation "odious and outrageous."[5] That same year had brought a major change in discipline in the navy with the abolition of flogging. The army had abolished corporal punishment in 1812, and there had been attempts to do the same in the navy. In 1820 Samuel Foot had introduced a resolution in the House of Representatives requesting that the Committee on Naval Affairs look into abolishing flogging as punishment in the navy, but the resolution failed to pass; and a bill abolishing flogging outright failed to win approval in 1844. Finally, in 1850, a bill advocated by Senator John P. Hale, assisted by former navy captain, now senator, Robert F. Stockton, passed Congress.

Foote agreed with the vast majority of U.S. Navy officers that the threat of corporal punishment was necessary in order to maintain naval discipline. He had ordered the lash used twenty-eight times aboard the *Perry* before he received word of its termination as punishment, but this was about half the average number of floggings per ship for the navy in this period. Although he was initially skeptical of the wisdom of abolishing flogging, Foote resolved to give what he referred to as the "experiment" a fair trial. He continued to believe that liquor was the cause of three quarters of the naval discipline problems necessitating flogging.[6]

Now that corporal punishment was no longer available, Foote believed that an end to liquor aboard ship was essential if discipline was to be maintained. In a letter to the *Sailor's Magazine*, Foote pointed out that there had been no problems on the *Perry* after flogging had been prohibited, but he attributed this to the fact that the ship was alcohol free. Foote repeated the same arguments in an open letter sent to a number of congressmen and in a speech delivered to a meeting of the Pennsylvania Seamen's Friend Society.[7]

Now, back onshore for an extended period, Foote flung himself into reform activities. In his free time he was a frequent public lecturer on such topics as temperance, improving conditions for sailors, suppressing the African slave trade, and support for overseas missionaries and the American Colonization Society in Liberia.[8] Although a northerner and a Whig, Foote had never been an abolitionist and regarded southern slavery as a rather benign institution. He found little of merit in African civilization and culture and believed that blacks had themselves begun the process of slavery in Africa by enslaving one another. He returned from Africa, however, convinced that the way to end slavery was to support efforts at colonization in Liberia. Foote joined the American Colonization Society and became one of its most ardent backers. In speeches he told of his firsthand knowledge of the effectiveness of the Liberian experiment. Foote was impressed with Liberia's leaders, especially President Joseph J. Roberts, and he was convinced that the country would soon become rich with an economy based on agriculture, mining, and trade. Liberia showed that blacks had capacities beyond those most whites were prepared to concede, and that they needed to be judged on their own merits; it could be a beacon for the rest of Africa. Privately Foote expressed the view that if he were black he would want to live in Liberia. Even if they were no longer slaves, he believed, blacks would still be in bondage to the white power structure and white racial attitudes as long as they remained in America.[9]

Foote was particularly concerned over the possibility that the African Squadron might be disbanded. There was much talk in Congress that U.S. warships were no longer necessary off Africa and that the squadron was a financial drain. Secretary of the Navy Graham was one of those who favored disbanding the African Squadron and allocating its vessels to the Home and Brazilian Squadrons. Foote opposed this possibility in a letter to Graham, in public speeches, and on trips to Washington that included conversations with Senator John M. Clayton of Delaware and even President Millard Fillmore.[10]

In April 1853 Foote received a letter from navy captain James L. Lardner of the *Dale,* who had just returned from Africa where his ship had captured two slavers. Lardner congratulated Foote on his 19 December 1852 promotion to commander and then went on to criticize the squadron's activities, noting that it seemed that "many of our naval officers are more afraid of slavers than the rascals are of them." This lack of action, he believed, had led to an increase in slaving, much to the shame of the U.S. Navy and the American flag.[11]

Lardner's letter may have been the final impetus for Foote, who in mid-1853 began work on what would be the first and only serious writing effort of his life, a book about Africa and the activities of the U.S. Navy's African Squadron. Foote knew that a book would reach a far wider audience than his speeches, and he saw it as a means both to persuade those in government to continue the effort to suppress the African slave trade and to publicize the experiment in Liberia. He also hoped to secure personal recognition. Increasingly concerned about his health and aware that because of the seniority system he might finish his naval career as a commander, Foote saw the book as his possible legacy.[12] Foote had ample time to write. His only navy duty during this period was to serve as judge advocate in the courts-martial of three officers held at nearby navy yards.[13]

At home, Foote recovered his health and wrote. His family now consisted of his daughter Josephine, sixteen; sons Augustus and William, aged six and five; and the newest addition to the family, daughter Emily, born in November 1852. Like Foote, Emily developed an eye disease, but hers was more severe; she lost her sight. Perhaps in part because of their shared eye problems, Emily was Foote's favorite child.[14]

In 1854 Foote published *Africa and the American Flag*. Dedicated to his friend Commodore Smith, the book is a well-written, sometimes eloquent account that stresses the contrasts of Foote's African experience:

> It is difficult in looking over the ship's side to conceive the transparency of the sea. The reflection of the blue sky in these tropic regions colors it like an opaque sapphire, till some fish startles one by suddenly appearing from beneath, seeming to carry daylight down with him into the depths below. One is then reminded that the vessel is suspended over a transparent abyss. There for ages has sunk the dark-skinned sufferer from "the horrors of the middle passage," carrying that ghastly daylight down with him, to rest "until the sea shall give up its dead," and the slaver and his merchant come from their places to be confronted with their victim.[15]

The first two-thirds of the book treat African geography, botany, climate, and zoology; the culture of western Africa; and Western efforts, including those of the United States, to halt the slave trade. This section contains much conjecture, but it also contains a history of Liberia and the operations of the American Colonization Society, whose records Foote relied on heavily in his writing.

The last third of the book, its most important part, records Foote's own experiences in Africa with the U.S. squadron. In this section he praised the Colonization Society and made a strong case for maintaining the U.S. African Squadron, arguing that it was necessary in order to protect a growing American trade with Africa from both slavers and illegal searches by Royal Navy warships. He also pointed out that the U.S. squadron had helped reduce the slave trade because slavers could no longer hide behind the U.S. flag, immune from British search. Finally, the squadron would assure the continuing success of Liberia and the spread of Christianity in Africa. He suggested alleviating some of the problems that faced the squadron by moving its base from Porto Praya to a location closer to the actual U.S. cruising station and adding fast steamers.[16]

Foote made clear the horror of the slave trade and heaped contempt on those who profited from it. One day they would have to answer to God for "the theft of living men, the foulness and corruption of the steaming slave-deck, and the charnel-house of wretchedness and despair."[17] Navy officers, educators, leaders in the colonization movement, Protestant clergy, and newspapers across the country all praised Foote's book, which was soon also published in London. Certainly it established Foote as a leading figure within the African colonization movement.

It is hard to determine the exact impact of the book on decision making in Washington regarding the African Squadron. Foote did send copies, along with covering letters, to influential friends in the capital, and during congressional debate on the issue Senator Clayton read from a letter Foote had written. But sentiment in favor of maintaining the squadron had already begun to grow when the new secretary of the navy, James Dobbin, had come out in favor of its continuation the year before. As it turned out, Congress did not change the status quo; the African Squadron continued its operations.[18]

On 9 March 1854, Dobbin assigned Foote to definite shore duty. He would resume his former post as executive officer of the Philadelphia Naval Asylum, where he would serve for the next fifteen months. Although the Asylum no longer housed midshipmen, it did still house the naval hospital and more than a hundred pensioners. Foote was probably posted to the Asylum because there had been disciplinary problems there, especially in the smuggling in of liquor. On the first day of his arrival Foote delivered a temperance speech, and soon thereafter he organized a temperance society. He also ended the smuggling of liquor.[19]

This time Foote's tenure at the Asylum was a happy one. His family joined him there, he received lavish praise for his book, and he and his wife enjoyed Philadelphia's social activities. Foote also was much in demand as a speaker on a variety of reform topics, and Philadelphia's proximity to Washington allowed him to meet with naval friends and political allies when necessary.[20]

In the capital the capable James Dobbin pushed naval reform. The U.S. Navy in the mid-1850s had about seventy ships, and Dobbin was determined to both modernize this force and increase its numbers. His powerful congressional contacts were of great help in enabling him in 1854 to secure funds to construct at least six first-class, propeller-driven steam frigates. Two sailing frigates, the *Santee* and *Sabine*, were to be modernized and an old ship of the line, the *Franklin,* converted into a first-class steam frigate. This was a significant increase in U.S. naval strength, as each of the new ships would be capable of carrying fifty guns.

Dobbin also supported the efforts of Foote's good friend Lt. John Dahlgren to improve U.S. Navy gunnery and to introduce new ordnance. Stationed at the Washington Navy Yard, Dahlgren conducted ranging of the existing navy guns and carried out a series of ordnance experiments. These led him to develop a new boat howitzer and to propose new 9- and 11-inch shell guns that would constitute a new system of ordnance for the U.S. Navy. Because of Dahlgren's numerous political contacts, his presence in Washington was a considerable advantage to Foote.[21]

No less pressing in Dobbin's view than strengthening the navy through more ships and improved ordnance was reform of its organization and administration. Dobbin secured congressional approval for a system of assimilated rank between line officers and the growing number of staff officers. In 1855 Congress agreed to a revision of the navy's penal code that embodied a number of officer recommendations, including allowing ship commanders to order summary courts-martial that could inflict minor punishments such as confinement in irons on bread and water, stoppage of pay and liberty, and dishonorable discharge. This ended the issue of reviving flogging.[22]

But above all else in importance was the matter of the seniority system. Dobbin noted in 1853 that "the great evil in our present system is,
that neither merit, nor service, nor gallantry, nor capacity, *but mere seniority of commission* [emphasis in original], regulates promotion and pay."[23]
A growing chorus of voices from both inside and outside the navy had
been urging replacement of the seniority system with a merit-based
promotion system. The main argument for the seniority system had
been fear of favoritism in appointments, leading to an aristocratic officer corps and a possible threat to the republic. The number of officers
in each rank had been fixed by law, but decades of indiscriminate midshipman appointments had led to a bloated officer corps in which those
holding lower ranks had little chance of promotion and with the upper
ranks completely filled by older men. In 1854 the navy had sixty-eight
captains, the youngest of whom was fifty-six years old. There were
ninety-seven commanders, of whom seventy-four were between the ages
of fifty and fifty-five. The navy's 327 lieutenants were between thirty and
fifty years old; and its 198 passed midshipmen ranged in age from twenty-
one to thirty-seven. This meant that a lieutenant could expect to be promoted to commander at age fifty-three, and a commander could expect
to reach captain at age seventy-four.[24]

Since the mid-1840s secretaries of the navy had established a system
whereby officers who were incapacitated by age and reason of health
would not be sent to sea but given nominal shore duty or no duty at all
while on leave-of-absence pay. But this did not have much effect on promotions because the officer corps was so bloated in its higher ranks.[25]
Justice and efficiency demanded the situation be changed. Dobbin wanted
President Franklin Pierce to appoint a commission consisting of officers
of different ranks to examine the whole promotion system and develop a
list of those officers who should be retired and those to be promoted. This
would then be subject to presidential approval, reversal, or modification.
Senator Stockton had introduced such a bill in the Senate in January
1853; later it was championed by Senator Stephen Mallory of Florida,
chairman of the Senate Committee on Naval Affairs and a powerful
voice for naval reform.[26]

Foote was keenly interested in the creation of such a board; certainly
he had a vested interest in culling some of the deadwood from the service. After all, he stood ninety-second among the ninety-seven commanders, in spite of the fact that he was one of the most experienced officers

in the service. More to the point, for twenty years Foote had advocated reform of the seniority system. Now, from Philadelphia, he wrote letters to members of Congress urging passage of Dobbin's proposal. It is unclear if Foote's lobbying had any effect, but on 28 February 1855, Congress passed "An Act to Promote the Efficiency of the Navy." This legislation created a review board of fifteen officers: five captains, five commanders, and five lieutenants.[27]

At this time Foote had been actively seeking a command at sea. In particular, he wanted to command the expedition to locate American Arctic explorer Elisha Kent Kane, who had set out in the spring of 1853 to find English Arctic explorer Sir John Franklin, who had disappeared along with his two ships. Kane had also vanished, and there was public support for an expedition to find out what had become of the two explorers and their men. Commodore Smith in Washington warned Foote to be ready for imminent orders. But others went north to the Arctic while Foote was ordered south to Washington to serve on the new review board.[28]

Commander Samuel F. Du Pont headed the Naval Efficiency Board, as it was called. Du Pont had been the most vocal navy advocate of such a board, and he told Dobbin that it should be made up of those in the navy who were outspoken advocates of reform—all of whom were his close friends. Along with Du Pont, the board's most influential members were Commos. William B. Shubrick and Matthew C. Perry. Foote had known Du Pont for twenty years and was a natural choice to serve; Du Pont offered him one of the five spots reserved for commanders.[29]

Officially appointed by President Pierce on 5 June 1855, the board was to convene in Washington as soon as possible. Du Pont considered it an act of moral courage to serve on the board, and all of its members, including Foote, were well aware of the risks it entailed. Despite the danger to his career, Foote welcomed the challenge.[30] Dobbin instructed the board to determine the capacity of all officers to perform all duties afloat and ashore. It would then decide those individuals in every grade who should be retained on active duty, those to be placed on the inactive list with leave pay, those who should be on furlough pay, and those who should be retired altogether. To assist in the board's deliberations he agreed to make available all Navy Department records.

Between 20 June and 26 July 1855 the board examined the careers of 712 officers and determined that 201 of them were incapable of performing all duties afloat and ashore. Of these, it placed 71 on leave-of-absence pay and

81 on furlough pay; it discharged 49 altogether. While he did not agree with all the board's decisions, Dobbin believed that on the whole they were fair, and he was confident that any errors could be corrected. He endorsed the report and sent it on to President Pierce, who consulted with Du Pont, Shubrick, and Dobbin, and then approved it on 12 September.[31]

As might be expected, there was an immediate and sharp outcry from within the navy. Dobbin himself noted: "Perhaps no event, either legislative or executive, touching the history of the Navy, has attracted more earnest attention, or created a more profound sensation, than the action of the late Naval Board."[32] Unfortunately, in his zeal to push for reform Dobbin had undermined his own efforts. In subsequent congressional debate it came to light that the board had deliberated for only 140 hours, or an average of only thirteen minutes on each officer's career. It had also failed to keep records of its deliberations and voting, and its members refused to disclose the bases of its decisions. All of this enhanced a feeling of paranoia in the navy and heightened charges of conspiracy, which helped diminish the board's accomplishments. But the publicity also exposed the serious problems in the seniority system and the need for reform and a retirement program. Although the board did break the logjam in promotions, many of those initially dropped were ultimately restored, thus swelling once again the list of active duty officers.[33]

Foote found his service on the board "exceedingly unpleasant," but he was also certain that it was necessary and that the results were on the whole fair (although he did give advice for an appeal to at least one friend retired by the board, and he also wrote Dobbin to request that he restore a former shipmate to active duty). Foote also wrote to fellow board members suggesting that they might testify before Congress to explain how decisions were reached, but none supported the idea.[34]

Although some officers did harbor resentment toward those who had served on the board, Foote seems to have largely escaped censure. As one of his biographers has noted, Foote was popular with his fellow officers because "he never allowed his personal ambition to manifest itself as jealousy or envy. He rarely spoke ill of another and always appeared genuinely happy in the success of others. If his religious sense of duty, and his obligation to the service, gave him an immutable drive to push naval reform, no one doubted his sincerity or earnestness."[35]

Foote soon resumed his normal routine. He escorted his eldest daughter, Josephine, to Washington, where the seventeen-year-old made her debut. In October Caroline gave birth to the couple's fourth child, and Foote's fifth: Maria Eudocia. But despite his contentment in his family, Foote longed to return to sea duty. He had now been ashore four years.[36]

In November 1855 Secretary Dobbin assured Foote that he would soon get a sea assignment. Foote had hoped for the Mediterranean station, perhaps even to command one of the navy's new steam sloops. He wanted to return to sea as soon as possible, however, and the first opportunity turned out to be a command in a different ocean altogether. On 5 April 1856, Dobbin ordered Foote to take command of the sloop *Portsmouth* and join the East India Squadron.[37]

~7~

CHINA SERVICE

oote was soon busy preparing the *Portsmouth* to join Commo. James Armstrong's East India Squadron. Rated as a first-class sloop but at 1,022-tons actually a big corvette, the *Portsmouth* was the second ship in the U.S. Navy to bear that name. The newest *Portsmouth* was constructed at the Portsmouth Navy Yard, launched in October 1843, and commissioned a year later. Considered a fast sailer, the sloop was 151 feet, 10 inches between perpendiculars; 38 feet, 1 inch in beam; 17 feet, 2 inches in depth of hold; and shipped 210 officers and men.[1]

The *Portsmouth* was one of the first ships in the navy to mount the new shell guns developed by John Dahlgren. Lighter in weight in ratio to their projectiles than the shot guns they replaced, they were designed to project large shells at a relatively low velocity. For centuries, solid shot was the principal projectile at sea. But wooden ships could sustain a tremendous amount of punishment, and even a shot penetrating a ship's side might leave only a small hole on the outside because the wooden fibers tended to close back again after a shot had passed through. Even if the hole was near the waterline, a carpenter could usually fill it with a wooden plug. In any case, it took a tremendous number of shots to sink a vessel. Most vessels lost in battle were not sunk but instead disabled by damage to masts and spars or succumbed to too many personnel casualties or to boarding.

The new shell was designed to lodge in the side of its target vessel and explode, producing greater personnel casualties but also causing large, irregular holes that would be difficult to patch. Shell offered the opportunity actually to sink an opposing ship. For this cruise the *Portsmouth*'s initial mixed battery of four 8-inch (64-pounder) shell guns and eighteen 32-pounders was replaced by a single-gun battery of eighteen 8-inch, 63-cwt (hundredweight, or 112 pounds) shell guns.[2]

It took time to mount the new battery; then there was difficulty securing sufficient crew to man the ship; by late March the *Portsmouth* was still short a hundred men. Foote did what he could to get crewmen, working his contacts in Washington. Adding to his problems was a brief bout with scarlet fever.[3]

Secretary Dobbin was anxious to have the *Portsmouth* sail as soon as possible to augment the American naval presence in the Far East. This region of the world, particularly Japan and China, was of increasing importance to the United States. Japan had been virtually isolated from the West since the seventeenth century, but in 1852, concerned about the well-being of shipwrecked Americans and anxious to open commercial relations, the Fillmore administration had sent a squadron to Japan under Commo. Matthew C. Perry. The commodore had returned to Japan in 1854 with seven ships to sign a treaty of friendship and commerce with that country.[4] China was now the immediate concern. American trade there was rapidly expanding, and Dobbin instructed Foote to protect "our valuable trade with China" as well as American whalers in the Far East. He was also "to enlarge the opportunities of commercial enterprise."[5]

The *Portsmouth* sailed from Norfolk on 4 May 1856. Once at sea, Foote drilled the crew on the new guns and worked to establish the same discipline system based on temperance and religion that he had employed so successfully aboard the *Perry*, although this time there could be no resort to the lash as final enforcement. Before sailing, Foote had gotten almost all the men to agree to forgo their spirit ration, and no alcohol was served during the Atlantic crossing. This helped solve another problem aboard ship—a shortage of space occasioned by the larger shells of the all 8-inch battery. The now-empty spirit room provided a place for these. Later, some of the crew broke their pledge so that the *Portsmouth* was no longer an all-temperance ship, but by then there were also fewer shells to store.[6]

Once the *Portsmouth* was at sea a serious problem arose. In the course of a gale and thanks to a faulty seal, some five thousand gallons of fresh water washed out of the tanks, leaving only about sixteen thousand gallons aboard. Foote regained some water by having the men stretch a large awning to catch rainfall, but this did not make up the shortage. On 27 July the *Portsmouth* was still thirty-four hundred miles from the East Indies and down to only three thousand gallons of fresh water. But Foote was one of the best seamen in the navy and the *Portsmouth* was a fast ship. On 2 August the ship entered the Sunda Straits, and after ninety-five days at sea, on the seventh made landfall in Batavia, where the Dutch authorities were quick to help. Foote replenished the ship's water and food, and after several days the *Portsmouth* sailed for Hong Kong, headquarters of the U.S. East India Squadron, by way of Macao. The sloop reached Hong Kong on 29 August; the journey from the United States had taken 116 days. Commodore Armstrong, who was at Shanghai while his flagship, the steam frigate *San Jacinto,* was undergoing repairs, directed Foote to remain at Hong Kong until he returned.[7]

China was then in chaos. The principal Western nations were trying to take advantage of China's weakness following its crushing defeat in the First Opium War (1839–42) to advance their own positions. According to the August 1842 Treaty of Nanking, China ceded Hong Kong to Britain and agreed to open treaty ports in Canton, Amoy, Foochow, Ningpo, and Shanghai. The United States soon demanded concessions as well, and in the 1844 Treaty of Wangxia forced China to grant it the same commercial status enjoyed by the British.

The Chinese imperial government in Beijing was seriously handicapped in dealing with the foreigners because it was waging a two-front war: against the Western governments seeking commercial and political concessions, but also a ferocious internal civil war, the great Taiping Rebellion (1850–64). Perhaps the single most destructive war of the entire century, the rebellion directly and indirectly claimed some twenty million lives.

In October 1856 fighting broke out again between Britain and imperial China at Canton (today Guangzhou) in what became known as the Second Opium War (sometimes called the Arrow War). The immediate cause of the war was the seizure at Canton of the lorcha *Arrow* and the arrest of its crew on smuggling charges. The Chinese-owned *Arrow* was registered in Hong Kong and flew the British flag. The incident brought an immediate demand from the British for the return of the lorcha and its crew. Chinese officials released a few members of the crew but claimed the British lacked jurisdiction because the Hong Kong registry of the *Arrow* had expired.

British officials consulted with Adm. Sir Michael Seymour and decided on an ultimatum with a twenty-four-hour deadline. Despite last-minute concessions by the Chinese, on 23 October Seymour's men stormed ashore and captured the four barrier forts, Canton's main defenses, located on both sides of the Pearl River by Whampoa Island, some twelve miles from the city proper. The British spiked the guns and burned the interior buildings, but made no effort to dismantle the thick stone walls.[8]

On 6 October Commodore Armstrong reported that Chinese revolutionaries were headed toward Canton and ordered Foote to be ready to assist in protecting Americans and their property there. This would mean moving the *Portsmouth* to Whampoa, but Armstrong left it up to Foote's "discretion and judgment how and when to act in the matter." On the tenth, Foote weighed anchor at Hong Kong and moved his ship seventy miles up the Pearl River to Whampoa.[9]

The U.S. consul in Canton, Oliver H. Perry (son of Commo. Matthew C. Perry), warned Foote that the British might attack Canton and asked that he take steps to protect American lives and property in the "factories" area on the outskirts of the city. Foote received the message at 2:30 A.M. on 22 October. At 3:00 A.M. he ordered "all hands" and had the sloop's boats hoisted out. At 6:20 A.M. Foote led ashore eighty seamen and marines armed with muskets and the sloop's boat howitzers. The factories were essentially a compound where foreign merchants lived and which contained their business and manufacturing concerns. Foreign merchant vessels were also supposed to load and offload their Canton cargoes there. The Americans arrived at the Canton factories at 9:00 A.M. and quickly took up positions to protect the compound, including the nearby French consulate, against a Chinese attack.[10]

Meanwhile the Chinese governor, Yeh Ming-ch'en, ordered all foreigners to leave Canton. Antiforeign sentiment was at the boiling point, and Yeh pointed out that the Chinese had difficulty telling the difference between British and Americans and their two flags. Indeed, the Chinese had fired on the *Cum Fa* (also *Kum Fa*), a small steamer traveling from Macao to Canton that had been flying the U.S. flag.[11]

After the British attacked Canton, Foote ordered fifteen additional seamen from the *Portsmouth* to his position at the factories. He also sought assistance from Cdr. William Smith, captain of the U.S. Navy sloop *Levant,* which had arrived in Hong Kong on 24 October. Smith traveled to Canton by boat ahead of his vessel, bringing with him 69 officers and men. This gave Foote 160 men to guard the compound. Smith also brought an order from Armstrong dated 17 October. No longer concerned about the movement of Chinese revolutionaries to Canton, he ordered Foote to take the *Portsmouth* on a four-month cruise along the south China coast, visiting ports and gathering intelligence that might be useful to Washington. Foote chose to disregard the order until Armstrong could be made aware of recent events in Canton.[12]

The Americans were uneasy over the gunfire and fires in Canton. On 27 October the British began shelling the city, and two days later British troops breached a section of the city wall and moved into Canton, ransacking Yeh's residence before they withdrew. Undermining Foote's efforts to preserve U.S. neutrality was a report that the U.S. consuls to Canton and Hong Kong, Oliver Perry and James Keenan, had accompanied the British assault. A drunken Keenan had carried a large American flag, which he waved over the city walls and then raised at Commissioner Yeh's residence. Reportedly he and Perry had also participated in the looting of Yeh's house. Keenan always denied these stories, but they circulated widely and Foote believed they were true. In any case the reports were a source of both concern and anxiety for the American sailors and marines at the foreign compound. Within hours of receiving the news, on 29 October Foote issued in his own name a circular in which he disavowed the American diplomats' actions, reaffirmed his government's neutral stance, and specifically prohibited any unauthorized use of the American flag. With this action Foote sought to reassure the Chinese that he was at Canton only to preserve American lives and property.[13]

Consul Keenan immediately sent Foote a sharp reproof protesting the circular and its criticism of his actions. He informed Foote that he planned to lodge a formal protest of what he regarded as a usurpation of his authority. Foote did not back down, informing Keenan that he alone would determine when and where the American flag was to be displayed. He also reported to Armstrong that the Chinese had not threatened the Americans and that Yeh had been courteous and correct in his communications. Further, Keenan's actions in joining the British assault with an American flag had seriously compromised American neutrality. Apparently Keenan thought better of protesting Foote's position; he and Foote both agreed to withdraw their letters.[14]

Meanwhile the situation at Canton remained stalemated. The British did not have the force to subdue the city and resorted to sporadic bombardment. They also cleared the river of sunken vessels and abandoned the barrier forts altogether. Commissioner Yeh, meanwhile, made no move against the Western factories. But with fires visible at Canton, Foote was undoubtedly relieved to have the *Levant* arrive at Whampoa.[15] While Foote was awaiting the arrival of Armstrong and the *San Jacinto* so that the commodore could decide whether or not to evacuate the Americans from Canton, Chinese soldiers twice fired on American sentinels and Foote ordered his men to return fire. Although no casualties were reported, the incident had led Foote to order the *Levant* from Whampoa to Canton. The *Levant* drew less water than the *Portsmouth,* and Foote believed its presence might ease the threat to Americans. If not, he would have available its firepower, and he could also use the sloop to evacuate Americans should that be necessary. At the same time Foote sought to avoid any act that might draw the United States into the fighting. He ordered his men not to fire unless fired upon, and even then they were first to shoot over the heads of their assailants. He warned his men that they were there only to protect American lives and that "any fire upon the Chinese who are not invading the rights of Americans is a murderous and wanton sacrifice of human life and will be severely punished."[16]

On 8 November Armstrong arrived at Hong Kong in the *San Jacinto.* That same day Foote sent a report to the commodore in which he noted that although no Americans had died in the nearly two and a half weeks of fighting, Yeh had requested that the Americans leave Canton for their own safety, along with their protective military force. Foote told Armstrong that he would keep his men in place until the situation no longer required them or Armstrong ordered him to leave. Somewhat surprisingly, Foote concluded his letter by saying that Yeh had failed to explain why the Chinese had fired on the *Cum Fa,* and that if a satisfactory response was not forthcoming and Armstrong did not arrive soon, he would "take such action as circumstances may require, in vindication of the insult offered to our flag."[17]

Foote also reported to Armstrong that Admiral Seymour, no doubt anxious to involve the United States in the fighting, had offered Royal Navy protection should an evacuation of Americans prove necessary.

Seymour had also offered to assist in revenging the insult to the American flag in the *Cum Fa* incident, but because the *Levant* was expected, Foote had declined. Foote said that otherwise he would have accepted Seymour's offer. Showing his pro-British bias, Foote wrote a naval friend whom he believed to be an anglophobe that the United Kingdom was "a nation altogether in advance, of any European, in promoting Christian civilization and the highest interests of mankind."[18]

On arriving at Hong Kong, Armstrong met with the American commissioner to China, Peter Parker, and then decided to investigate the situation for himself. He proceeded upriver in the *San Jacinto* and arrived on 12 November at Whampoa, where he received Foote's letter of 8 November and immediately ordered marine reinforcements to Foote. He also wrote to Secretary of the Navy Dobbin, informing him of the situation and expressing strong approval of Foote's actions. Foote, he said, had "taken every measure and precaution that prudence can suggest for the protection and safety of our countrymen and their property."[19]

On 14 November Foote traveled downriver to Whampoa to confer with Armstrong. The British had by then removed some of their force from Canton; this, and his fear that even the mere presence of U.S. forces at Whampoa might somehow draw the United States into the fighting, caused Armstrong to order Foote to withdraw his land force from the foreign compound. The two men agreed that the *Levant* would remain offshore to protect the factories and provide a place of refuge for Americans if the need should arise.[20]

On 15 November Foote and his party set out for Canton in a ship's boat to carry out the planned evacuation. Despite the fact that the boat prominently flew a U.S. flag and was unarmed, Chinese gunners in one of the four barrier forts opened fire on it from point-blank range. The Chinese fired two shots: the first fell a short distance from the boat, the second struck nearer and ricocheted on beyond it. The Chinese action has never been satisfactorily explained, but it was the work of local commanders who probably mistook the Stars and Stripes for the Union Jack. Foote returned the fire with the only weapon available, a pistol. As the Americans pulled back out of range, a second fort opened fire on the boat with a mixture of solid shot and grape, also without effect, although the shots were quite close. In all, the Chinese fired on the boat five times. Foote now returned to the *San Jacinto* to report the incident to Armstrong.[21]

The previously cautious Armstrong wasted no time in demanding that this insult to the flag be swiftly avenged without recourse to diplomacy. He ordered Foote and Capt. Henry H. Bell of the *San Jacinto* to secure several steamers to tow the *Portsmouth* and *Levant* into position in order to shell the barrier forts.[22] The four forts appeared to be formidable structures; their massive stone walls contained a total of 176 guns—many of which were of 8-inch caliber or larger—and they were manned by some five thousand Chinese. But these were also the same forts the British had occupied and partially neutralized earlier.

On the morning of the sixteenth Armstrong sent a steamer to Canton to remove most of the men who had been guarding the factories there. He also sent Lt. James Williamson in an armed cutter with a pilot to sound the channel near the forts. When this boat came within a mile and a half of the forts it too came under Chinese fire. This time the Chinese gunnery was more accurate; Coxwain Edward Mullen was decapitated by a cannonball while heaving the sounding lead.[23]

The men from Canton arrived at the American anchorage by noon, and the ships were now up to complement. Armstrong then ordered the steamers *Willamette* and *Cum Fa* to tow the *Portsmouth* and *Levant*, respectively, to the forts. The *San Jacinto* drew too much water to be able to participate, so Armstrong transferred his flag to the *Portsmouth*, leaving Lieutenant Williamson behind with a skeleton crew of sixty men. The other men Armstrong divided between the *Portsmouth* and the *Levant*.

It took the steamers several hours to maneuver the American warships into position up the narrow Whampoa Channel, but by 4:20 P.M. the *Portsmouth* was positioned some five hundred yards from the first fort. The *Levant*, however, had grounded about a mile away and was unable to join in the attack. Before the *Portsmouth* had even dropped anchor the Chinese opened fire. Foote quickly responded with his shell guns, concentrating on the nearest and largest fort. Over a two-hour period the *Portsmouth* fired 230 shells and some grapeshot. The Chinese gunners, who fortunately had only solid shot, hulled the *Portsmouth* six times during the exchange, but the only American casualty was one marine seriously wounded. At nightfall the Chinese guns fell silent. In his official report to Dobbin, Armstrong commended Foote for his "coolness and skill in handling the *Portsmouth* under fire." A veteran of the War of 1812, Armstrong also had high praise for the sloop's crew and reported that he had never seen such steadiness in battle or precision of fire. Interestingly, this was Foote's first time under fire in his thirty-four years in the navy.[24]

That night a rising tide helped refloat the *Levant,* which was moved into position near the *Portsmouth,* although the river's swift current made it difficult for the Americans to maintain their firing position. In the morning, when the tide dropped, the *Portsmouth* grounded in turn. Worse, it was in such position that only one of its guns could be brought to bear on the forts. For much of the day the *Portsmouth* remained in this exceedingly vulnerable position, but, for whatever reason, the Chinese failed to take advantage of the situation to renew their fire. A rising tide in the afternoon freed the *Portsmouth* and Foote was then able to bring it into position so that its port broadside guns could bear on the other forts.

When the Chinese did not resume shelling the American ships in the morning, Armstrong departed for Whampoa to demand an explanation of the attack from Chinese authorities. After conferring with Commissioner Parker on the eighteenth, Armstrong sent a note to Yeh demanding a formal apology and warning that if none were forthcoming within twenty-four hours he would take whatever steps he thought necessary. Yeh failed to respond within the time limit specified, and when he did answer merely requested that in the interest of safety the Americans withdraw their ships from the river. Armstrong took a bellicose stance; his reply accused Yeh of waging war against the United States.[25]

Before he departed, Armstrong had ordered Foote to remain in position near the forts but not to open fire unless he was first fired upon. In a message sent to Foote by fast steamer, Armstrong said that he hoped that negotiations would defuse the crisis, but he warned Foote to be vigilant. If attacked, Foote was to "spare them not, take their forts and level them to the ground." There were then only sixty men onboard the *San Jacinto,* and Armstrong requested the return of forty of the crew to help defend his flagship if that should prove necessary. This would leave Foote with some five hundred men on the *Portsmouth* and *Levant.*[26]

Foote informed Armstrong that the Chinese were reinforcing their positions and placing new batteries so they could fire on the American ships. Foote was increasingly apprehensive about Armstrong siphoning off his men to the flagship. When Foote received orders from Armstrong on 18 November to return Commander Bell and an additional twenty men to the *San Jacinto,* Foote immediately sent off a rather abrupt note to his superior in which he reminded Armstrong that he had relinquished the command to Foote. While he himself had made no overt move, Foote wrote, the Chinese were reinforcing. He could not spare one more man. He had only the bare minimum necessary to take the forts; any fewer would make it impossible. He asked that Armstrong either "come here yourself and in person resume command of the forces, or give me authority to proceed in the operations which were so effectively prosecuted for three hours after we took up our position against the enemy."[27] After Foote had sent off his reply someone noticed that Armstrong had added a postscript to his letter telling Foote that if he saw that the Chinese were strengthening their positions, he could act on his own discretion. Foote immediately informed Armstrong that had he seen this, "I should not have bothered you at all on the subject."[28]

Fortunately for Foote, Armstrong was not angered by his overhasty remarks. Indeed, he told Foote to keep the men in question. He also repeated his earlier instructions and reminded Foote that he was to prevent the strengthening of the forts "in the most expedient and efficient manner your judgment and means may warrant, even though you may be led to the capture of the forts."[29] Foote responded quickly, apologizing again for overlooking Armstrong's earlier postscript and telling him that it fully addressed his own concerns. He then informed Armstrong that since he was unable to prevent the Chinese from strengthening their defenses he would react by attacking the barrier forts as early as the next morning. Armstrong replied to this with a strong vote of confidence.[30]

At 6:30 A.M. on 20 November, with the *Portsmouth* and *Levant* in position, Foote ordered the crews beat to quarters, and at 6:45 they opened fire on the two nearest forts. Five minutes later the Chinese returned fire, but it slackened after about an hour. Foote then personally led ashore the columns of boats with a party of 287 officers, sailors, and marines supported by four Dahlgren boat howitzers. The men landed about three quarters of a mile from the fort and immediately began a flanking movement. They dragged three of the howitzers on field carriages through rice paddies and across a waist-deep creek around behind the fort to attack it from the rear. It was necessary to pass through a village, and some shots were fired on the Americans until they used howitzer fire to clear the streets. On reaching the fort the Americans found its defenders in full retreat; the marines shot down many of them as they attempted to escape across a nearby creek. In all, some fifty Chinese were killed. On the U.S. side, two apprentice boys were killed during the landing by the accidental discharge of a rifle. By 11:00 A.M. the fort was secure and flying the American flag.

When Chinese in the second fort across the river opened fire on the Americans in the first fort, Foote ordered his men to reposition some of the fort's fifty-three cannon and silence the guns of the second fort without actually having to capture it. During the exchange of fire the Chinese sunk the *Portsmouth*'s launch, which, however, was recovered and refloated. Foote ordered the rest of the men to spike the remaining Chinese guns, destroy the magazines, and fire any remaining buildings. By noon the work was finished, and the men settled down to a lunch of confiscated ducks and chickens roasted over fires in the burning fort. A Chinese land force from Canton that Foote estimated at nearly three thousand men attempted to assault the fort, but marine rifle fire twice drove them back. That night, after spiking the remaining Chinese guns, much of the assault force returned to the two ships, although Commander Bell and the men from the *San Jacinto* remained ashore.[31]

At 3:00 A.M. on 21 November an 8-inch shell from one of the Chinese forts hit the *Portsmouth*. Its guns returned fire and quickly silenced the fort. At 4:00 A.M. Bell and the men from the *San Jacinto* returned to the American ships, and at 6:00 Foote ordered gunners on his two ships to open fire on the remaining three forts. A brisk action then ensued, during which one American was mortally wounded aboard the *Levant*. After silencing the guns in the nearest fort, at 7:00 A.M. Foote again led an assault force ashore. This time the little steamer *Cum Fa* towed the boats, which came under heavy Chinese fire. A 64-pound ricochet shot hit the *San Jacinto*'s launch, killing one man, mortally wounding two, and seriously wounding seven. Despite this the Americans repeated their tactics of the day before, landing away from the fort and advancing on it from the rear to take it by storm. One marine was severely wounded in the attack, which took place within view of some one thousand Chinese troops just out of howitzer range. The Americans then turned some of the forty-one guns in the second fort on another fort on an island in the river that had joined in the firing and was now silenced in turn. The storming party spiked the guns in the fort, burned their carriages, and destroyed everything they could. At 4:00 P.M. a detachment of marines stormed and took a battery of six guns on the riverbank. Two companies of sailors then used boat howitzer fire to repel hundreds of Chinese soldiers advancing toward them from two directions.

That same afternoon, again using a boat assault, the Americans landed on the island with the third fort. This too was taken, along with its thirty-eight guns. As the men completed their destruction of this fort, the Chinese in the one remaining fort on the Canton side opened fire. Again the Americans used captured guns against that fort along with fire from their howitzers. Foote then suspended further operations until the next day. Chinese preparations that night indicated that they planned a spirited defense.

At daybreak on the twenty-second, Foote ordered the *San Jacinto's* first lieutenant, left behind with a small detachment in the third fort during the night, to use howitzer fire to cover the final American landing. Foote hoped this diversion would draw fire from the remaining fort away from his landing party, but the ruse did not work. Foote, in the *Portsmouth's* launch, now led three columns of boats that rowed toward shore. Despite rapid and effective fire from howitzers in the launch and from the Americans in the third fort, the Chinese maintained a brisk fire against the boats. Fortunately for the attackers, the guns were too elevated, and most of the Chinese shot and grape passed over the boats without harm; only three shot struck close, two of them hitting oars. This time the Americans made right for the fort instead of trying to come at it from behind. The boats could not reach the shore, so the landing party jumped out and waded to land, charged the fort, and quickly captured it. The defenders fled. This fort mounted thirty-eight guns, which the Americans spiked before they withdrew to their ships. Foote was back onboard the *Portsmouth* by 10:30 A.M., to be greeted by cheers from the crew. He then sent word to Armstrong of the completion of his nearly flawlessly executed operation.[32]

Both Armstrong and Foote agreed that simply taking the forts was not sufficient and that something should be done so that they would not be a problem in the future. The next day Foote set his men to demolishing the four forts. They knocked sections from the walls, hard work because the walls were thick and much of the work had to be done by hand, and also because Chinese snipers provided constant harassment. The crews also employed some 6,250 pounds of black powder. Unfortunately, on 3 December a spark from an iron bar striking a stone while preparing a place for demolition ignited a premature blast that killed three Americans and seriously wounded nine others. The work of destruction took two weeks and was finished by 6 December.[33]

Armstrong was still awaiting an apology from Commissioner Yeh, who
for some time had refused to budge. At the same time the commodore
rejected British requests that the Americans cooperate with them in
other military operations against the Chinese, determined not to embroil
the United States any more deeply in the fighting than it already was. He
informed Foote that taking and destroying the forts had avenged the
insult to the American flag, eliminated a threat to the American ships,
and strengthened the American bargaining position; but this was as far
as he intended to go.[34]

In his 26 November report on the capture and destruction of the forts
Foote told Armstrong that some rumors placed Chinese casualties at as
many as five hundred men but he thought the correct figure was probably half that number. The Americans lost seven dead, all sailors, and
twenty-two wounded, of whom six were marines. Chinese shot had struck
the *Portsmouth* eighteen times and the *Levant* twenty-two times but
without serious injury to either vessel.[35]

Finally, on 5 December, Commissioner Yeh yielded slightly. In a letter
to Armstrong he assured the commodore that there was no cause for
strife between their two nations. He also asked for an explanation of how
American ships using the river would display their flags. Although this
was not an apology, Armstrong took it as probably the best response he
would receive and used it to bring matters to an end. Armstrong stead-
fastly refused to adopt the course many American merchants would have
preferred: common cause with Britain in order to wrest concessions
from the imperial government.[36]

In his reports to Washington Armstrong was again lavish in his praise
of Foote. He wrote that he could not "but express my admiration of the
gallantry of, and the services rendered by Commander Foote, whose conduct from the commencement of the troubles at Canton up to the completion of the object of the expedition, has been indefatigable and judicious."[37] The British were pleased and complimentary as well. When
Foote returned his two warships to the Whampoa anchorage, seamen
aboard the two British ships there manned the rigging and cheered while
their bands played "Hail Columbia" and "Yankee Doodle." In their official reports British civilian and military officials also commended the
Americans for their gallantry and skill.[38]

Foote had no doubt that he had acted correctly in taking the barrier
forts, but he was nonetheless concerned over how the events would be

perceived back in the United States. Most American newspapers simply reported the events as they had occurred; only a few took sides. The *New York Times* and the *Boston Daily Advertiser* approved of the action, but Horace Greeley's *New York Tribune* held that Foote had acted with unnecessary severity. More hurtful was criticism from an unexpected source, the Reverend James C. Beecher of Canton, in the form of a letter published in the *Boston Weekly Journal* on 24 August 1857.

When Foote received a copy of this article a year later, he confronted Beecher onboard the *Portsmouth* at Hong Kong. He pointed out numerous misrepresentations in what Beecher had written and demanded an apology. Beecher asked to see what had been published and two days later wrote Foote that the report had been a confidential and carelessly written letter to a friend and that he had not intended that it be published. Nevertheless he refused to back down because he found nothing in the article that he considered wrong. He believed that the fighting between the Chinese and the British need not have involved the Americans and that sending the ships to Whampoa had led directly to the destruction of American property and had risked American lives. Chinese firing on U.S. vessels should have been expected, given the fighting in progress and the long-standing Chinese hatred of foreigners. Beecher concluded by saying that while he disagreed with what the navy had done, he still held Foote in esteem.[39]

In a stinging and lengthy reply written on 18 November 1857, Foote wrote Beecher what even his sympathetic biographer James Hoppin characterized as an "indignant and caustic" response. In what he said would be their last communication, Foote pointed out that the United States had done nothing to provoke the conflict. The Chinese had not fired at French vessels or those of other nationalities; these had been allowed to pass. Foote found Beecher's views "to be as crude as they are perverse where the honor of your country's flag is involved."[40]

Foote need not have worried about the official reaction in Washington. When he learned of the events Secretary Dobbin fully endorsed the actions taken and instructed Armstrong to commend the officers and men of the East India Squadron for "the brave and energetic manner in which the wrong was avenged." At the same time, he reminded Armstrong that the United States sought friendly relations with China. Secretary of State William L. Marcy, informed of developments by Commissioner Parker at Hong Kong, concurred with Dobbin's assessment, but he, too, stressed the need for the United States to maintain amicable relations with China and not to compromise its neutrality.[41]

In China, an uneasy standoff continued between the Chinese government and the American squadron. Events soon rendered the squadron's presence in Canton unnecessary, however. On 14 December 1856 a fire, probably set by Chinese, swept through and destroyed the foreign factories outside Canton, causing some one million dollars in damage. Afterward the only foreigners left at Canton were British troops. Foote was at Hong Kong supervising repairs to the *Portsmouth* when he received the news. The British governor in Hong Kong, Sir John Browning, met with him and urged him to press Armstrong into common military action against the Chinese. Foote informed Armstrong that he had told Browning that the United States could not base its policies on rumor and speculation.[42] This turned out to be the correct response. The Chinese authorities and U.S. government now took the position that both the slight to the American flag and the destruction of the forts were isolated incidents that should not be allowed to impede normal relations between China and the United States. Indeed, despite the drama of the action, Foote's taking of the barrier forts had little impact on the long course of Chinese-American relations, although it did help preserve American interests in China and pave the way for subsequent treaties negotiated by U.S. envoy William B. Reed.[43]

No doubt Foote was relieved when on 24 December Armstrong ordered him to take the *Portsmouth* to visit ports in northern China. He was also glad to get to sea because a number of the crew had fallen sick with typhoid and dysentery. Three men died at the end of November and in early December, and at one time a quarter of the sloop's crew was sick. Foote was also chagrined that some of the crew had broken their temperance pledge and were demanding their grog ration. It cannot have been many—the *Portsmouth* received only thirty-eight and a half gallons of whiskey from the *San Jacinto* for the upcoming cruise—but it was still a blow to Foote.[44]

The *Portsmouth* sailed from Hong Kong on 1 January 1857. The passage through the Formosa Strait was rough, and the weather did not improve until the sloop arrived at Shanghai, China's most populous city, on 28 January. Foote allowed his again-healthy crew liberty ashore. After its call at Shanghai the *Portsmouth* headed south to Ningpo, where the governor assured Foote that he would protect American property. At both Shanghai and Ningpo, Foote renewed acquaintances with missionaries and merchants.[45] The *Portsmouth* next visited Foochow and Amoy. The one-day stop at Amoy was not on Armstrong's itinerary. Foote wanted to call there simply because he had recently exchanged letters with the leader of its Christian community, the Reverend Elihu Doty, whom he had met eighteen years before while he was a lieutenant on the *John Adams*.[46]

On 14 March 1857 the *Portsmouth* returned to Hong Kong. Foote assured Armstrong that whatever was happening elsewhere, the northern Chinese ports were quiet. This was not true in the south, however, where animosity against the British had turned into a campaign against all foreigners.[47] Armstrong was by this time in very poor health, and on 11 April, after the situation had calmed somewhat, he sent Foote and the *Portsmouth* in his place to Singapore to look into a salvage case involving a Dutch vessel, the *Henrietta Maria*, that had been abandoned at sea and brought into port by an American ship, the *Coeur de Lion*. Although the British questioned the Americans' right to the ship, Foote was able to resolve the case in favor of the Americans.[48]

Armstrong had also entrusted Foote with delivering to Bangkok the U.S. consul, Dr. Charles Bradley, along with the newly ratified commercial treaty between the United States and the Kingdom of Siam. The *Portsmouth* sailed from Singapore on 21 May, arriving at Siam six days later. In early June Foote traveled up the Menam River in the royal steam yacht to visit the Siamese capital of Bangkok with some of his officers and Bradley. Siam then had a dual monarchy with two kings, the younger of whom was considered the heir apparent. Foote met both and immediately became close friends with the latter, who was fluent in English, gregarious, and interested in Western technology. Especially knowledgeable about artillery, he queried Foote about the *Portsmouth* and its armament. Foote invited him to tour the ship, and although no Siamese king had ever before visited a foreign warship, he accepted. The royal entourage spent most of a day aboard the *Portsmouth*. The king even returned early the next day with most of his retinue and went for a short cruise aboard the sloop during which Foote exercised the sloop's guns and fired a royal salute for the visitors.[49] Foote liked what he saw in Siam. The country was rich in agricultural resources, and he found the Siamese generally "manifesting the habits of industry and thrift." He gave considerable credit for this to American missionaries in Siam and went out of his way to show his support for them.[50]

The *Portsmouth* arrived back in Hong Kong on 26 June. Armstrong had taken the other ships in the squadron to Shanghai, and Foote's sloop was the only American vessel there. Armstrong had received a report that the Taiping rebels were moving against Foochow and wanted Foote to investigate. He instructed Foote that if U.S. lives and property were threatened, he was not to land troops but simply to evacuate the Americans.[51]

Foote quickly wrote Armstrong and asked permission to bring the *Portsmouth* to Shanghai instead. He reminded the commodore that the last time the sloop had been to Foochow its deep draft had almost caused it to ground in the shallow anchorage. More important, the sloop had been on station for a year and badly needed repair to the copper hull plating, which was deteriorating. Without copper plating, the *Portsmouth* would be extremely vulnerable to worms. At Shanghai the ship could be put into dry dock and repaired.

Armstrong agreed and sent the *Levant* to Foochow instead. Foote took the *Portsmouth* out of Hong Kong on 4 July; the ship arrived in Shanghai nine days later and was soon in dry dock. With the *Portsmouth* undergoing repairs, Foote gave the crew extensive time ashore. The restraints of shipboard discipline were loosened in the process, and in his last weeks in Shanghai Foote presided over a number of courts-martial for drunkenness and overstaying leave ashore.[52]

While he was in Shanghai Foote suggested to Armstrong that the *Portsmouth* sail to Japan. Since the 1854 visit of Commo. Matthew Perry's squadron, only one U.S. Navy warship had called there, Armstrong's *San Jacinto* in 1856. Foote believed it was important for U.S. vessels to exercise treaty provisions and visit Japanese ports on a regular basis, and he thought it wise to look in on Consul Townsend Harris at Shimoda (Simoda). As a final argument Foote told Armstrong that he believed a short cruise was necessary for the health of his crew. An unstated reason was Foote's desire to see Japan, a place he had not yet visited. On 20 August Armstrong agreed to Foote's suggestion and issued orders for the *Portsmouth* to call on the Japanese treaty ports.

The "long and dreary" passage to Japan was not without danger. A week after setting out, and only about thirty-five miles southwest of Shimoda, the crew of the *Portsmouth* sighted and narrowly avoided running onto some previously uncharted breakers. As Foote noted, had these been encountered at 3:00 A.M. instead of 3:00 P.M. the sloop's cruise "would have come to an abrupt termination." These were promptly named the "Portsmouth Breakers."

The next day, 8 September, the *Portsmouth* arrived at Shimoda. Consul Harris was delighted; he had not seen an American or received any communication from the United States since Armstrong had brought him to Japan a year earlier. Foote met with Harris and entertained him onboard the sloop. He also met with local Japanese officials. Foote was much impressed by the intelligence, courtesy, sophistication, frugality, and cleanliness of the Japanese. He found them more civilized than the Chinese and concluded they were "the best developed, most intelligent, healthy and happy-looking people, we have seen on this side of the Cape of Good Hope."[53]

Armstrong had asked Foote to make a survey of Shimoda harbor, but poor weather made this impossible. Foote also concluded that the harbor was not satisfactory for trading purposes. The inner harbor was safe but too small; the outer harbor was totally exposed and unsafe. And while coal was available locally, there were few export goods of interest to the U.S. market to make trade worthwhile. While he was ashore Foote and the other Americans shopped at a local market and bought a large quantity of lacquerware. Before the *Portsmouth* sailed Harris presented Foote with one of two little dogs that the Japanese had given him the year before. Foote noted that the Japanese seemed genuinely to admire Americans and appreciate U.S. power, and he professed satisfaction that God was "evidently causing the portals of hitherto impervious, heathen and uncivilized lands, to be thrown open wide for the introduction of Christian civilization."[54]

After four days at Shimoda, on 12 September the *Portsmouth* departed for the other Japanese treaty port of Hakodate. During the five-day passage Foote began a long letter of his impressions of Japan and the Japanese that he intended to mail to friends in the United States on his return to China. Foote also began a journal detailing his Japanese experiences.[55] He was most impressed with Hakodate's large, protected harbor, which he estimated as capable of holding two hundred ships. The climate was excellent and the nearby area was rich in agricultural products and iron ore. Foote wrote Armstrong that Hakodate was a much better port than Shimoda, and he strongly recommended it for the location of a naval depot. It was, he said, the "most desirable place, in point of health and enjoyment, for a man of war that I have ever visited."[56]

While at Hakodate Foote met with U.S. consul Elisha Rice as well as local Japanese officials. The latter were most courteous, and the only problem Foote encountered was in a request for beef. The Japanese informed him that they were unable to comply, probably because of a shortage of beef for food in the area. Foote reminded them of the treaty that guaranteed visiting American ships whatever provisions they required and stated that he expected a bullock to be delivered at 10:00 A.M. the next day. The next morning the Japanese had not one but two bullocks waiting. When the same thing happened the next week, Foote decided not to press the matter. But several weeks later, just before the sloop sailed, Foote received word that the imperial government in Yedo (Tokyo) had decided that a herd of cattle would be kept near Hakodate to be available for the Americans in the future. Foote, always the stickler for U.S. rights, noted that even "beef sometimes involves a principle."[57]

Perhaps believing he had gone too far, Foote worked to minimize this incident in the interests of improving overall Japanese-U.S. relations during the remainder of his stay in Japan. On 26 September he welcomed the Japanese governor and his entourage aboard the *Portsmouth* with a thirteen-gun salute. The Americans also served the visitors a meal that surprisingly, given Foote's temperance inclinations, included champagne. On 10 October the *Portsmouth* sailed from Hakodate and arrived at Hong Kong sixteen days later.[58]

Foote was to have rendezvoused with Armstrong at Hong Kong before November, but when the *Portsmouth* arrived there, Armstrong and the *San Jacinto* had not yet returned. The *Levant* was there, however, and Foote met with Cdr. William Smith, from whom he obtained a shipment of one thousand cigars that he had ordered the previous spring and that Smith had brought back from the Philippines. While awaiting Armstrong's return to Hong Kong Foote met with British officials and caught up on his correspondence, responding to letters from both kings of Siam. He also wrote to Christian missionaries in south China and sent them a number of gifts. He was particularly pleased that the missionaries were interested in his long letter detailing his experiences in Japan and the possibility that Japan might soon be open to Christian missionary activity. On 15 December 1857, Foote gave permission for his letter to be read before the Shanghai Literary Society; six months later it was published in an English journal there.[59]

Ten days after the *Portsmouth* reached Hong Kong the USS *Minnesota* arrived. Captained by Foote's friend Samuel Du Pont, the *Minnesota* carried the new U.S. commissioner and minister plenipotentiary to China, William B. Reed. A few days later, on 10 November, the *San Jacinto* also arrived at Hong Kong, giving Foote a chance to report on his Japan trip to the commodore. Four days after that, Armstrong put the *Portsmouth* at Reed's disposal and the U.S. diplomat asked to visit Portuguese Macao. On 22 December, when British and French forces began another assault on Canton, the *Portsmouth* returned to Macao to protect American property there.[60]

Armstrong had been in poor health for some time, and on 15 January 1858, Josiah Tatnall, bearing the newly created rank of flag officer, arrived at Hong Kong by mail steamer to assume command of the East India Squadron. The federal government in Washington, concerned about the worsening situation in China, ordered the squadron increased by the addition of the new steam frigate *Mississippi*, which soon arrived to join the other ships.[61]

The increase in the size of his squadron allowed Tatnall to send some ships to other stations while still maintaining a major presence in south China. He now ordered Foote and the *Portsmouth* to join him and the *San Jacinto* at Manila, and the *Portsmouth* arrived there on 17 February. Not long afterward, Tatnall received unexpected orders from Washington for the *Portsmouth* to return to the United States with the squadron's sick. This was logical because the two-year enlistments of most of the crew would soon expire. Foote quickly prepared the *Portsmouth* for the long voyage home, and the ship sailed from Manila on 5 March 1858.[62]

The return trip, accomplished without incident but slowed by lighter than usual winds, took three months by way of St. Helena. Foote did not relax shipboard discipline and drilled the men regularly. Unless he was unwell he also conducted Sunday services, and he oversaw the education of the young naval apprentices onboard, about whom he reported in a letter to Secretary of the Navy Isaac Toucey. On the afternoon of 13 June the *Portsmouth* sailed into Portsmouth harbor, concluding a cruise that had lasted more than twenty-five months.[63]

~8~

THE BROOKLYN NAVAL YARD

*I*mmediately on his return to the United States Foote put the *Portsmouth*'s crew to work preparing the ship for inspection. He also sent reports to Secretary of the Navy Isaac Toucey praising the crew and to naval constructor John Lenthall of the Bureau of Construction and Repair reporting that the *Portsmouth* was badly in need of work, including replacement of rotten wood, rusted iron, rigging, and water casks.[1]

After relinquishing command of the *Portsmouth* Foote hurried to New Haven to be with his family. He needed to catch up on his correspondence, and he wanted to visit Washington to assess the situation there and meet with his friends in the Navy Department. Foote was especially concerned about reactions to his role in the taking of the Canton barrier forts. Fortunately, any criticism was offset by the general public perception that the navy's response, while perhaps too forceful, had been limited and short-lived. The United States had averted participation in a prolonged conflict that now involved Britain and France. Secretary Toucey, in his annual report to Congress, unequivocally stated his own strong support for Foote's action at Canton. Even so, Foote's subsequent efforts and those of his friends Commodore Smith and Commander Dahlgren to secure official recognition and some vote of thanks from

Congress were unsuccessful. Too many individuals in influential places, including President James Buchanan, preferred simply to forget the matter. In any case pressing domestic concerns soon caused Chinese affairs to recede into the background.[2]

On 26 October 1858, Secretary Toucey appointed Foote executive officer of the Brooklyn Navy Yard, a post he would hold for three years. A plum shore assignment, the yard was also only a short train ride from Foote's home in Connecticut. Foote's daughter Josephine was now twenty-one; his four other children ranged in age from eleven to three. In June 1859, at age forty-two, his wife, Caroline, gave birth to their last child, a boy, whom they named John Samuel.[3] Foote's health seemed more precarious than ever. In addition to the frequent headaches that had plagued him for so long, he also suffered from lameness in his legs. To this was now added a painful case of the piles.[4]

Although Capt. Samuel Breese, Foote's former commander in the Cumberland, was the yard's commander, Foote actually ran the day-to-day operations. The Brooklyn Navy Yard was the second largest of the navy's nine yards; only Gosport in Norfolk was larger. Brooklyn and Gosport had the navy's only dry docks, and Brooklyn was also a center for the navy's growing steam warship construction.

Foote needed all the administrative skills he had learned in his stints at the Boston Navy Yard and the Philadelphia Naval Asylum to manage the Brooklyn Yard, which had been poorly organized and run before he arrived. There were no published regulations, and no guard stood at the gate to prevent workmen from leaving at their pleasure. Political patronage determined purchasing, the workers were indolent, and there was little oversight. The energetic Foote soon installed a porter at the gate who noted down the times that individuals arrived and left. Foote also reorganized the administration, discharged many workers, put naval officers in charge of all the important projects, and even instituted fire drills.[5] And somehow he found time to renew acquaintances with fellow naval officers, especially his close friend John Dahlgren, who was busy at the Washington Navy Yard developing a new ordnance system for the U.S. Navy. Their friendship was such that Dahlgren dedicated his 1856 book, Shells and Shell Guns, to him. Dahlgren and Commodore Smith at the Bureau of Yards and Docks remained Foote's two closest friends in Washington.[6]

Foote soon was deeply involved in promoting morality and Christianity. While he was at the Brooklyn Yard he regularly attended a Congregational church, but he gave generously to all Christian faiths, including Catholic missions. He spoke frequently about the overseas Christian missions and China. But most of his effort to promote Christianity was expended at the navy yard. Soon he had established a program of religious instruction and mission schools for yard workers and their families. He also promoted nightly prayer meetings, which were held regularly aboard the yard's receiving ship, the old ship of the line *North Carolina*. Foote was so confident of success in this endeavor that he thought it might be the beginning of a major revival in the New York area.[7]

Known for his personal integrity and fairness, Foote was in demand to serve on courts-martial involving naval personnel, and he often presided. Humane and inclined to favor the sailors, especially in issues involving moral peccadilloes, Foote was seen by some of his fellow officers as too lenient and endeavoring to curry favor with the men, which they believed undermined naval discipline.[8] Foote also continued to press for changes in the navy that would benefit its seamen. After examining the *General Admiral,* for example, a new steam frigate being built by Isaac Webb for the Russian navy, Foote wrote Secretary of the Navy Toucey a detailed report in which he extolled the ship's toilet facilities and baths and pointed out that installation of these in U.S. Navy vessels would greatly improve crew morale and health. It is hard to believe that other naval officers would have made that a major point.[9]

Foote also again involved himself in temperance activities. He helped organize a three-day national convention in November 1859 in New York City that brought together chaplains, ministers of churches working with sailors, and others interested in the welfare of seamen. In the course of their meeting the delegates called on Foote to draw up a petition asking Congress to abolish the grog ration. Foote quickly produced such a document, and the convention unanimously adopted it.[10]

Foote also continued to speak out for African colonization efforts and vigorous U.S. action to suppress the slave trade. In July 1859 he sent Secretary Toucey a long letter on the subject in which he reiterated the reasons for zealous enforcement. Foote argued for a supply depot to support operations off the southern African coast and, in contrast to many of his fellow officers, also for cooperation with the Royal Navy as the best way to end the trade. He also believed that a strong U.S. presence off the African coast would help promote the success of Liberia. Foote saw his own best chance to secure a niche in history in helping to suppress the African slave trade, and he hoped to help accomplish this in person in command of one of the navy's new light-draft steamers.[11]

When Foote's lobbying for an African Squadron billet was not successful, he sought another position that would enable him to continue his reform work: that of superintendent of the Naval Academy. Established in 1845 at Annapolis, the academy was still controversial; many naval officers clung to the belief that practical experience at sea was the best schooling system for officers. Foote, however, supported the academy and its concept of a technical education in the classroom as a preparation for experience at sea. He had also shown himself much interested in furthering scientific knowledge.[12]

In March 1860 Lt. Edward Simpson, a gunnery instructor at the academy who had served under Foote in the *Portsmouth*, wrote to urge Foote to seek the superintendency. Capt. George Blake, who had served in the post for three years, was expected soon to step down. Undoubtedly the idea appealed to Foote, for he sought the advice of his influential friend Capt. Samuel Du Pont, who had served on the naval board that organized the academy. Du Pont gave his enthusiastic assent.[13]

As Foote waited for word from Annapolis regarding the superintendency, events elsewhere in the nation removed all possibility of his obtaining the post. The country was fast moving toward civil war. When Abraham Lincoln won the 1860 presidential election, leaders of the lower South let it be known that they would not agree to the inauguration of a "black" Republican president. Between the time of Lincoln's election and his inauguration, South Carolina, Georgia, Mississippi, Florida, Alabama, and Texas organized the Confederate States of America and began taking control of federal government properties within their borders. The two notable exceptions were Fort Pickens at Pensacola, Florida, and Fort Sumter in the harbor of Charleston, South Carolina.

President Buchanan opposed secession but believed he lacked the constitutional powers to suppress it, and he was reluctant to antagonize Virginia and other states and perhaps push them into the Confederacy. Several cabinet members resigned to protest Buchanan's failure to act, but Toucey was not among them. When Buchanan finally concluded that he would have to send supplies to Maj. Robert Anderson at Fort

Sumter, the southerners in the cabinet resigned, leaving it in the hands of conservative Democrats from the North and the border states. Toucey, Acting Secretary of War Joseph Holt, and General in Chief Winfield Scott sent a merchant vessel, *The Star of the West,* from New York for the purpose of relieving Sumter, but on 9 January 1861 South Carolinians fired on the ship and it withdrew without unloading.

Buchanan believed that the responsibility for dealing with the secession of the Deep South rested with Congress, not with the president. Toucey agreed and came under much criticism for his failure to concentrate the navy's vessels so as to prepare them for war; in fact, he further dispersed them by sending many to foreign stations as if there were no crisis at home. He also accepted without question the resignation of many southern officers from the navy. By the time Toucey resigned on 4 March 1861, more than one hundred officers had left the service. All of this led to much criticism at the time and later to Toucey's censure by Congress. After the Lincoln administration took over, Toucey left office and returned home to Connecticut.[14]

Foote was among the navy officers who disagreed with Toucey's policies. As he helped outfit the *Star of the West* for its trip to Fort Sumter, Foote must have known that an unarmed merchant ship could not accomplish such a mission. He must also have been depressed by news on 12 January that Florida had seceded and sent troops to occupy the Pensacola Navy Yard. Although there was little danger of a repeat of these events at the Brooklyn Yard, Foote was determined to protect federal property under his care. By mid-January he had the yard under the tightest possible security.[15]

Many in the U.S. Navy despaired at the failure in leadership. In a January 1861 letter to Foote, Captain Du Pont summed up the thoughts of many officers. He criticized the drift in Washington and bemoaned the fact that nothing was being done to halt the secessionist movement. Du Pont had visited Annapolis and thought that "the course was clear" for Foote to become superintendent when Blake left, but he feared that there might not be any academy to go to because Maryland was strongly secessionist. He also regretted the fact that Armstrong had been at Pensacola rather than Foote.[16]

While many old friends resigned from the navy to join the Confederacy, Foote was certain of his own course. Committed to his God and to the U.S. Navy, Foote as a Christian hated slavery, and as a naval officer was fiercely loyal to the United States. He made this clear to his older brother, John, who visited him during this troubled period and later related that the two had lengthy discussions about what might occur. During one such discussion Foote asked, "John, will you fight?" His brother replied that he did not know what he would do. Foote then said, "I will fight in this case; my life is in my hands, and if you will not fight, don't talk quite so loud."[17]

On 4 March 1861, Abraham Lincoln was inaugurated as president of the United States. In his inaugural address he renewed his pledge to respect slavery in the states where it existed and to enforce the Fugitive Slave Law, but he made it clear that he would not permit secession. Among Lincoln's key cabinet appointees was Gideon Welles, Foote's childhood friend, as secretary of the navy. Although they seldom met, Welles and Foote had remained good friends. Foote's only concern about the appointment must have been his fear that Welles was still upset over Foote's role in trying to keep Welles, a civilian, from heading the Bureau of Provisions and Clothing in 1846. Foote promptly sent Welles a congratulatory letter and followed this with a March visit to Washington. Foote was not disappointed; Welles received him warmly.[18]

Welles must have been cheered by the presence of an old and loyal friend in the midst of so much disaffection. Many of the Navy Department's clerks were openly hostile to the government; and some of the key commanders were of dubious loyalty, including the chief of the Bureau of Ordnance, Capt. George Magruder, and the commander of the Washington Navy Yard, Capt. Franklin Buchanan. Also the navy was far from ready for war. In early 1861 it had about ninety ships designed to carry a total of 2,415 guns, but only forty-two ships were in commission and Toucey had scattered most of these on foreign station. The Home Squadron numbered only twelve vessels carrying 187 guns.[19]

Foote gave Welles frank assessments of his fellow navy officers. Although Welles believed that on occasion Foote let friendships color his judgment, he valued Foote's honesty and came to rely on his opinions. Foote did not abuse their friendship to seek undue personal advantage. Indeed, on more than one occasion when Welles sought to expand their social relationship, Foote rejected this as improper with a superior. Foote must have been pleased to discover that Welles was convinced he was the right man to head the Naval Academy. This, of course, was contingent on the United States averting civil war, which was not to be.[20]

Welles himself came to believe that he was the key in advancing the careers of both Foote and David Farragut. The secretary noted in his diary in 1864:

> Had any other man than myself been Secretary of the Navy, it is not probable that either Farragut or Foote would have had a squadron. At the beginning of the Rebellion, neither of them stood prominent beyond others. Their opportunities had not been developed; they had not possessed opportunities. Neither had the showy name, the scholastic attainments, the wealth, the courtly talent, of Du Pont. But both were heroes.[21]

President Lincoln, who was anxious to avoid antagonizing the border states, for weeks did nothing that might upset them. By this time in the South only Fort Pickens off Pensacola and Fort Sumter off Charleston remained in federal hands. Sumter's situation was the more precarious. Ringed by South Carolina artillery, its garrison was almost out of provisions. Given this, the simplest course of action would have been to hold on to Pickens and evacuate Sumter.

On 30 March Lincoln ordered Welles to prepare a relief expedition for Fort Sumter based on a plan drawn up by Gustavus Fox. The expedition was to be ready to sail by 6 April, with Lincoln to make the final decision at that point. This ran against the advice of a majority of the cabinet, including Secretary of State William Seward, who argued that it would probably lead to war and cause Virginia to secede; Seward proposed evacuating Sumter and holding on to Pickens.

Fox suggested running boats with supplies and men to the fort under cover of darkness, protected by Sumter's guns and those of nearby ships. Key to this plan was the steam frigate *Powhatan* at the Brooklyn Navy Yard. The frigate had just returned from a lengthy cruise in poor repair and had been ordered decommissioned and its engines disassembled. Welles now revoked those orders. The *Powhatan* was to be put back together and pressed into service for the relief of Fort Sumter.

Lincoln was still vacillating on 1 April when Seward, accompanied by Capt. Montgomery Meigs of the U.S. Army and Lt. David Dixon Porter of the navy, presented his plan to reinforce Fort Pickens. It too involved the *Powhatan*. Porter assured Lincoln that if he were given command of the frigate he could guarantee success. Lincoln agreed to the plan and personally signed the orders for Meigs and Porter to proceed. Seward and Porter convinced Lincoln to bypass Welles. If the Navy Department was notified, they asserted, the South would know of the plan immediately through the department's disloyal clerks and any chance to save Fort Pickens would be lost. This was a serious breach of naval procedure, both in bypassing Welles and in giving Porter command of a ship that would never in normal circumstances have been entrusted to a lieutenant.[22]

Lincoln also signed an order to the commandant of the Brooklyn Navy Yard ordering that the *Powhatan* be outfitted with all speed and secrecy. Under no circumstances was Welles to be notified until the frigate was at sea. Porter wasted no time, and the next morning, 2 April, he was at the Brooklyn Navy Yard. Commodore Breese was on leave, so Porter presented himself to Foote, who only the day before had received separate orders from Lincoln and Welles to prepare the *Powhatan* for sea. Foote was immediately suspicious of Porter and thought his orders might be a ploy to turn the frigate over to the South. Foote insisted on first notifying Welles, but Porter finally convinced him not to do so by what he later described as a mix of flattery, promise of recognition, and the threat of a charge of treason if he refused to obey.[23]

Once convinced, Foote energetically threw himself into readying the *Powhatan.* He sent for the ship's officers and began putting together a crew. That was the easy part. In addition to the normal tasks of readying any ship for sea, there were the daunting challenges of rerigging the entire vessel and reassembling the engines and boilers. In shifts around the clock, workmen at the yard accomplished this in only four days, by 6 April.[24]

Welles, blissfully unaware of Seward and Porter's subterfuge, was busy assembling a squadron for his planned operation off Charleston. Several telegrams from Welles now convinced Foote that the secretary really did not know what was planned for the *Powhatan.* Foote tried to cover himself with Welles by informing him that work had started but that the orders had not come direct. In another telegram he told Welles that he was executing orders given him by army and navy officers. This immediately aroused Welles's suspicions because he knew that the army was not involved in the operation planned for Sumter. Welles then approached Lincoln, who merely reconfirmed his orders.

On 5 April Foote informed Porter and Meigs that Welles had ordered a delay in the *Powhatan*'s sailing. Porter tried to convince Foote that Welles's telegram was a forgery. At the same time Porter telegraphed Seward to complain about Welles, and this brought matters to a head.

That night in Washington, Seward stormed into Welles's room at the Willard Hotel and demanded an explanation for his interference with the Porter expedition. The bewildered Welles claimed that there was no Porter expedition and insisted on going to Lincoln to resolve the matter. At about midnight they found Lincoln still at work at the White House. At first confused by the conflicting orders, Lincoln ordered the *Powhatan* restored to the Sumter expedition. Seward protested to no avail.

Seward continued his duplicitous ways, however. Instructed by Lincoln to notify the Brooklyn Yard immediately, he delayed sending the telegram until 2:30 the next afternoon and did not note that it was by Lincoln's order. Foote did not get the telegram until 3:00 P.M., a half hour after the *Powhatan* had departed. The frigate was still in the East River, however, and Foote immediately sent an aide in a tug to overhaul it. At about 5:00 P.M., near Staten Island, Porter received the telegram but refused to obey, stating that his orders came directly from the president and that it was too late for him to change his plans. The *Powhatan* then continued out into the Atlantic and south toward Fort Pickens. Fox's relief expedition to Sumter sailed without the frigate two days later. In retrospect, it seems unlikely that the *Powhatan*'s presence would have changed the outcome at Sumter.[25]

Confederate officers at Charleston, given wide latitude by Confederate president Jefferson Davis and informed that the Union expedition had sailed, now demanded Sumter's surrender. On receiving an unsatisfactory reply, they ordered shore batteries to open fire before the expedition could arrive. At 4:30 A.M. on 12 April the first shot of the Civil War boomed out across Charleston harbor. Sumter surrendered the next day.

Foote was angry about having been duped, and he later told Porter that he should have been tried and shot for taking the *Powhatan*. Foote also had to have been quite concerned about how Welles would view his role in the affair. Fortunately the secretary was preoccupied with more pressing concerns, and in any case he considered Seward and Porter the principal offenders. Welles's only advice to Foote, sent through Commo. Hiram Paulding, was that in the future he should honor only those orders that came directly from him. In a respectful letter to Welles, Foote reminded the secretary that he had detained the *Powhatan* "as far as I had authority to do so and until Captain [Samuel] Mercer, my superior officer, informed me that he should transfer his ship to Lieut. Comd'g Porter, who would sail with her, as he did." There was little Foote could have done to prevent the frigate from sailing. Welles agreed, and there the matter ended.[26]

With the outbreak of the war Foote hoped for a sea command, but for the next few months he was busy at the Brooklyn Navy Yard. Lincoln's formal proclamation of a blockade of the southern coasts would require rapid expansion of the navy, through both purchase and conversion of merchant ships and the construction of new warships. Much of this activity took place at the Brooklyn Yard, now the navy's most important facility after the loss of the Gosport Yard following the secession of Virginia. Foote played a key role in organizing this activity, and although charges were later leveled at others at the yard, including naval constructor Samuel P. Pook, for paying vast sums for obsolete vessels to be converted into warships, Foote was never implicated. Throughout his life no one questioned Andrew Foote's integrity.[27]

June brought two significant events in Foote's life. His eldest child, Josephine, then twenty-four, married; and on the twenty-ninth Foote was promoted to captain, then the highest rank in the U.S. Navy.[28]

Foote continued to work for abolition of the grog ration aboard navy ships. Several factors assisted him in his effort, one being the strength of the temperance movement in the North. Southern officers, a high percentage of whom had now left the service, had been among its most outspoken opponents, and officers now at war on station had written Foote not to slacken his efforts. Gideon Welles also favored ending the grog ration. A teetotaler, he had become well aware of the problems caused by alcohol during the time he had headed the Bureau of Provisions and Clothing. Later, Assistant Secretary of the Navy Gustavus Fox was another strong advocate for naval temperance.[29] The new chairman of the Senate Committee on Naval Affairs, John P. Hale, promptly introduced a bill that called for no spirits to be given to anyone under age twenty-one and authorized a commanding officer to suspend a seaman's grog for drunkenness. Sailors would still get their gill of spirits, but a half pint of wine could be substituted for it if necessary. For those unable to draw the spirit ration or who voluntarily relinquished it, the navy offered an extra four cents a day. The bill became law on 18 July.[30]

Foote still hoped to receive command of one of the navy's powerful new steam warships under construction, or at the least one of the steam frigates now returning home from overseas. Certainly few in the navy had his experience in coastal operations and riverine warfare. On 23

August 1861, however, Welles called Foote to Washington to offer him not a frigate but command of Union naval forces on the upper Mississippi. At this early stage of the war, Welles and other leaders in Washington were preoccupied with operations along the eastern seaboard, principally in establishing the naval blockade of the southern ports. The West, however, was an important theater, and controlling its great rivers would be vital if the Union was to win the war. The army claimed jurisdiction over all western riverine operations. The navy's job would be to assist the army by winning superiority on the rivers. Once that was done the navy could tighten the blockade and maintain lines of communication.

The great western rivers of the United States were for the most part too shallow and winding for sailing vessels with their traditional broadside batteries. The situation called for river gunboats: broad-beamed, shallow-draft vessels mounting as many as four guns forward and two aft and others in broadsides. The South lacked the shipyards, skilled workers, adequate marine engines, and industrial works to make the heavy iron plate required for such ships. Utilizing its superior manufacturing resources, the North could place a larger number of better-built gunboats onto western waters and get them there first.

In early May 1861 the commander of the Department of the Ohio, Maj. Gen. George B. McClellan, recommended to General in Chief Winfield Scott the construction of three gunboats to support federal troops occupying Cairo, Illinois. Cairo, located where the Ohio and Mississippi Rivers meet, was an important strategic site that offered direct access to the river traffic of Illinois, Kentucky, and Missouri. From it Union gunboats could control both the Ohio and the upper Mississippi.

Scott had already foreseen the need for gunboats as a part of his "Anaconda Plan" to strangle the South. Also lending his support to a naval presence in the West was an important Missouri political figure, Attorney General Edward Bates. On 17 April Bates wrote his friend James B. Eads of St. Louis, a civil engineer who had been part owner of a salvage business employing twin-hulled, steam-driven salvage vessels on the western rivers, to come to Washington and lend his expertise. On 29 April Eads wrote to Welles urging that Cairo be made the main base for a Union gunboat operation to command the Mississippi and Ohio Rivers. Eads proposed converting the powerful steamers used to pull snags from the river into river gunboats. These "snagboats" would become floating batteries protected against enemy fire by bales of cotton. Eads then traveled to Washington and met with Welles and Fox. He also attended a cabinet meeting in which he spelled out his ideas for gunboats on the western waters. Welles referred Eads's suggestions to the War Department, "to which," he said, "the subject more properly belongs." Later Welles would maintain that the army had insisted on jurisdiction over naval forces on western rivers.[31]

On 16 May 1861, Welles ordered Cdr. John Rodgers to report to McClellan at Cincinnati and assist in "establishing a Naval Armament on the Mississippi and Ohio rivers . . . with a view of Blockading or interdicting communication and interchanges with the States that are now in insurrection." Excepting men and guns, the army was to furnish whatever Rodgers needed. Rodgers would be subordinate to McClellan but would report to the Navy Department.[32] Rodgers seemed an excellent choice for the assignment. An experienced officer familiar with steam propulsion who came from a distinguished naval family (his father was Commo. John Rodgers of War of 1812 fame), Rodgers also had excellent political connections; his brother-in-law, Brig. Gen. Montgomery Meigs, was the army quartermaster general. Since the army would pay for the flotilla, Welles assumed this connection would prove valuable. But like most deepwater sailors, Rodgers knew nothing about riverine warfare.[33]

Any concerns Rodgers may have felt about serving under an army general fourteen years his junior were soon allayed because McClellan gave him a free hand. Over the next few months Rodgers made great strides in creating an inland navy for the Union. On his own initiative he purchased three side-wheel steamboats and converted them into gunboats, known as "timberclads" for the five-inch-thick oak planking installed as protection. In mid-June he traveled to Washington, where he secured cannon to arm them, and at the end of the month he began recruiting crews to man them.

Rodgers was anxious to test his new gunboats and quiet the skeptics. On 15 August, although they were not yet fully manned, two of the timberclads, commanded by Lt. Seth Phelps, made a trial run down the Mississippi almost to New Madrid, Missouri. The two chased two Confederate gunboats to New Madrid, but Phelps thought it prudent not to proceed farther and expose his lightly armed gunboats to Confederate batteries there.[34]

Rodgers's days in the West were now numbered. In late July, McClellan, his chief supporter, was called back east and Gen. John C. Frémont arrived to command the newly created Department of the West at St. Louis. Although he had excellent political connections and a national reputation as "The Pathfinder" for his earlier explorations of the West, Frémont lacked aptitude for higher command. He and Rodgers soon quarreled. Frémont was worried about the threat of possible Confederate gunboats and, while waiting for Eads's ironclads to be finished, followed Eads's recommendation and purchased *Submarine No. 7*. Rodgers strongly opposed this move. Frémont thought Rodgers was spending too much time with the newly operational timberclads and not enough supervising construction of the ironclads; and he feuded with Meigs, adding to the pressure on Rodgers. Frémont demanded Rodgers's removal and was supported in this by his friend Postmaster General Montgomery Blair. The official Navy Department explanation for Rodgers's removal was that the riverine force had grown to the point that an officer more senior than a commander should be in charge. Welles hoped that this senior officer would be more successful than Rodgers in dealing with Frémont. His choice for the post was Foote.[35]

Foote must have had serious reservations about accepting the assignment. It was not the sea command he desired, and in any case the western flotilla was still building. He would lack a navy yard, supplies, and financial support. But Welles convinced him, believing that in Foote he had the right combination of an aggressive commander with previous experience in amphibious operations, a careful administrator, and a seasoned diplomat. Foote was outspoken, and not always diplomatic, but he was certainly uniquely qualified for the job. Foote feared failure but he never shrank from responsibility. On 26 August Welles detached him from the Brooklyn Navy Yard and four days later handed him orders appointing him commander of naval operations on western waters.[36]

The task before him was daunting. Foote would be a naval officer essentially without resources and subject to army control; and he was well aware that his government's priorities lay with coastal operations. Then there was the lesson of his predecessor. Foote would need all his professional assets as well as his formidable resources of resolution and faithfulness to duty to do this job, as well as the ability to get along with army officers.

The day after receiving his new orders Foote got together with friends in Washington, including Charles Davis, Dahlgren, Lt. Henry Wise, and Wise's friend, British war correspondent William H. Russell. The latter, who had been quite critical of U.S. Army operations early in the war, was impressed with Foote and noted, "it will run hard against the Confederates when they get such men at work on the rivers and coasts, for they seem to understand their business thoroughly."[37] Foote set out for his new post a day later, and on 6 September he arrived at St. Louis.

❧ 9 ❧

THE WESTERN FLOTILLA

*T*he next eight months were the shortest and yet most challenging assignment of Foote's naval career. The relationship between the U.S. Army and Navy in the West was initially quite difficult. Joint operations were rare, and Foote was breaking new ground. He owed much to Rodgers's hard work, and Rodgers had every reason to be bitter over being replaced just as his command gave promise of being an important one. There had been no advance notice of his arrival, and Foote found himself with the unpleasant task of informing Rodgers that he was being replaced. Foote reported to Fox that Rodgers "behaved well, officer-like and gentlemanly." Nonetheless, Rodgers complained bitterly to Secretary Welles that "when the plant thus watered and cultivated gives its first prematurely ripe fruit, the crop is turned over to another with cold words."[1]

A week after his arrival at St. Louis, on 12 September 1861, Foote celebrated his fifty-fifth birthday. Contemporary accounts describe him as of medium size but square built and compact. His face, although not handsome, showed both strength and fixity of will. He had keen black eyes, an erect posture, quick movements, and was soft-spoken.[2] Cdr. Henry Walke, who served under him during this period, wrote of him:

He was slow and cautious in arriving at conclusions, but firm and tenacious of purpose. He has been called "the Stonewall Jackson of the Navy." He often preached to his crew on Sundays, and was always desirous of doing good. He was not a man of striking physical appearance, but there was a sailor-like heartiness and frankness about him which made his company very desirable.[3]

With his blunt manner and implacable resolve, Foote was absolutely the right man for this appointment. Commo. C. R. P. Rodgers said of him, "Foote had more of the bulldog than any man I ever knew. . . . [W]hen the fighting came, then he was in his element—he liked it."[4] Like Ulysses S. Grant, Foote believed the way to defeat the enemy was to attack him. Brave and determined in battle, he was also a brilliant organizer who got on well with his fellow officers. The Union's success in the West would owe much to his efforts.

The western theater was a vast area bounded by the Appalachian Mountains to the east and the Mississippi River to the west. Kentucky, Georgia, and Tennessee were its battlegrounds; and Tennessee, the last state to join the Confederate States of America, was its key. Tennessee's railroads and rivers were important routes west and south. If the Union could control these, the way to the lower South and trans-Mississippi region would be open. When Foote arrived in the theater Rodgers had the three timberclads—the *Tyler, Lexington,* and *Conestoga*—ready for service, but the ironclad program was still in its infancy. Construction on nine ironclad gunboats and thirty-eight mortar boats was going on around the clock, seven days a week. In addition to the seven ironclads contracted for with Meigs, Frémont had authorized Eads to purchase and convert two snagboats to ironclads: the 633-ton *Submarine No. 7,* which as the *Benton* (named by Frémont in honor of his father-in-law, Thomas Hart Benton) became Foote's flagship and mounted sixteen guns; and the 355-ton *New Era,* renamed the *Essex* by its captain, Cdr. William D. Porter, in honor of his father's ship, with five guns. Although he did make some contributions to the design of the ironclads, Foote's principal achievement with the flotilla was in its administration. He worked hard to bring order out of chaos and secure the resources needed for the flotilla's smooth functioning in battle. Considering the new technology being incorporated into the boats and the inevitable delays and cost overruns, this was a considerable accomplishment.

Indeed, Foote regarded the creation of the flotilla as the greatest achievement of his life and the fighting of it only secondary. In November 1862 he characterized his efforts as "a work of almost insuperable difficulty." Foote wrote Assistant Secretary of the Navy Fox, "I only wish that you could have spent one day here for the last six weeks, as no imagination can fancy what it is to collect materials and fit out western gunboats with western men without a navy yard, in the west, where no stores are to be had."[5]

Welles provided a captain for each new gunboat. Foote put Commander Walke in charge of the timberclads at Cairo while he remained at St. Louis to push work on the ironclads under construction there. Remaining there would also keep him in close touch with Frémont. On 5 October Foote assigned another new officer, Cdr. Roger Perry, to take charge of ordnance, quartermaster, and commissary duties. Foote established a floating depot at Cairo for repair and replenishment of his Mississippi flotilla, then later ordered a ten-acre navy yard to be built at Mound City just above Cairo.[6]

The need to build and arm his river flotilla did not prevent Foote from seeking to impose his own moral principles on those under his command, and he soon issued orders that "all persons connected with the flotilla" were to carry out "a strict observation of Sunday" in which officers and men would "abstain from all unnecessary work" and be given the opportunity to attend church services: "It is the wish of the commander in chief that on Sunday the public worship of Almighty God may be observed on board of all the vessels composing the flotilla." He also insisted on strict observation of a ban on all "profane swearing" and went on to conclude that "discipline to be permanent must be based on moral grounds, and officers must, in themselves, show a good example in morals, order, and patriotism to secure these qualities in the men."[7]

Frémont gave Foote virtually a free hand, telling him, "Use your own judgment in carrying out the ends of government." He also instructed Foote, "Spare no effort to accomplish the object in view with the least possible delay."[8] Foote effected improvements in plating and arming of the gunboats and urged the speedy casting of their ordnance, which Rodgers had already arranged. Much of the work on the gunboats was slipshod, and it was delayed by a lack of money, carpenters, and supplies. Foote was unable to secure boat howitzers because ships in the blockading squadrons along the Atlantic had first call on new production. There

were also problems getting the mortars, and at least some of the flotilla's
main battery guns were castoffs. Some of the first 9-inch guns sent to
the West had been cast in 1855 and previously rejected as unsafe. Later
Foote would have problems with old army rifled 42-pounders blowing up
and injuring their own crews.[9]

Foote was particularly concerned about the mortar boats. He feared
their engines were not powerful enough to propel them against fast-moving
currents. On 11 January 1862, he sent Fox a private telegram:

> I only wish you could see them. Their magazines are merely square holes in
> the timbers, banded together, forming the boat, and of course most of them
> leak. The mortar-boats would require, if all fitted out, about eight hundred
> men. There are no conveniences for living aboard. They will leak more and
> more. Some of our best officers have no better opinion of these rafts or boats
> than I have; still this is unofficial. It is my business to let the Government
> judge and I am to obey orders and while I can not consider these boats as well
> adapted to the purposes for which they were designed, still, as I said to Gen-
> eral Meigs, so much has been expended upon them, they ought not to be cast
> aside, or words to that effect, and I certainly would not presume to throw
> obstacles in the way of having them fitted, armed, and equipped.[10]

Frémont's replacement, Maj. Gen. Henry Halleck, halted construction of the mortar boats after he assumed command in November 1861.
Foote later stated that had Halleck not stopped him, he could have had
the mortar boats ready by the first of the year. Only after Lincoln became
intensely interested in them did Halleck change his stance, but too late
for the mortar boats to participate in the battles at Forts Henry and
Donelson.[11]

Foote had difficulty securing pay and rations for his men, but his
hardest task was securing trained crewmen. This was in part because of
higher wages in the merchant service (thirty dollars a month, as opposed
to eighteen for the navy) and the lack of ready cash, which precluded
paying an advance. By mid-October Foote had only about a hundred
men shipped for the gunboats. Rodgers had tried recruiting in Cincinnati, Louisville, and St. Louis. Foote opened recruiting offices as far
away as Chicago, Detroit, Milwaukee, and Cleveland. He also enlisted
volunteers from those aboard the timberclads. But none of these efforts
secured sufficient men. Appeals to the Navy Department brought five
hundred men, sent out in November; and some were also secured from

the Great Lakes. But crewmen remained in short supply, for the needs of the blue-water navy along the Atlantic seaboard were always met first. On 17 December Fox shifted to the army the responsibility for finding men to man the gunboats. That same day General McClellan directed General Halleck to send eleven hundred men from "unarmed regiments" to gunboat duty, and Halleck informed Foote that he had eleven to twelve hundred men available if he wanted them.

But Halleck also insisted that officers must accompany the enlisted men and that army personnel be regarded as "marines" subject only to the authority of the gunboat captains. Foote replied that he had filled his officer requirements and there were in any case no accommodations aboard the gunboats for additional officers; he needed "men to fight the guns and work the boats." Foote presumed that volunteers from the army would be discharged and then shipped aboard the gunboats, and on 31 December the army agreed to detail enlisted personnel without their officers. McClellan authorized Halleck to discharge any soldiers volunteering for gunboat service. Nevertheless, at the end of January 1862 Foote was short seventeen hundred men: one thousand for the gunboats and seven hundred for the mortar boats. Finally Welles secured the release from certain Massachusetts regiments of up to six hundred men with seafaring experience.

Despite his difficulties in finding men, for political reasons Foote rejected African Americans in the flotilla. He informed Lt. Leonard Paulding that "as there are objections or difficulties in the Southern country about colored people, we do not want any of that class shipped."[12] Many of the men he did enlist were untrained. As historian John D. Milligan has observed, "by and large, the crews acquired the skills of river and war by the same trial-and-error methods which had brought the gunboats themselves into being."[13]

Another problem was financial. Congress had appropriated one million dollars for the army Quartermaster's Department expressly for the western navy. This money was to have been disbursed to the contractors at regular intervals, but the government failed to meet its obligations. Eads soon exhausted his credit and was running up large debts to keep the work going; at one point he threatened to stop work altogether. Meigs admitted that the problem lay with his department, which had failed to understand the great demands of modern war. Even so, the problem was a long time in being solved. Payments to Eads were still in arrears at the time the gunboats were commissioned. Technically the gunboats that saw action at Forts Henry and Donelson were still his property.[14]

On 12 October 1861, the *St. Louis* slid down the ways. First of the City-class gunboats to be launched, it was also the first U.S. ironclad. During the next three weeks all of the remaining ironclads of the original contract were launched—either near St. Louis into the Mississippi or at Mound City into the Ohio. The *Benton* went down the ways at Carondelet the second week in November. The river was falling and Foote was anxious to get all the ironclads to Cairo and complete the remaining work on them there. He made arrangements for navy officers and some seamen to take the gunboats to Cairo, apparently with the workmen still aboard. Their transit was not without incident. The *Pittsburg* ran aground near Cape Girardeau, Missouri, and a following transport smashed into it. The *Benton* also ran aground, seventy miles from Cairo, and it took ten days and four steamers to free it.

During the passage to Cairo problems were discovered with the boats' steam engines. In an effort to protect the vulnerable steam drums, these had been crowded into the holds; as a result, water as well as steam went into the engines. It took four weeks to relocate the drums on top of the boilers. Only the *Benton* had both steam drums and boilers fully protected in its hold. Exposed machinery would later lead to disaster for two of the ironclads and some two hundred of their men.[15]

On 15 January 1862, a team composed of Cdrs. Roger N. Stembel and Alexander M. Pennock and Master Carpenter James R. McGee inspected the seven City-class ironclads and determined that Eads had completed the work to his contract's specifications, except for the time in which they were to have been delivered at Cairo. Foote accepted the report and put all the gunboats save the *Benton*, which was found to be deficient in power, in commission the next day.[16]

Foote's lack of appropriate rank undermined his authority. Army officers as far down the ranks as lieutenant colonel—the rank the army then equated with a naval captain—constantly obstructed his orders. "We suffer a great deal for my want of rank," Foote wrote to Fox.

> I want, for the efficiency of the fleet, the appointment of flag-officer. . . . I am considered merely as a captain, and I find I want rank in order to render my command more effective. My own boat will carry 16 heavy guns . . . nearly the armament of a frigate—and there will be 12 boats, also 38 boats, in addi-

tion, if we get them ready, which will constitute a large squadron, and am I not under the law entitled to the rank and to the appointment of a flag-officer? Now, when afloat, there is nothing to distinguish my vessel from the others. Here I am embarrassed on all sides for want of rank.[17]

Frémont had tried to alleviate the rank problem when on 11 October he placed under Foote's command all craft and shipping "belonging to the entire floated expedition down the Mississippi River."[18] But Halleck, Frémont's replacement, was a prickly personality covetous of his prerogatives, and Foote no longer had the free hand with him that he had enjoyed with Frémont. A promotion would certainly help. Congress had authorized the permanent rank of flag officer, equivalent to major general in the army, and Foote was promoted to that rank on 11 November 1861, and thereafter signed his name with the title "Flag-Officer, Commanding Naval Forces, Western Waters."[19]

Foote proved adroit in dealing with his army counterparts. When Fox wrote in December asking about the desirability of transferring the flotilla to the Navy Department, Foote responded that while he wished it had been done in the beginning, he was by that time so dependent on the army for so many services that "I hope that no change will be made disturbing or changing materially our present organization as I greatly fear that such change would seriously impair our efficiency for good service." In fact, Congress did not transfer the authority of warships on inland waterways from the army to the navy until October 1862, at which time the Mississippi flotilla formally became the Mississippi Squadron.[20]

Certainly Foote needed all of his diplomatic skills in dealing with Halleck, a man for whom he had little respect. Foote referred to him as a "military imbecile" and thought he might make a good clerk. Halleck's appointment as Frémont's replacement had induced Foote to request a transfer to another command; which, however, Welles rejected. But the aggravation of dealing with Halleck and trying to find men and supplies for his command exacted a toll. Foote later wrote Fox that the experience of preparing the squadron had added ten years "to my age of constitution."[21]

The task was nonetheless critical. Control of the West's great rivers—the Mississippi, the Ohio, the Tennessee, and the Cumberland—was in fact vital to both sides in the war. In 1861 they were immensely important avenues of communication in a region of insufficient railroads and poor roads. Both sides shipped food and war materials by water, and it

MISSISSIPPI
THEATER OF
OPERATIONS

was often considerably quicker to move troops by that means than by marching them overland. The Union relied on this vast river system to bring men, food, and supplies from the East and Midwest and intended to use it as a means to invade the South.

Tennessee was the cornerstone on which this strategy rested. Critical to the Confederacy, it was a major food-producing area, and its capital, Nashville, was a key rail center and one of the Confederacy's most important arms centers, producing artillery, small arms, percussion caps, cartridges, and sabers. Nashville facilities also made uniforms and leather goods. Along the Cumberland River northwest of Nashville lay the South's largest gunpowder mills. Tennessee also held two-thirds of the Confederacy's mineral wealth, including one of its largest iron-producing regions, located between the Tennessee and the Cumberland Rivers, and 90 percent of its copper. Tennessee also supplied more soldiers to the Confederacy than any other state save Virginia.[22]

At the beginning of the war few leaders, North or South, sensed the full importance of Tennessee and there was no precise military plan for taking the state. Old Union general in chief Winfield Scott's Anaconda Plan called for the navy to strangle the South by naval blockade along the Atlantic and Gulf coasts while a strong army supported by twelve to twenty steam gunboats split the Confederacy in two along the Mississippi River. President Lincoln favored a two-pronged attack: from Cairo on Memphis and from Cincinnati on east Tennessee. Tennessee had been the last state to leave the Union, indicative of divided loyalties there. Indeed, Senator Andrew Johnson and Representative John Maynard, both from eastern Tennessee, remained in Washington to represent their antisecession constituents. Lincoln hoped that a strong military effort in the state might lead to the establishment of a pro-Union government there. Maj. Gen. George B. McClellan, Scott's successor as general in chief, was interested in the railhead of Nashville and proposed sending eighty thousand troops there in conjunction with an Atlantic coast pincer from Charleston toward Augusta. Later, he proposed operations to secure Missouri, a thrust down the Mississippi, and operations in eastern Tennessee to seize railroads from Memphis to the east. McClellan, who had been in the railway business before the war, understood the importance of railroads in moving troops and supplies; securing southern railroads could paralyze the Confederate army and win the war for the North. He evolved a plan calling for several armies to move south from Ohio to reunite at Chattanooga and then march on Atlanta in conjunction with expeditions against Charleston and New Orleans.[23]

The first major Union foray in the western theater came in October 1861 when Gen. William "Bull" Nelson carried out what became little more than a raid into eastern Kentucky. The commander of the Department of the Cumberland, Brig. Gen. William Tecumseh Sherman, did not encourage a thrust into Tennessee. He informed McClellan that his seventy-thousand-man force was "too small to do good and too large to sacrifice." Confederate defenses were reportedly well developed and the lack of good roads and adequate rail lines presented serious difficulties.[24]

In early November 1861, with Missouri largely secure, Lincoln had reorganized the Western Department. After consulting with McClellan, Lincoln assigned Maj. Gen. Henry Halleck to command the newly designated Department of the Missouri to embrace Missouri, Iowa, Minnesota, Illinois, Arkansas, and Kentucky west of the Cumberland River. The ambitious and scholarly Halleck (he was known in the army as "Old Brains") was an administrator rather than a field general, and also a man who sought to wear the laurels earned by others. Halleck immediately preoccupied himself with bringing order out of the administrative chaos he inherited from the incompetent Frémont. At the same time Brig. Gen. Don Carlos Buell replaced Sherman as commander of the Department of the Ohio, which embraced Ohio, Michigan, and Indiana. The dividing line between the two departments was drawn so as to give Buell, considered one of the best generals in the Union army, access to the Cumberland River for a thrust against Nashville. Although federal armies were never bound to their geographical designation, the command structure in the West eventually led to problems and was a serious mistake.[25]

Once the reorganization was accomplished, Lincoln pressed his new commanders to get on with the task at hand. At the beginning of 1862 Union forces in the West outnumbered the Confederates two to one. Halleck at St. Louis had thirty thousand men. His subordinate, thirty-nine-year-old Brig. Gen. Ulysses S. Grant, commanded the Cairo Military District and twenty thousand men. Among these were units at the mouths of the Tennessee and Cumberland Rivers under sixty-year-old Brig. Gen. Charles F. Smith. The highly regarded Smith had been one of Grant's instructors at West Point and was three times breveted for bravery during the Mexican War. Buell, commander of the Department of the Ohio with headquarters at Louisville, had seventy thousand men (of whom perhaps fifty-seven thousand were effectives).[26]

Buell and Halleck, citing logistical problems and insufficient resources, delayed taking the offensive. The two commanders bickered back and forth and communicated frequently with McClellan. Lincoln wanted simultaneous attacks to put maximum pressure on Confederate defenses, but each of his two commanders in the West sought priority for his own plan. Buell wanted to attack Bowling Green, Kentucky, but only if supported by Halleck; Halleck favored a thrust up the Tennessee

River, but only if Buell was in a supporting role. Each, anxious to outdo the other, feared risking failure.[27]

The Confederates, on the other hand, had a unity of command. On 15 September 1861, Gen. Albert Sidney Johnston assumed command of the Confederate Western Military Department. Although he had never commanded a major army in the field, many in the South considered him the Confederacy's ablest general. A close friend of Confederate president Jefferson Davis, Johnson at the outbreak of the war was a brevet brigadier general in command of the Department of the Pacific. He declined a high Union command and resigned his post when his adopted state of Texas seceded. Davis, who called Johnston "the greatest soldier, the ablest man, civil or military, Confederate or Federal,"[28] made him a full general, second on the army list only to Adj. Gen. Samuel Cooper. Johnston's new command was one of the most difficult of the war—defending the broad, river-threaded Mississippi Valley against vastly superior Union land and naval forces.[29]

The Confederates had hoped to fix their northern frontier on the Ohio River, but Kentucky's proclamation of neutrality precluded this. Kentucky did, however, provide a shield for the defense of Tennessee, which the Confederates now proceeded to undo. On 4 September, before Johnston's arrival, Maj. Gen. Leonidas Polk of the Confederate army committed one of the major blunders of the war: He ordered Brig. Gen. Gideon J. Pillow to fortify Columbus, Kentucky, on the Mississippi River twenty miles below Cairo. This violation of Kentucky's neutrality gave the Union an excuse to intervene in that state. Two days after the Confederates seized Columbus, General Grant, acting on his own initiative, took Paducah, an important Ohio River town forty-five miles from Cairo at the confluence of the Tennessee and Ohio Rivers, to prevent the Confederates from moving in. This operation, carried out on the morning of 6 September, just as Foote was arriving at St. Louis, was made possible by transports escorted by the *Tyler* (commanded by Commander Rodgers) and *Conestoga* (Lieutenant Phelps). A few days later Grant positioned troops at Smithfield at the mouth of the Cumberland. The Union now controlled access to the Ohio, Tennessee, and Cumberland Rivers. On 11 September the Kentucky legislature ordered Confederate forces to leave the state.[30]

The Confederate defense of Tennessee rested on a line centered on the Tennessee and Cumberland Rivers, with the two flanks in advance of the center. Confederate forces were operating on the outside of the

arc, or exterior lines, while Union forces enjoyed the advantage of interior lines. The Confederates' awkward defensive position was partially
offset by their control of the railroad from Bowling Green to Columbus.

Columbus is close to where the Ohio River is joined by its two main
tributaries, the Cumberland and the Tennessee. The 650-mile-long Tennessee River rises in eastern Tennessee a few miles above Knoxville,
flows through northern Alabama and a corner of Mississippi, returns to
Tennessee, and then flows north into Kentucky west of Bowling Green
to join the Ohio at Paducah. The circuitous seven-hundred-mile-long
Cumberland River rises in eastern Kentucky and joins the Ohio at
Smithland, a few miles above Paducah.

Johnston regarded Columbus as the key to the western theater and
vowed to construct there a "Gibraltar of the West." Polk soon emplaced
guns on the high bluffs overlooking the river for some twenty miles in
either direction; by the end of October he had ten thousand troops there
and ultimately a large number of guns. Columbus became the most important Confederate fortification on the great river. The ever-cautious Halleck
wrote McClellan on 20 January that "Columbus cannot be taken without
an immense siege train and a terrible loss of life. I have thoroughly studied
its defenses—they are very strong." But Columbus could be flanked. As
Halleck noted, "it can be turned, paralyzed, and forced to surrender."[31]

While Foote was busy overseeing construction of the more powerful
ironclads, he kept his three wooden gunboats out singly or in pairs ply-
ing the rivers in a series of small excursions. They gathered intelligence,
bolstered Unionist sentiment by showing the flag, and carried out small
attacks, sometimes in conjunction with the army. Cdr. Henry Walke had
operational command of the three timberclads. Walke, who had been a
midshipman with Foote, was an experienced officer and an accomplished artist who had seen action during the Mexican War. Lieutenant
Phelps's *Conestoga* made regular runs up the Tennessee and Cumberland Rivers to report on Confederate military activity. The *Tyler* (Walke)
and *Lexington* (Commander Stembel) kept guard on the Mississippi
below Cairo and reported on the Confederate buildup at Columbus. On
4 September the latter two boats steamed downriver to reconnoiter
Columbus carrying some of General Grant's staff and a hundred Union
soldiers. Off Columbus the *Tyler* fired eight to ten 8-inch shells into the
Confederate works and then retired. Soon the Union gunboats impressed
even army skeptics.[32]

One early expedition planned in conjunction with land forces resulted in the 10 September 1861 Battle of Lucas Bend. Confederate troops had established themselves at Norfolk, Missouri, about eight miles below Cairo, and Grant was determined to remove them. Toward that end he sent a land force and utilized the *Conestoga* and *Lexington* to cover their advance. The troops traveled only about three miles before running into Confederate pickets. The two steamers had preceded the troops, and Phelps's *Conestoga* came upon a Confederate force of cavalry and perhaps sixteen artillery pieces on the Missouri side of the river at Lucas Bend. Phelps immediately opened fire, and the Confederates returned fire. On hearing the noise, Stembel brought up the *Lexington* to join the fight. Union shell apparently had a considerable effect against the Confederate cavalry. About 1:00 P.M. the two timberclads retired upriver, hoping to draw the Confederates toward the Union troops moving overland in their direction. At the same time two Confederate steamers, one of them the *Yankee,* appeared from Columbus. Phelps engaged the *Yankee* at long range, managing to hit it with a shot in ricochet. The *Lexington* also scored a hit on the Confederate vessel with a shell from its 8-inch gun at extreme elevation that hit the *Yankee*'s wheelhouse. With only one engine working, the *Yankee* hauled off to the safety of the Confederate shore batteries at Columbus. The two Union gunboats then resumed firing on the Confederates ashore and forced them to retire. There was only one Union casualty, a man aboard the *Conestoga* hit by small-arms fire from shore. Phelps had his men fire canister at the thicket from which the shot had come and quickly cleared it of Confederates, some of whom were also shot by small-arms fire from aboard the steamer.[33]

In October, at the request of General Smith, Phelps began making reconnaissance trips to Fort Henry on the Tennessee River and Fort Donelson on the Cumberland. On the eleventh the *Conestoga* went up the Tennessee and anchored for the night several miles downriver from Fort Henry. The next morning Phelps took his ship in closer and examined the fort through a spyglass. The *Conestoga* received small-arms fire from along the bank, but Phelps reported that a shot from the *Conestoga* "put an end to further demonstrations of the kind." Phelps also told Foote that he had reliable reports that the Confederates were converting three steamers into gunboats and planned to use the extensive ironworks along the river to produce their iron plate. The largest of these gunboats was the *Eastport,* said to be one of the finest and fastest steamers in the West.

On the fourteenth the *Conestoga* entered the Cumberland and ascended sixty miles until the water became too shallow to proceed farther, then dropped back downriver to Eddyville, Kentucky. That town was largely secessionist, and southern sympathizers had driven out many of the Unionists, but the steamer's arrival there reversed the circumstances and sent the secessionists fleeing. On the seventeenth the *Conestoga* was again on the Tennessee, where Phelps seized a steam ferry, the *Henry*, and took it to Paducah.[34]

On 26 October the *Conestoga* escorted the steamer transport *Lake Erie* to Eddyville with three companies of the Ninth Illinois Regiment. The troops went ashore early the next morning and marched to a Confederate camp at Saratoga, some four miles from Eddyville. The Union troops charged and scattered the Confederate force, killing seven men, including the commander; the Union side suffered only three wounded. The Union troops then reembarked with their booty. The raid netted twenty-four prisoners, a number of horses and mules, and a quantity of small arms.[35]

On 10 December Lieutenant Phelps, one of Foote's most energetic officers, confirmed that the Confederates were building gunboats on the Cumberland, one at Clarksville and another at Nashville. He also reported that the *Eastport* was undergoing conversion up the Tennessee beyond Fort Henry. Phelps recommended immediate operations on both rivers.[36]

On 1 November 1861, Grant carried out a demonstration against Columbus in order to mask a Union effort in southeastern Missouri and prevent Polk from sending reinforcements there from Columbus. The next day Grant took 3,114 men (five infantry regiments, two artillery pieces, and two cavalry companies) down the Mississippi in six transports escorted by the *Lexington* and *Tyler*. Grant apparently had no precise plans when he set out, although one of his biographers contends that he clearly intended to fight rather than merely stage a demonstration.[37] Grant certainly knew that Columbus was too powerful for him to assault. Early on the seventh he landed 2,500 men to attack a Confederate force of 2,700 men encamped at Belmont, Missouri, across the Mississippi from the Confederate Gibraltar. The Union troops went ashore some three miles above Belmont, then moved to attack it while, at Grant's request, Commander Walke took the two timberclads to bombard Columbus as a diversion.

While the gunboats circled and exchanged broadsides with the heavy Confederate guns in the upper batteries at Columbus, Grant's force defeated the Confederates ashore. But when they gained the Confederate camp, the Union troops stopped to loot, enabling the Confederates to regroup. Polk, meanwhile, had sent reinforcements across the river, protected by the lower batteries at Columbus, with the plan of cutting off Grant's men from their transports.

Walke kept his timberclads moving constantly to avoid the Confederate gunfire. His gunboats engaged the Columbus batteries three times, and he was able to take advantage of his enemy's overshooting to close to within 450 yards. Most of the Union rounds fell short, however, and the only serious damage to the Confederate side occurred when one of their own guns burst. By now the Confederate batteries had the range, and Walke quickly removed his vessels, but not before shot from a 24-pounder entered the *Tyler,* decapitating one seaman and wounding two others. Walke now brought the timberclads back to the landing to pick up Grant's troops.

Shortly afterward, Grant's now-outnumbered forces managed to cut their way through the rebel forces. As the last federals were hurriedly reboarding the transports, the Confederates struck in strength and were met by fire from the timberclads. As Walke noted, "Our gunboats being in good position, we opened a brisk fire of grape and canister and five shells, silencing the enemy with great slaughter." A few miles up the river the timberclads encountered the Union transport *Chancellor* with Brig. Gen. John A. McClernand aboard. He informed Walke that some Union troops had been left behind and asked the gunboats to return to get them. Walke agreed and was able to secure most of the men, along with about forty Confederate prisoners.[38]

The Battle of Belmont was costly for both sides: 610 Union casualties and 642 Confederate. Each side claimed victory. Confederate general Polk referred to it as "this signal triumph of our arms and the defeat of the machinations of our enemies," attributing it to "the favoring providence of Almighty God."[39] Belmont was not an engagement Grant could point to with particular pride. Indeed, many of his officers and men saw it as a blunder reflecting poor generalship. The Confederates had won the battlefield, but Polk had failed to capture Grant and his expeditionary force. Had he done so, it would have had great consequences for both western riverine warfare and the entire war in general.

The northern press celebrated Belmont as a victory. Certainly it delighted Lincoln, who saw in Grant a general willing to fight. Although it was hardly the beginning of a great thrust down the Mississippi as it was pictured in the northern newspapers, Belmont did help bring about Union control of Missouri and provided valuable combat experience for Grant's troops. It also spread a near panic in the South over possible future Union amphibious operations. Polk requested additional men and artillery and was now reluctant to heed General Johnston's calls for manpower. In this sense Belmont was perhaps a critical diversion for the subsequent Union operations against Forts Henry and Donelson. Certainly Foote had every reason to be pleased; his timberclads had demonstrated that they could speedily move both men and supplies; operate with surprise and flexibility; and, at minimum cost to themselves, provide effective artillery support for troops ashore.[40]

Throughout the rest of November and December the Union flotilla was busy with river patrol duties. On 19 November, Nathan Bedford Forrest and three hundred Confederate soldiers laid a trap at Canton, Kentucky, letting it be known that there was a quantity of supplies there and hoping to lure a party ashore. The *Conestoga* set out, but Phelps was warned by a German man on the shore a few miles from their goal. When the Confederates opened up from a wooded area with small arms and a 12-pounder, Phelps fired his 32-pounders, which had already been charged with canister. These acted like giant shotguns and soon ended the engagement without significant damage to the timberclad.[41]

In January 1862 McClellan ordered Grant, through Halleck, to stage a "demonstration" threatening Nashville. McClellan believed that Buell was about to begin his long-delayed offensive on that city and hoped that the "demonstration" would keep Confederates from Columbus or Forts Henry and Donelson from reinforcing Brig. Gen. Simon Bolivar Buckner's command at Bowling Green and blocking Buell's path.

Grant immediately ordered Brig. Gen. C. F. Smith at Paducah to send troops up the western bank of the Tennessee River to threaten Fort Henry. At the same time Grant accompanied six thousand men of Brigadier General McClernand's division from Cairo and Bird's Point into western Kentucky to threaten Columbus. The weather was cold with rain and snow; the roads, never good in the best of times, were horrible. Despite the elements, this mission of more than a week provided further training for the Union soldiers and prevented Confederate troop movements.

Foote's gunboats supported these operations; the *Conestoga* and *Lexington* lent aid to Smith from the Tennessee, while the *Essex* and *St. Louis* did the same for Grant and McClernand on the Mississippi. On 11 January the latter two gunboats fought an hour-long battle with three Confederate gunboats that came up from Columbus and drove off the rebels.[42]

Meanwhile, Buell and Halleck were still at loggerheads over strategy, with Buell opposing any large-scale attack by Halleck against Fort Henry. Buell informed both Halleck and McClellan that he could support Grant only by marching his entire army against Bowling Green, something he was not prepared to do. Anything less, he said, would be unsuccessful and would be regarded by the Confederates as a mere demonstration.

Under pressure from both McClellan and Lincoln to mount an assault into eastern Tennessee, Buell finally sent Brig. Gen. George H. Thomas with four thousand men in a thrust toward Knoxville. The Confederate generals defending the Cumberland Gap, Maj. Gen. George B. Crittenden and Brig. Gen. Felix Zollicoffer, soon learned of this and took steps to stop them, but Zollicoffer maneuvered into a position north of the flooded Cumberland from which he was unable to retreat. Under these circumstances, Crittenden decided to attack. This led to a Union victory in the Battle of Mill Springs, Kentucky (or Logan's Crossroads) on 19 January 1862. It also cost Zollicoffer his life, shattered Johnston's right flank, and changed Union strategy in the West.

Crittenden retreated across the Cumberland toward Knoxville, abandoning eastern Kentucky to Union control. Buell, citing poor roads and supply difficulties, did not follow up the victory by advancing into eastern Tennessee. Thomas moved his army to Burkesville, Kentucky, about seventy-five miles northeast of Nashville on the Cumberland. Both he and Buell wanted Foote's gunboats to push up the Cumberland past Fort Donelson and join them in a Union attack on Nashville, a move they believed was preferable to an operation under Halleck against Fort Henry. After McClellan rejected this proposal, Buell suggested a full-scale attack against Bowling Green in conjunction with Halleck's descent on Fort Henry; but Buell's troops did not move from Burkesville until 6 February, far too late to effect the strategic concentration sought by Halleck.[43]

Halleck, who opposed multiple lines of operation, favored concentrating in middle Tennessee with Buell within supporting distance. He wanted to attack Fort Henry while Buell moved against Fort Donelson. Concentrating Union strength in the two-rivers area would also mean that Halleck could bypass Columbus without having to attack that stronghold. McClellan agreed that securing control of Confederate rail lines running east was much more important than taking Columbus or Memphis.[44]

While the two department commanders were communicating with McClellan rather than each other, General Smith's column, accompanied up the Tennessee by the *Conestoga* and *Lexington,* got close to Forts Heiman and Henry. The *Lexington,* with Smith and his staff aboard, steamed to within two miles of Henry before coming under fire from its batteries.[45] Smith was not convinced that the Confederate forts were vulnerable to a combined land and river operation. Fort Heiman occupied high ground commanding Fort Henry from the other side of the Tennessee River. Grant believed that

> its possession by us, with the aid of our gunboats, would insure the capture of Fort Henry. This report of Smith confirmed views I had previously held, that the true line of operations for us was up the Tennessee and Cumberland rivers. With us there, the enemy would be compelled to fall back on the east and west entirely out of the State of Kentucky.[46]

Grant was eager to get on with a major campaign. He wrote his sister that he now commanded more men than Winfield Scott had in Mexico and that he hoped to "retain so important a command for at least one battle."[47] On 6 January he secured permission from Halleck to visit him in St. Louis in order to discuss important military matters; his intent was to persuade Halleck to launch an immediate offensive in which troops would be moved by river against Fort Henry and then invade the Tennessee River valley. Grant wrote later that Halleck authorized the visit grudgingly and received him with "so little cordiality that I perhaps stated the object of my visit with less clearness than I might have done, and I had not uttered many sentences before I was cut short as if my plan was preposterous. I returned to Cairo very much crestfallen."[48]

A number of individuals later claimed credit for the river offensive against Forts Henry and Donelson. Commander Porter had reported the vulnerability of Fort Henry to naval attack, and Lieutenant Phelps had long urged an assault on both the Cumberland and Tennessee Rivers. Buell had also advocated such a strike, and Smith had pointed out the vulnerability of Fort Henry. But the most persistent advocates of such a campaign were Grant and Foote, who consulted often. Grant later said that Foote "agreed with me perfectly as to the feasibility of the campaign up the Tennessee."[49] Foote recalled it differently. He wrote in November 1862 that he "proposed to General Grant . . . that with four of the boats and 6,000 troops we should ascend the Tenn. and attack Fort Henry. The General preferred the Cumberland and Fort Donelson, as the more appropriate points of attack, but yielded to my views if Genl. Halleck's assent could be obtained."[50]

As individuals, Foote and Grant could hardly have been more different. One was a God-fearing abolitionist teetotaler; the other may have feared God, but he was certainly indifferent toward slavery and hardly abstemious. Yet they worked together splendidly. The subsequent successful Union river campaign in Tennessee owed much to this, as well as to their initiative, leadership, and lack of ego. Unlike many other commanders in history, Foote well understood the necessity of close army-navy cooperation. He told his brother John that the two were "like blades of shears—united, invincible; separated, almost useless."[51]

On 22 January 1862, Grant received Smith's formal report concerning the vulnerability of Forts Heiman and Henry to attack.[52] Convinced that he was correct, Grant on the twenty-eighth renewed his call for a Union offensive and telegraphed Halleck: "With permission, I will take Fort Henry, on the Tennessee and establish and hold a large camp there." Foote also sent a telegram to Halleck: "General Grant and myself are of the opinion that Fort Henry, on the Tennessee River, can be carried with four ironclad gunboats and troops, and be permanently occupied. Have we your authority to move for that purpose when ready?"[53] Halleck still withheld permission, and the next day Grant sent a detailed proposal by letter.

Halleck's decision was influenced by his desire to counter Buell's success in Kentucky. Lincoln was also applying pressure. On 27 January, using his authority as commander in chief of the nation's armed forces, Lincoln had issued General War Order 1, decreeing that all Union armies begin an advance on 22 February (George Washington's birthday and Jefferson Davis's inauguration day). But what finally prompted Halleck to act was a report that Richmond was sending Confederate reinforcements west. As he put it to Grant, "A telegram from Washington says that [Gen. P. G. T.] Beauregard left Manassas four days ago with fifteen regiments for the line of Columbus and Bowling Green. It is therefore of the greatest importance that we cut that line before he arrives. You will move with the least delay possible."[54] Unfortunately for Johnston and the South, the reinforcement was limited to Beauregard and a handful of staff officers.

On 30 January Halleck wired Grant: "Make your preparations to take and hold Fort Henry. I will send you written instructions by mail."[55] The Union expedition set out on 2 February. Johnston's bluff was about to be called.[56]

~✕ 10 ✕~

FORT HENRY

*A*fter Tennessee seceded from the Union, Gov. Isham G. Harris sent Brig. Gen. Daniel S. Donelson to select sites along the Tennessee and Cumberland Rivers for fortifications. Although Donelson was not happy with any of the locations he investigated, he chose two. The site on the Tennessee River was named Fort Henry for Gustavus A. Henry, the state's senior Confederate senator. The other, on the Cumberland, was named for the general himself.

In the summer of 1861 Col. Adolphus Heiman and the 720 men of his Tenth Tennessee Regiment began work on the Tennessee River site. Fort Henry covered some three acres of ground in a solidly built, five-sided earthwork parapet about eight feet high. Rifle pits extended to the river and above the main work on the water side and from outside Fort Henry's perimeter some two miles to the east toward Dover and Fort Donelson.[1]

In December 1861 Brig. Gen. Lloyd Tilghman assumed command of Forts Henry and Donelson. An 1836 West Point graduate, Tilghman's only previous active military duty had been during the Mexican War. He and others who served at Fort Henry were as one in criticizing its location.[2] Although it lay in a bend of the Tennessee River and commanded a straight stretch of water some three miles long, Fort Henry was on low ground that was overwashed by the river and easily commanded by higher terrain on both sides. When Johnston's military engineers finally examined Fort Henry, they reported that the site was badly chosen and confirmed that it could be dominated by high ground across the river. Johnston ordered that high ground to be held and fortified. Tilghman later called Henry "a wretched military position":

> The entire fort . . . is enfiladed from three or four points on the opposite shore, while three points on the eastern bank completely command them both, all at easy cannon range. . . . The history of military engineering records no parallel to this case. Points within a few miles of it, possessing great advantages and few disadvantages, were totally neglected, and a location fixed upon without one redeeming feature or filling one of the many requirements of a site for a work such as Fort Henry. . . . An enemy had but to use their most common sense in obtaining the advantage of high water, as was the case, to have complete and entire control of the position.[3]

But Tilghman did little to rectify the situation. By January he had barely started to fortify the heights on the west bank, known as Fort Heiman after Henry's second in command. Johnston, who had ordered the work done months before, was furious. Although he telegraphed Tilghman to push efforts to entrench Fort Heiman, the work there was still unfinished when the Union forces arrived in February 1862. Fort Henry mounted seventeen heavy guns: twelve faced the river and five guarded the land approaches. The fort had eight 32-pounders, two 42-pounders, one 128-pounder columbiad rifled gun, five long 18-pounder siege guns, and a 6-inch rifled gun (also described as a 24-pound caliber throwing a 68-pound shot). There were also six old 12-pounders. Suspicious of the latter, the defenders tested two, which blew up, and promptly discarded the others.[4]

Compounding problems for the Confederates, in early February 1862 both the Tennessee and the Cumberland were in flood. At Fort Henry the water came near to flooding the magazines and even to within a few feet of the guns themselves, and some of the land within the fort's perimeter was two feet underwater. The Confederates had no ammunition for their 42-pounders, leaving only nine guns able to contest a water approach. And Tilghman had only 2,610 men in two brigades under Colonels Heiman and Joseph Drake. Many of these were raw recruits who had only shotguns and hunting rifles; the Tenth Tennessee Regiment was armed with flint-locks from the War of 1812.[5]

On 30 January Lieutenant Phelps took the *Conestoga* and *Lexington* on a last reconnaissance of Fort Henry and invited Brig. Gen. Lew Wallace to join him. The gunboats anchored in the middle of the Tennessee at Panther Island that night. The next day the *Conestoga* approached the fort and Phelps and Wallace examined it through a spyglass. The defenders did not fire. Phelps reported that the river was probably mined and that the Confederates anticipated an attack and were "prepared to defend the post at all hazards."[6]

Foote reported to Gideon Welles from Paducah that the transports had been delayed but he was "ready with the seven gun-boats to act offensively whenever the Army is in condition to advance; and have every confidence, under God, that we shall be able to silence the guns of Fort Henry and its surroundings." Foote did complain about the lack of trained men. Although the army had produced more volunteers than the number required, they were untrained and fewer than fifty of them were with the flotilla.[7]

On 2 February the Union movement from Cairo to Fort Henry began. Although great effort had been made to ready the ironclads for service, only four were available when the expedition set out: the *Cincinnati* (flagship, Commander Stembel), *Carondelet* (Commander Walke), *Essex* (Commander Porter), and *St. Louis* (Lieutenant Paulding). The three timberclads—the *Conestoga* (Lieutenant Phelps), *Lexington* (Lt. James W. Shirk), and *Tyler* (Lt. William Gwin)—assisted in escorting the troop transports. Two trips would be necessary to transport all of Grant's seventeen thousand men.[8]

Despite his doubts regarding them, Foote had hoped to employ his new mortar boats in the assault, but this proved impossible. Fort Pitt Foundry was slow in delivering their mortars, and so they were left behind. Lincoln, who had become quite interested in the western navy, and especially the mortar boats, was furious, and Fox reported to Foote that the president was determined to remove the chief of the Bureau of Ordnance, Col. James W. Ripley. On 31 January Lincoln authorized Foote, through Lieutenant Wise, to purchase two steamers to act as tenders and to quarter their crews. He also expressed the hope that when the mortar boats were ready to attack Columbus, Kentucky, that they would "rain the rebels out" because he wanted to "treat them to a refreshing shower of sulphur and brimstone." Through Wise, Lincoln also commended Foote for "the energy you have displayed in the matters intrusted to your charge."[9]

Once the transports were in place the ironclads led the advance up the Tennessee, with the more vulnerable timberclads bringing up the rear; Phelps commanded the latter division. Grant placed General McClernand in command of the expedition while he followed in one of the later boats. McClernand's force halted some six miles below Fort Henry.[10] Thanks to the torrential rains, the river was about twenty-five feet above low water. The strong river current made for slow and dangerous progress, but it did sweep away a number of Confederate mines (known as "torpedoes"), whose presence had been inadvertently revealed by the wife of a Confederate captain at the fort in conversation with some of Grant's scouts. Foote immediately set Phelps's division to work sweeping for them. Using the *Conestoga* and *Tyler*, Phelps dragged the river in the channel off Panther Island where the mines were now known to be located. The torpedoes were sheet-iron cylinders five and a half feet long and pointed at each end; each contained about seventy-five pounds of gunpowder and was fired by contact-type detonators. Phelps used cutters to bring the mines to the surface with lines and grappling hooks. That day they recovered six mines, soaked and harmless. The next day they removed two more.[11]

The Confederates were aware of the Union advance. At 4:00 P.M. on the fourth a courier arrived at Fort Donelson with word from Colonel Heiman at Fort Henry that at 4:30 A.M. signal rockets from a picket at Bailey's Landing on the Tennessee had announced the Union advance. Tilghman, who had been overseeing the work to improve Donelson's defenses, immediately left to direct Fort Henry's defense. Lt. Col. Jeremy F. Gilmer, chief engineer of the Western Department, who had been sent by Johnston to try to remedy deficiencies at Henry and Donelson, went with him, as did some Confederate cavalry. Meanwhile Capt. Jesse Taylor, commanding Fort Henry's artillery, recalled, "Far as eye could see, the course of the river could be traced by the dense volumes of smoke issuing from the flotilla—indicating that the long-threatened attempt to break our lines was to be made in earnest."[12] Tilghman telegraphed General Polk to request reinforcements and on the next day, the fifth, optimistically stated that "there was a glorious chance to overwhelm the enemy." No reinforcements arrived.[13]

Upon his arrival at the federal anchorage Grant wanted to determine how close he could land his men to Fort Henry without having them come under fire. He boarded the *Essex* and proceeded upriver past the mouth of Panther Creek, which flowed westward into the Tennessee. Because the creek was a torrent, Grant hoped to land south of it and save his men the difficult crossing. The *Essex* soon came under fire but the shot fell short. Grant had decided that he could indeed land south of Panther Creek when the Confederates opened up with a rifled gun that outranged those aboard the ironclad.[14] James Laning, second mate aboard the ironclad, described what happened:

> When about two, or two and a half miles distant, the fort fired a rifle shot, which passed over our boat to the right and cut down a number of saplings on shore. In a few moments, another shot, fired with more precision, passed over the spar-deck among the officers; through the officers' quarters, visiting in its flight the steerage, commander's pantry and cabin, passing through the stern; doing, however, no damage except breaking some of the captain's dishes, and cutting the feet from a pair of his socks, which happened to be hanging over the back of a chair in his cabin. These shots reaching us at so great a distance, rather astonished us, as the enemy intended they should.[15]

The second shot barely missed both Grant and Porter, and Porter immediately ordered the *Essex* back. In the end, Grant had his troops debark north of the creek, at Bailey's Ferry, three miles from the fort and just beyond the range of its guns, and then left for Paducah with the transports to hurry along Smith's division. He returned the next day with Smith's advance elements.[16] Late on the fifth, three of the Union gunboats steamed into view of Fort Henry and opened a "vigorous and well-directed fire" that killed one defender and wounded three others. It also prompted the Confederates to fire six shots in return, at which point the gunboats withdrew.[17]

The Union troops did not finish debarking until the night of the fifth, when it rained heavily. Although he did not yet have all his men in place, Grant believed that the Confederates would quickly move to reinforce Fort Henry, and that "prompt action on our part was imperative." That evening, hopeful all his men would have arrived in time, Grant ordered the advance to begin at 11:00 A.M. the next day.[18] Later that night a heavy thunderstorm moved through the area, causing a further rise in the river, and trees, fences, and other debris threatened to sweep the boats in the river downstream. Coal heavers aboard the gunboats were hard at work to keep steam up and paddlewheels churning to hold the boats anchored in the river.[19]

While Grant was making his preparations, Foote inspected his ships and admonished the men. James Laning remembered that Foote told the crew of the *Essex* "to be brave and courageous, and above all to place their faith in Divine Providence." He instructed Laning, who had charge of the gunboat's battery, to make every shot count and told him that his "greatest efforts should be to disable the enemy's guns, and to be sure you do not throw any ammunition away. Every charge you fire from one of those guns cost the government about eight dollars. If your shots fall short you encourage the enemy. If they reach home you demoralize him, and get the worth of your money."[20]

Grant planned simultaneous land and water attacks. During the night of the fifth he sent General Smith with two of his brigades along the west bank of the river to prevent any reinforcement from that direction, to cut off any Confederate escape, and to seize the high ground at Fort Heiman for possible artillery emplacement. When they reached Fort Heiman, Smith's men discovered that the Confederates had already evacuated it. The main Union land effort was to be made on the east bank of the river by McClernand's division with a brigade from Smith. But the area's wretched roads, dense woods, and swampy conditions delayed their arrival at Fort Henry.

On the night of the fifth, realizing the strength of the opposing forces, Tilghman had called together his principal officers. All were pessimistic, believing they could not withstand an attack by an enemy estimated to number at least twenty-five thousand men. Tilghman asked Taylor if his guns could "hold out for one hour against a determined attack." When Taylor replied in the affirmative, Tilghman ordered his commanders to have their men ready to move at a "moment's notice."

At ten o'clock on the morning of the sixth, before the Union attack began, Tilghman ordered all but the artillery company manning the batteries to go to Fort Donelson. This left only about a hundred defenders at Fort Henry, including those too sick to move. Tilghman saw the troops on their way to safety and then returned to the fort to share its fate. His intention was to delay the attackers long enough for his command to escape. By the time Tilghman returned to Henry the naval attack was already under way.

Just before 10:00 A.M. Foote had met with his captains onboard the *Cincinnati,* encouraged them, shook hands with each, and asked God to look after them. The captains then returned to their vessels, and at 10:20 Foote signaled the flotilla to prepare for battle; at 10:50 he ordered the ships to get under way. At 11:35 the four ironclads formed in line abreast: the *Essex* on the right, then the *Cincinnati, Carondelet,* and *St. Louis.* Because of the narrowness of the river the latter two gunboats were lashed together and remained so during the battle. A half mile behind them came Phelps's timberclads.[21] The gunboats moved slowly forward, using Panther Island as a shield for as long as possible. In passing the island the ironclads were almost close enough together for a man to have walked from one to another. They then spread out again. As the Union flotilla neared Fort Henry there was no sound from shore and no sign of the Union troops, and Foote decided to begin the battle without them. As the flotilla continued upriver, the fort, with its Confederate flag waving defiantly, huts, and earthworks, soon came into view.

At 11:45 A.M., the *Cincinnati* fired a shot from about seventeen hundred yards' range, signaling the other gunboats to commence fire. When the Union flotilla had approached to within a mile, Taylor ordered the fort's water battery to respond, and firing then became general. The gunboats used only their bow guns, initially elevated at seven degrees with shell fuses set to explode in fifteen seconds. They continued to fire while they closed to within six hundred yards of the fort, when their guns were depressed to only three degrees and shells were at five-second delay. Phelps's division remained at long range, lobbing shells into the fort. The timberclads were positioned toward the left bank to avoid firing over the ironclads.[22]

Captain Taylor assigned each Confederate gun crew to a particular vessel and ordered them to keep their pieces "constantly trained" on that target. The Confederates had the advantage in knowing precise ranges to their targets, and their fire was both lively and accurate. Although Fort Henry had only nine guns that could respond, the gunners succeeded in hitting all the gunboats many times (fifty-nine hits in all), but most of the damage was slight, save to the *Essex.* About two-thirds of the way through the battle, and after the *Essex* had fired seventy-two shots from its two 9-inch Dahlgren shell guns, a Confederate shell tore into the ironclad's middle boiler. The blast and steam killed or wounded thirty-two men, including Commander Porter. Badly scalded, he managed to escape through a port;

a seaman clinging to the side of the vessel held him up until he could be brought back aboard. The gunboat drifted out of control downriver but was towed to safety by a tug. A seaman was also killed and nine others wounded onboard the *Cincinnati*; Foote briefly had the wind knocked out of him by a shot against the pilothouse but was otherwise uninjured.[23]

The damage to the fort was more extensive. From the beginning Union fire was quite accurate and the crews could see shell explosions throwing up earth around the rebel guns. At 12:35 P.M. the fort's 6-inch rifled gun blew up, killing or wounding all its crew, and a priming wire stuck in the vent of the 10-inch columbiad, effectively spiking it. Two 32-pounders were then struck at almost the same time, and as Taylor noted, "the flying fragments of the shattered guns and bursted shells disabled every man at the two guns." The Confederate gunners were dispirited, and even Tilghman's example of working one of the guns himself failed to elicit much enthusiasm.[24]

Lieutenant Colonel Gilmer and some others now also left for Donelson. At 1:50 P.M., with only four guns able to return fire, Tilghman mounted the parapet and waved a flag of truce. Heavy smoke prevented Union gunners from seeing it, but five minutes later Captain Taylor and a sergeant succeeded in freeing the halyards on the flagpole, which had been hit by Union fire, and lowered the Confederate flag. Taylor reported that by then the gunboats were only two hundred yards from the fort and sweeping it with their fire.

Tilghman sent his adjutant out in a small boat to the *Cincinnati*, and the crewmen of the flagship let out a loud cheer. Foote later wrote his wife, "I had to run among them & knock them on the head to restore order. The surgeon hollered and bellowed & I told him that he ought to be ashamed of himself."[25] Foote then sent Commander Stembel and Lieutenant Phelps ashore to raise the U.S. flag. Phelps accepted the surrender from Taylor for Tilghman. Later, at Foote's request, Tilghman went aboard the flagship.[26] Foote later told a friend that Tilghman arrived aboard the *Cincinnati* deeply distressed,

> wringing his hands and exclaiming, "I am in despair; my reputation is gone forever." I replied, "General, there is no reason you should feel thus. More than two thirds of your battery is disabled, while I have not lost less than one third of mine. To continue the action would only involve a needless sacrifice of life, and under the circumstances, you have done right in surrendering. Moreover, I shall always be ready to testify that you have defended your post like a

brave man." I then added, "Come general, you have lost your dinner, and the steward has just told me that mine is ready;" and, taking him by the arm, we walked together into the cabin.[27]

Tilghman had, moreover, accomplished his aim of saving the garrison. Two hours had been gained for the escape. Indeed, only ninety-four men, including Tilghman and sixteen aboard the Confederate hospital boat *Patton,* surrendered at Fort Henry. Confederate personnel losses from federal fire were remarkably light: five dead, eleven wounded, and five missing. The victors did capture the fort's heavy guns, supplies, and equipment abandoned by the garrison, which had retreated to Donelson on foot without wagons.

The Union troops played no part in the battle. McClernand had moved out on schedule at 11:00 A.M. with his division, followed by Smith's Third Brigade. Grant had ordered him to bestride the road to Fort Donelson and Dover in order to prevent Confederate troops from reinforcing Fort Henry or evacuating it. McClernand was then to await Grant's orders and be ready to storm Henry if need be. Poor road conditions—the track was mired in mud—delayed the troops' arrival, but they cheered the sound of the naval bombardment. At 3:00 P.M. McClernand learned that the Confederates might be evacuating the fort and sent cavalry ahead to verify it. The cavalrymen pursued the retreating Confederates, slowed by muddy roads, for some three miles and captured six guns and thirty-eight stragglers. After the battle McClernand gave Fort Henry a new name: Fort Foote.[28] The first Union troops did not arrive at Fort Henry until about an hour after its surrender. Commander Walke, whom Foote had placed in charge, then turned the fort over to Grant. McClellan was delighted to learn that Henry had fallen. He wired Halleck: "Please thank Grant and Foote and their commands for me." His request was carried out only with respect to Foote.[29]

Foote reported to Welles that the gunboats "after a severe and rapid fire of one hour and a quarter, have captured Fort Henry and have taken General Lloyd Tilghman and his staff, with 60 men, as prisoners. The surrender to the gunboats was unconditional, as we kept an open fire upon them until their flag was struck."[30]

Significant though this victory was, its circumstances were unlikely to be repeated: the high river had worked very much to Union advantage, as had the low position of the batteries facing the gunboats, and a number of the Confederate guns had been disabled by accidents. Tilghman well understood this. In a report to Richmond he detailed the damage inflicted on the Union ironclads and then noted:

> The weak points in all their vessels were known to us, and the cool precision of our firing developed them, showing conclusively that this class of boats, though formidable can not stand the test of even the 32-pounders, much less the 24-caliber rifled shot, or that of the 10-inch columbiad. It should be remembered that these results were principally from no heavier metal than the ordinary 32-pounder, using solid shot, fired at point-blank, giving the vessels all the advantages of their peculiar structures, with planes meeting this fire at angles of 45 degrees. The immense area, forming what may be called the roof, is in every respect vulnerable to either a plunging fire from even 32-pounders or a curved line of fire from heavy guns.[31]

Immediately after the capture of Fort Henry, Grant called together his officers to discuss the possibility of taking Fort Donelson. "The question for consideration, gentlemen, is," Grant informed them, "whether we shall march against Fort Donelson or wait for reinforcements. I should like to have your views." All declared themselves in favor of moving against Donelson as soon as possible.[32]

The Sunday after the battle Foote preached at a church in Cairo on the text John 14:1, "Let not your hearts be troubled; ye believe in God; believe also in me." One of the crew of the *Benton* who attended described it as "a real good plain common sense sermon, with which everyone seemed pleased."[33]

❧ II ❧

FORT DONELSON

Fort Donelson was located on the west bank of the Cumberland River two miles north of the little county seat of Dover. Larger and better placed than Fort Henry, it occupied a steep bluff as much as a hundred feet above the Cumberland and overlooked a straight stretch of several miles of the river. Because the Cumberland was then in flood, Hickman's Creek to the north and Indian Creek to the south of Donelson, both of which emptied into the Cumberland, were filled with deep water and were much wider than normal. This aided the defenders by providing a natural barrier, but it also worked to the advantage of attackers in that they would not have to extend their longer, exterior, line to cover these points of the line. Further, the backwater up Indian Creek bisected the Confederate position and made communication with Dover difficult.

The fort itself covered only about fifteen acres. Constructed by troops and slaves over some seven months, it had earthen works at least six feet high. The garrison had built some four hundred log cabins as barracks. The outer works covered about one hundred acres. Immediately after the fall of Fort Henry the Confederates accelerated work on extending the land defenses. This included digging rifle pits that reached out some two miles toward Fort Henry and clearing timber to secure unobstructed fields of fire and constructing entrenchments. The ground was hilly and generally wooded. Beyond the entrenched line over about half of its length was a ravine running north and south that opened onto Hickman's Creek. On the line's fort side the defenders cut down trees about chest high, leaving them attached to their stumps with the tops pointed outward from the entrenchments to form a crude abatis in front of most of the line.

Donelson's two river batteries were cut into the slope of the ridge facing downriver. The most important of these was the lower battery to the north, which commanded the Cumberland beyond the extreme range of its guns. It was dug into the hillside and sat thirty feet above river level at the time of the battle. Excavated dirt was mounded up on the lower side of the slope to make a rampart some twelve feet high. Sandbags added to its height and were placed so as to leave narrow embrasures for the guns. These could be slight because the river targets against which the guns would fire would be on a narrow front. The trench was also arranged so that each gun was protected from the one next to it, insuring that an explosion at one gun would not damage the others. The battery contained the defenders' largest gun, a 10-inch columbiad on a barbette mount, and nine 32-pounders.

The upper battery, to the south of the first battery and directly east of the fort, also could fire upriver. It had three guns: a 10-inch columbiad bored and rifled as a 32-pounder and two 32-pounder carronades. The fort itself had eight additional guns. In his *Naval History of the Civil War*, David Porter described Donelson as "the strongest military work in the entire theater of war."[1]

The day after Fort Henry fell, Brig. Gen. Bushrod R. Johnson assumed command of Donelson. The garrison then numbered only about six thousand men, including the two brigades of infantry that had fled Fort Henry under Colonel Heiman and had arrived the night of 6 February 1862. General Johnston, assumed that Grant would move next on Donelson and that the fort was doomed. In a report to Richmond Johnston predicted that

> the slight resistance at Fort Henry indicates that the best open earthworks are not reliable to meet successfully a vigorous attack of iron-clad gunboats, and, although now supported by a considerable force, I think the gunboats of the

enemy will probably take Fort Donelson without the necessity of employing their land force in co-operation, as seems to have been done at Fort Henry."[2]

When Generals Johnston, Beauregard, and William J. Hardee met to consider options after the fall of Fort Henry, all agreed that Donelson could not be held. Johnston wanted to extract his forward defenders so his army could fight under more favorable circumstances. He would give up Kentucky for the time being. Confederate forces at Bowling Green, the eastern anchor of his defensive line, would retreat on Nashville for a defense behind the Cumberland. And despite Maj. Gen. Leonidas Polk's opposition, Johnston decided to evacuate Columbus except for a small force and send its troops to Humboldt, Tennessee. The Confederates would try to hold Island No. 10 and Fort Pillow, both on the Mississippi and guarding upriver access to Memphis. Johnston reported to Richmond that all three generals agreed on these moves. Although there is no proof of this, Beauregard later claimed that he had urged Johnston to concentrate Confederate resources at Fort Donelson. On 14 February Beauregard did write prophetically: "We must give up some minor points, and concentrate our forces to save the most important ones, or we will lose all of them in succession."[3]

If Johnston believed Donelson was untenable, why did he send twelve thousand reinforcements there? This force was not sufficient to defeat Grant and merely upped the ante of possible losses through capture. The answer is simple. Johnston sent the reinforcements because he thought that strengthening the force at Donelson would keep Grant at bay until Johnston could withdraw the rest of his eastern forces to Nashville; in fact, he informed Jefferson Davis that he intended to fight for Nashville at Donelson. Thus as Union general Wallace noted, Johnston, despite his knowledge of the vast Union forces opposing him,

> persisted in fighting for Nashville, and for that purpose he divided his thirty thousand men. Fourteen thousand he kept in observation of Buell at Louisville. Sixteen thousand he gave to defend Fort Donelson. The latter detachment he himself called, "the best part of his army." It is difficult to think of a great master of strategy making an error so perilous.[4]

Historians have been hard on Johnston for his troop dispositions. T. Harry Williams noted that "the only explanation for these confusions and contradictions is that Johnston was moving temporarily in a fog of mental paralysis induced by the crisis he was facing."[5]

Grant certainly believed that Johnston had made a major blunder. He had expected Johnston to be a formidable opponent but later wrote: "After studying the orders and dispatches of Johnston, I am compelled to materially modify my views of that officer's qualifications as a soldier. My judgment now is that he was vacillating and undecided in his actions."[6] Such behavior could be fatal against an aggressive commander such as Grant.

If indeed he was determined to make a stand at Donelson, Johnston should have concentrated all his available forces there. Instead he sent half of the available men to Donelson and the other half to Nashville. Had Johnston concentrated his northern resources at Donelson he could have confronted Grant's fifteen thousand men with thirty thousand before Grant could be reinforced by Buell. With Grant defeated, Buell would have had to retreat back to the Ohio. But the Confederate high command failed to think of its separate detachments as parts of a whole.[7]

Johnston could also have left General Hardee to supervise the retreat from Bowling Green while he either went to Donelson himself or sent Beauregard to direct the defense. Instead he took charge of the retreat from Bowling Green and sent Beauregard to supervise the Confederate withdrawal from Columbus. One point worth remembering is that Johnston was able to shift so many men to Donelson because Buell was slow to move and too far north to be a threat. Certainly Johnston hoped that an active defense of Donelson would buy the time to allow him to shift from a strategy of dispersed defense to one of concentrated offense. He wanted to strike the invading Union forces at some point, which in fact occurred in the Battle of Shiloh. Sacrificing Donelson and its garrison was never a part of his plan.[8]

Johnston had begun sending men to Donelson even before he learned of Henry's fall. On 9 February Gen. Gideon Pillow and two thousand men arrived there from Clarksville. Pillow exhorted his men to "drive back the ruthless invaders from our soil and again raise the Confederate flag over Fort Henry. . . . Our battle cry, 'Liberty or Death.'"[9] Shortly thereafter Gen. Charles Clark came up from Hopkinsville with two thousand more men, followed by Brig. Gens. John B. Floyd and Simon Bolivar Buckner from Russellville with eight thousand men.[10] The Confederates were indifferently armed. Their weapons included English-manufactured Enfields, single- and double-barreled shotguns, hunting rifles, and flintlock muskets, some of which had been modified with percussion locks.[11]

Johnston's decision to place Floyd in command at Donelson was unwise, to say the least. He was not a willing combatant. As late as December 1860 Floyd, a former governor of Virginia, had opposed secession. President Buchanan had appointed him secretary of war in 1857, and Floyd served in that post through the end of December 1860. He did not want to go to Donelson, and Pillow had to travel to Clarksville to convince him to obey Johnston's order. As Grant noted, although Floyd "was a man of talent enough for any civil position, he was no soldier and, probably, did not possess the elements of one."[12]

General Pillow, the second in command at Donelson, was simply incompetent. A prominent Tennessee lawyer, he had played a significant role in the 1844 nomination of President James K. Polk, who had repaid him during the Mexican War by appointing him a brigadier general of volunteers. Later Polk advanced him to major general. Grant, who served with Pillow in Mexico, had only contempt for his military abilities.

Simon Bolivar Buckner was the one capable soldier among the three senior Confederates at Donelson. A native of Kentucky and graduate of West Point, he had served with distinction in the Mexican War but left the army in 1855 to enter business. He supported Kentucky's neutrality and was offered a commission as a brigadier general in the U.S. Army, but after federal troops moved into his home state Buckner accepted a comparable rank in the Confederate Army.

Floyd arrived at Donelson on the night of 12 February with the last of his command; Johnson became his chief of staff. By this time the Donelson garrison had swelled to some eighteen to twenty-one thousand men, including a cavalry regiment and six light artillery batteries. Buckner with six regiments and two artillery batteries held the Confederate right wing; Pillow commanded the Confederate left wing of six brigades and four artillery batteries. The Confederates braced for the Union attack.[13]

So confident had Foote been of victory at Fort Henry that on 2 February he had issued bold special orders to Lieutenant Phelps. On his own initiative and without even consulting others, Foote instructed Phelps on the fall of Fort Henry to take his timberclads up the Tennessee River, disable the key Memphis-to-Louisville railroad bridge twenty-five miles above Henry, and then raid into Confederate territory as far upriver as the depth of water would allow. Foote himself departed for Cairo with his ironclads to effect repairs; only the *Carondelet* remained behind to support Union troops ashore.[14]

Phelps's five-day mission upriver began a few hours after the surrender of Fort Henry and was a great success. The timberclads seized three Confederate steamers and destroyed six others. One of the captures, the *Eastport,* later became a Union ironclad of the same name. The expedition also secured a considerable quantity of lumber, iron plate and other stores, and small arms. Its psychological impact was great as well, spreading panic among Confederates while at the same time heartening Unionists, a surprising number of whom came forward to cheer the Union gunboats.[15]

As Phelps raided up the Tennessee, Grant was preparing to move against Donelson. In informing General Halleck of the victory at Fort Henry, Grant said that he expected to take Fort Donelson on the eighth. This proved overly ambitious. Heavy rain turned roads into quagmires, and much of the route from Henry to Donelson was underwater, making the movement of artillery and baggage trains there all but impossible. Then, too, the gunboats were still away. Halleck had been singularly noncommittal on the matter of Grant's plan to attack Donelson. Grant later wrote in his *Memoirs* that "General Halleck did not approve or disapprove of my going to Fort Donelson. He said nothing whatever to me on the subject."[16]

Strangely, Halleck's exhortations to take Donelson were made to Foote, on 11 and 12 February, rather than to his field commander. Halleck did, however, work to get reinforcements to the point of battle. Gen. David Hunter sent men from Kansas, and Buell, too late, sent Gen. William Nelson's large division. The War Department also ordered scattered fragments of companies in the West consolidated into regiments and sent to Donelson, although many of these men were virtually untrained and would have to learn on the job.[17]

Grant was convinced that Johnston would move quickly to reinforce Donelson, and he was anxious to attack as soon as possible. As he put it later, "I felt that 15,000 men on the 8th would be more effective than 50,000 a month later."[18] Grant urged Foote to take the gunboats left at Cairo up the Cumberland without waiting for those that had gone to Eastport and Florence. As it happened, the *Conestoga* and *Tyler* returned from their raid up the Tennessee soon enough to be available, as was Walke's *Carondelet.* Grant requested that they secure control of the Cumberland as close to Donelson as possible. The *Carondelet* was the first to arrive. Towed by the steamer *Alps,* it reached the vicinity of

Donelson at 11:30 A.M. on the twelfth. No Union troops were in sight, and the fort looked deserted. Walke ordered some ten rounds fired at Fort Donelson from long range "to unmask the silent enemy, and to announce my arrival to General Grant." There was no reply from the fort. Walke then took the ironclad downriver a few miles and anchored for the night.[19]

Foote, meanwhile, had been busy at Cairo. His remarks to his wife concerning the engagement at Fort Henry are candid and quite telling: "I never again will go out and fight half prepared," he wrote. "Men were not exercised & perfectly green. The rifle shots hissed like snakes. Tilghman, well he would have cut us all to pieces had his best rifle not burst & his 128-pounder been stopped in the vent."[20]

On the night of 11 February, as Grant moved McClernand's division a few miles east toward Fort Donelson to more solid ground, Foote left Cairo with a reconstituted flotilla to cooperate in the attack on Donelson. His earlier enthusiasm and impatience for battle had dissolved into serious reservations:

> I go reluctantly, as we are very short of men; and transferring men from vessel to vessel, as we have to do, is having a very demoralizing effect upon them. Twenty-eight men ran off to-day, hearing that they were again to be sent out of their vessels. I do hope that the 600 men will be sent immediately. I shall do all in my power to render the gunboats effective in the fight, although they are not properly manned, but I must go, as General Halleck wishes it. If we could wait ten days, and I had men, I would go with eight mortar boats and six armored boats and conquer.[21]

The *Essex* and *Cincinnati* could not be repaired in time to participate. Although he believed the flotilla was unprepared, Foote sailed on Grant's urging with the *St. Louis* (flagship; Lieutenant Paulding), *Louisville* (Cdr. Benjamin Dove), and *Pittsburg* (Lt. Egbert Thompson). On the twelfth the gunboats encountered the *Conestoga* and *Lexington*. Foote ordered the *Conestoga* to join his flotilla, but the *Lexington*, which had been damaged in an accident, continued on to Cairo for repairs. At Paducah the flotilla joined up with twelve loaded troop transport steamers. The gunboats arrived in the vicinity of Fort Donelson on the night of the thirteenth to find that Grant's troops had already invested the fort on the landward side. Many of the officers and men of the Union flotilla believed they would replicate their easy victory at Fort Henry, but Donelson would be different.[22]

Meanwhile, on the twelfth, the first Union reinforcements arrived at Fort Henry in the form of Col. John M. Thayer's brigade of two full regiments. Grant ordered them not to debark but to follow the gunboats from Henry down the Tennessee, up the Ohio, and then up the Cumberland to Donelson.[23] Also on the twelfth Grant started out overland for Donelson from Henry with McClernand's and Smith's divisions, eight artillery batteries, and part of a cavalry regiment. In all, Grant had fifteen thousand men in twenty-five regiments. The weather had turned unseasonably warm, and many of the men chose to leave behind their knapsacks, heavy overcoats, and blankets or cast them aside en route, an action they would soon have cause to regret.[24]

The Union troops met no resistance before running into Confederate pickets west of Fort Donelson. Grant ordered Smith to take the left, facing Buckner's right wing, and McClernand to oppose the Confederate left wing under Pillow. On that day and the next, fifteen thousand unentrenched Union troops confronted twenty-one thousand entrenched Confederates, who made no effort to engage them.[25]

Firing opened early on the thirteenth when Union sharpshooters sniped at Confederate soldiers working to improve their forward defenses. Union infantry extended their lines north and south to make the investment as complete as possible. Artillery also was brought into position, and batteries on both sides opened fire.[26] McClernand soon discovered that the Confederate line was too long for him to envelop. Moreover, near the extremity of the rebel left lay the Charlotte road, a resupply route and possible escape hatch to Nashville. Grant ordered up the twenty-five hundred men of General Lew Wallace's brigade of Smith's division, who had been left behind at Fort Henry, and they arrived at Donelson on the fourteenth. Up to this point Union troops had initiated the limited fighting that had occurred.[27]

Of the Union flotilla, only the *Carondelet* had arrived. On the morning of the thirteenth it returned and took up a post near Donelson. Walke received a message from Grant asking him to make another demonstration at 10:00 A.M. to divert the Confederates while his troops improved their lines. The *Carondelet* got under way and, masked by a heavily wooded point on the riverbank, fired 139 70- and 64-pound shells at the Confederate positions from long range. This time the Confederates returned fire. Most of their shot passed high, but two hit home. At 11:30 one of these, a 128-pound solid shot from the rifled gun in the upper battery, burst through the front casemate, wounding a half dozen members of the crew and slightly damaging the ship's machinery. The *Carondelet* halted fire briefly to transfer wounded to the *Alps* and then lobbed another 45 shells into the fort. It ceased fire only after expending almost all its ammunition. In the exchange one of the *Carondelet*'s shots struck a Confederate 32-pounder, disabling it and killing two men, including Capt. Joseph Dixon, an engineer who had assisted Lieutenant Colonel Gilmer in the construction of both Henry and Donelson. Five other defenders were wounded. According to some Confederates the *Carondelet*'s shelling on the thirteenth did more damage than the bombardment the next day from the entire flotilla.[28]

Thus far there had been no major fighting between the two armies. That changed shortly after noon on the thirteenth when, despite Grant's order not to bring on a general engagement, McClernand undertook to capture a Confederate battery that had been annoying his men. He sent three regiments to assault a position supported by the bulk of the Confederate strength. Despite three attempts, the Union assault failed. Losses were heavy on the Union side and Grant was displeased, but the attack did have the advantage, as one Union participant noted, of preventing the besieged "from suspecting the inferiority in numbers of the attacking force."[29]

That afternoon the weather changed dramatically from impending spring back to winter, and a driving wind brought sleet and snow and a temperature of only twelve degrees. There was much suffering on both sides.[30] At 11:30 that same night Commodore Foote arrived with his three ironclads, the timberclads *Tyler* and *Conestoga,* and the transports. Thayer's brigade went ashore the next morning and Wallace's brigade arrived from Forts Heiman and Henry about noon. Grant then restored Wallace's brigade to Smith and gave Wallace command of what became known as the Third Division, composed of Thayer's brigade and two other brigades of reinforcements that had also arrived with Foote. This new division now took over the Union center.

Except for an area along the Cumberland River above Dover, the Confederates were now completely invested. Floyd had let a splendid opportunity slip away. Had his troops attacked on the thirteenth, they might have pushed Grant back to Fort Henry and, as Wallace noted, "more than offset Foote's conquest."[31] After the fourteenth that was no longer possible.

On the morning of the fourteenth, as Grant strengthened and extended his lines, the senior Confederate commanders decided to try to break out before increasing Union reinforcements made it impossible. Pillow was to lead an attack against the Union right flank with Buckner's forces covering the rear. Early that afternoon, however, Floyd countermanded the order on the insistence of Pillow, who thought it too late for an attempt that day.[32]

Grant, meanwhile, called on Foote to mount a naval attack. His plan was to hold the Confederates within the fort from the land side while the Union flotilla attacked at close quarters and reduced the water batteries. If possible, some of the gunboats would run past Donelson and get south of Dover, cutting off Confederate resupply by the river.[33] Although Foote would have preferred to delay until he could make a personal reconnaissance, he complied with the request. On the morning of the fourteenth the crews placed chains, lumber, bags of coal, and other hard materials on the upper decks of the gunboats and around their boilers to protect them from plunging shot. The preparations were completed by the afternoon, and the boats began their assault shortly before 3:00 P.M., using the same formation as at Fort Henry: the *St. Louis, Carondelet, Louisville,* and *Pittsburg* in front, and the vulnerable timberclads *Tyler* and *Conestoga* about a thousand yards astern and beyond the range of Donelson's guns.

Surprise was impossible; the Confederates had an excellent field of fire up the long, straight stretch of the Cumberland, while at the same time their earthen works were difficult to locate from the water side. At about 3:30 P.M. and fifteen hundred yards' range, the Confederates fired two shots against the advancing Union ships from the 10-inch columbiad. Both fell short. When it had closed to about a mile from the fort the *St. Louis* opened fire and the other gunboats followed suit. Foote attempted to reduce the accuracy of the Confederate fire by varying his speed from time to time. The Union ships fired rapidly until they were within two to four hundred yards of the battery.[34]

The firing continued for an hour and a half. The Confederates found that the height of their water battery and guns on the bluff permitted plunging fire that nullified the sloping Union armor by hitting it at right angles. This soon began to tell. As Commander Walke described it, the Confederate shot "knocked the plating to pieces, and sent fragments of iron and splinters into the pilots, one of whom fell mortally wounded, and was taken below . . . and still they came, harder and faster, taking flag-staffs and smoke-stacks, and tearing off their side armor as lightning tears the bark from a tree."[35]

The nearness of the Union fleet aided the inexperienced Confederate gunners by allowing them to bring more of their guns into action and fire more accurately. The Union gunboats, meanwhile, could use only their three bow guns, and the gunners found it difficult to locate the Confederate positions and to elevate their guns sufficiently to bring the enemy under fire.

Confederate shot soon took away the steering mechanisms of two of the Union warships and badly damaged the pilothouses of two others. The flagship *St. Louis* was hit fifty-nine times. Splinters from a shell explosion wounded Foote in the left foot; the same shell killed pilot F. A. Riley, who had been standing right next to him, and took away the ship's wheel. As the ironclad could no longer be controlled, Foote ordered Lieutenant Paulding to let it drift downriver. He then went down to the gun deck to have his wound tended to and to urge on the gunners. Another shell struck the vessel belowdecks, knocking down five of six men manning a gun and wounding Foote again, this time in the left arm. The *Louisville,* disabled by a shot that carried away its rudder chains, drifted out of action. Aboard the *Carondelet* a rifled gun, loaded too hastily, blew up on firing and wounded more than a dozen men. Two Confederate hits killed four men. More would have been casualties had not lookouts shouted warnings of incoming Confederate shot to allow the men time to duck. Nevertheless, Walke reported that there was so much blood on the decks "that our men could not work the guns without slipping."[36] The *Carondelet* sustained the most severe damage of all the gunboats when the *Pittsburg,* also in difficulty, crashed into it and broke its rudder. The *St. Louis* was disabled when the *Tyler* smashed into its steering gear. Three of the four ironclads were now hors de combat and drifting downstream. In the flotilla as a whole, eleven men were killed and forty-three wounded, half of these on the *Carondelet.* Confederate soldiers broke into cheers as the Union vessels withdrew.[37]

In reporting the engagement to Welles, Foote said he had taken his ships in against Donelson at the "urgent request of General Halleck and General Grant, who regarded the movement as a military necessity, although, not in my opinion properly prepared."[38] He also told the navy secretary that the flotilla's assault, if it had continued for fifteen more minutes, would have resulted in the capture of the two forts. "The enemy's fire had materially slackened and he was running from his batteries" when the *St. Louis* and *Louisville* were forced to retire.[39]

Both sides suffered misconceptions regarding the naval attack. Damage to the gunboats was not as severe as it at first seemed, although Foote described the ironclads as "badly cut up." The *St. Louis* was hit 59 times, the *Louisville* 36, the *Carondelet* 35, and the *Pittsburg* 30: in all, 160 hits. Some of these were serious but none was fatal. On the other hand, Foote's assertion to Welles that the attack on the fourteenth had "badly disabled" Donelson was simply not true.[40] This myth lingered; well after the war Hoppin claimed in his biography of Foote that "shot and shell from the fleet plowed into the lower batteries, dismounting guns and driving away the gunners." Then, just at the "critical moment . . . [with] victory . . . almost in their grasp," some of the gunboats were disabled. In fact, much of the Union fire had gone high and there had been no casualties among the Confederate defenders and no damage to the battery or its armament. Capt. B. G. Bidwell observed that the Yankees' "fire was more destructive to our works at 2 miles than at two hundred yards. They over fired us from that distance."[41] Even David Porter later wrote, "we feel obliged to say that all the credit for the capture of Fort Donelson belongs to the Army. . . . This victory belonged exclusively to General Grant."[42]

The Confederates, having defeated the Union land attack of the day before, now had another success, and river communication with Nashville remained open. Writing after the Civil War, Porter speculated that Foote might have sent his remaining gunboats past the fort that night and then taken Donelson under fire the next day from its more vulnerable upriver side as well as cutting off the Confederate garrison from escape across or up the river. But this is hindsight.[43]

The night of the fourteenth was again quite cold with wind, snow, and sleet. The weather greatly complicated life for both sides, but especially for the Union troops. Many of the defenders had huts for protection; the besiegers lacked even tents. Men at the front lines on both sides could not light fires for fear of giving away their positions, and Grant went to sleep without knowing whether or not he would have to settle in for a long siege and order up tents or instruct the men to build huts.[44]

At 2:00 A.M. on the fifteenth a message arrived at Grant's headquarters from Foote requesting a meeting. Foote said that his wounds prevented him from traveling, and he asked Grant to join him aboard the

St. Louis four miles downstream. Grant instructed his division commanders to hold their positions and not initiate any engagement unless they
received express orders from him, then left to meet Foote. Later he was
criticized for not designating a commander to act in his absence.

The bad weather slowed Grant on his trip to meet with Foote. When
he reached the shore near the *St. Louis* a small boat took him out to the
flagship, where Foote briefed him on damage to the squadron and suggested that Union troops ashore entrench while he took the two most
seriously damaged gunboats to Cairo for repairs. Foote told Grant he
would leave the other two ironclads behind to protect the transports at
the landing. He believed he could return in ten days, hopefully with the
powerful *Benton* and mortar boats, at which time they would renew the
attack. When the two men parted it was on the understanding that they
would follow Foote's plan, but as Grant put it later, "the enemy relieved
me from that necessity."[45] From this point on, in fact, the navy contributed little to the battle.

When he went to meet with Foote, Grant assumed that any new fighting at Donelson would be initiated by him, which is probably why he did
not designate someone to act in his absence. As historian James M.
McPherson noted, this reflected Grant's generalship: "he always thought
more about what he planned to do to the enemy than what his enemy
might do to him."[46] Grant had no reason to believe otherwise. The Union
had been the aggressor up to that point and had now greatly improved
its strength. During the first two days of the investment Grant had only
fifteen thousand men and no gunboats. Now he had six warships, Wallace's large division, and the twenty-five hundred men from Fort Henry.[47]

The Confederate commanders, however, were not willing to wait any
longer. They knew their position was untenable and that Grant was
steadily increasing his strength. On the night of the fourteenth, therefore,
Generals Floyd, Pillow, and Buckner met at the Dover Hotel to consider
their options. The Confederate commanders decided to implement their
earlier plan. Pillow's division, assisted by cavalry, would attack along the
west bank of the Cumberland River against McClernand's division on the
Union right flank. Pillow would open an escape route by rolling up Union
troops on his front and pushing them west. Buckner's men would then
strike the Union center. When the Union right flank had been rolled back
into the Union center, Pillow would lead the retreat to Charlotte, Tennessee. Buckner would hold the Union center at bay outside the entrench-

ments until the remainder of the Confederate garrison had escaped and then serve as its rear guard during the retreat.

The planning for this scheme was haphazard, and some regiments took neither knapsacks nor rations. That night Pillow's men assembled to the rear of the extreme left of the Confederate line without alarming the Union pickets; no doubt the howling wind helped.[48] The Confederate attack began at six o'clock on the morning of the fifteenth and caught the Union troops completely by surprise. In a hard-fought close action the Confederates drove the federals back, although in good order. At about nine o'clock, with the Union right wing being rolled up and giving way, Pillow ordered Buckner to advance. Buckner then sent three regiments forward. For a time the Union troops withstood the Confederate attacks, but they soon used up their ammunition and were forced to retreat.[49]

At the same time, Confederate cavalry led by Col. Nathan Bedford Forrest attacked the Union right. By eleven o'clock Pillow held the road to Charlotte and the area that had been occupied by McClernand's division. With the escape route open, all that remained was for Pillow to deploy his regiments in column and begin the march to safety. He threw away that chance. Imagining that he was now in position to defeat Grant and force the federals back to Fort Henry and to their transports on the Cumberland, Pillow ignored Floyd's orders and continued the attack. He now ordered Buckner to advance.

General Wallace, mindful of Grant's command not to move without express orders from him, refused McClernand's first appeal for assistance but sent an officer to Grant's headquarters for instructions. Grant's staff was unwilling to act in his absence, but with the Union flank now turned and the situation desperate, Wallace ordered a brigade forward. It was soon heavily engaged but, unsupported, was forced to retreat. Wallace then ordered his one remaining brigade forward. There was savage fighting, but the Union troops repulsed the Confederates. Pillow convinced Floyd that the Confederates should return to the entrenchments. Later Pillow sought unsuccessfully to shift the blame for this blunder to Buckner.[50]

Grant now intervened. On leaving the *St. Louis* he had been informed by an aide of the desperate situation. Riding as fast as he could, he reached Wallace's command post at about 1:00 P.M. Then, convinced that the Confederates were attempting to break out, Grant ordered his troops to retake the ground lost on the right flank. He also reasoned that in order to break through, the Confederates must have weakened their lines elsewhere. If General Smith could mount an immediate attack against the Confederate right wing before the rebels could redistribute their forces, the course of the battle might be reversed.[51] Smith's attack went forward swiftly, and Union troops using their bayonets breached the breastworks and drove back the defenders. Buckner's men came up and halted the Union advance but were unable to force the invaders from the works. The Union troops now held the high ground in the fort, placing the entire Confederate position in jeopardy.[52]

As General Smith's forces moved out on the left flank, General Wallace's Third Division retook the ground lost earlier. The Confederates retired back into the fort in good order and took with them six Union guns, several thousand small arms, and at least two hundred prisoners, but they were both disappointed and discouraged. That evening five additional federal infantry regiments reached the area in river transports. Union strength was now up to twenty-seven thousand men, and it was no longer possible for the bulk of the Confederates to escape.[53]

Foote had already departed for Cairo with the disabled gunboats on the fifteenth, leaving the *St. Louis* and *Carondelet* behind to protect the transports, when a dispatch arrived from Grant, who wanted the gunboats to keep up a show of force. At 2:30 P.M. Commander Dove in the *Louisville*, the senior naval officer present, received Grant's message and decided not to accompany the *Pittsburg*, which had started downriver fifteen minutes before. Instead, he immediately went onboard the *St. Louis* and *Carondelet* to consult with Paulding and Walke and ascertain the condition of their vessels. The *Carondelet* could not be moved, but Dove ordered the *St. Louis* into action, then followed behind in the *Louisville*. The two gunboats steamed upriver and the *St. Louis* lobbed a few shells into the fort. Toward dusk both vessels returned to the anchorage. Certainly this had little impact on the events that followed. The next morning Dove cleared both vessels for action and again got under way for Fort Donelson, although this proved unnecessary.[54]

That night Generals Floyd, Pillow, and Buckner met once again at the Dover Hotel to assess the situation, the meeting continuing into the early hours of the sixteenth. They agreed to attempt a retreat early the next morning over the ground Pillow had gained previously, but only if the federals had not reoccupied it in strength. They asked Forrest to send out scouts to determine the condition of the road next to the river and report on the presence of Union troops. The scouts returned with word that they had seen no troops but that about one hundred yards of road was under some three feet of water.

Pillow proposed that they attempt to cut their way out, but Buckner said that was no longer possible. The Union troops who had taken a portion of the Confederate right would almost certainly attack at first light, and his men would not be able to hold them half an hour. Besides, the men were in no condition to march. They were short of rations and their ammunition was nearly expended.[55]

Pillow and Floyd decided to escape rather than surrender. Buckner announced he would share the fate of the garrison and assumed its command. Pillow escaped by commandeering a flatboat to take him across the Cumberland. Floyd got away by taking over two steamers that arrived at daybreak, one bringing four hundred recruits from Nashville. Floyd used the vessels to rescue much of his brigade, leaving the recruits to surrender. Forrest managed to lead out his own cavalry regiment, some artillerymen on their horses, and two hundred men from other cavalry commands, perhaps five hundred men altogether. They forded a creek just south of Dover between the Union right flank and the river. In all, perhaps five thousand Confederates escaped.[56]

Early on the sixteenth Buckner asked for an armistice and terms of surrender. On General Smith's urging Grant replied: "No terms except unconditional and immediate surrender can be accepted. I propose to move immediately upon your works." Buckner, who had no choice, accepted "the ungenerous and unchivalrous terms which you propose."[57] As one historian has noted, "Grant had given the Civil War a new, grim, and determined character."[58] On the sixteenth Grant telegraphed the headquarters of the Department of the Missouri: "I am pleased to announce to you the unconditional surrender this morning of Fort Donelson, with 12,000 to 15,000 prisoners, at least forty pieces of artillery, and a large quantity of stores, horses, mules, and other public property."[59]

While northerners celebrated their first great victory of the war, Halleck immediately tried to claim much of the credit for himself and downplay Grant's contribution. Halleck wanted supreme command in the West, with his rivals Buell and John Pope, who had nothing to do with the victories, under his command. On 18 February Halleck congratulated General Hunter in Kansas for rapidly sending reinforcements to Grant, but his only communication to his field commander was an order to Grant not to let the gunboats go beyond Clarksville. Indeed, Halleck sought to credit the victory at Donelson to General Smith. His only recognition of Grant's achievement was a formal order, published that same day, in which he thanked Foote, Grant, and their men for the two victories. He made no effort to communicate his thanks to Grant directly.[60]

Lincoln, who was not taken in by Halleck's attempt to claim the glory for himself, at once sent the Senate his recommendation for Grant's promotion only, although shortly afterward Buell and Pope were also promoted to major general. In March 1862 Congress passed a resolution thanking Foote and "the officers and men of the Western Flotilla under his command." It was not until July, however, after other victories, that the gunboat commanders were also advanced one grade in rank and Foote was promoted to rear admiral.[61]

Andrew Hull Foote

Attack on the barrier
forts near Canton, China,
21 November 1856
*Original lithograph
courtesy of the
Franklin D. Roosevelt
Library*

The brig *Perry* apprehending the slaver *Martha* off Ambriz, West Africa, 6 June 1850

Union gunboats advancing up the Tennessee River, 6 February 1862

Attack on Fort Donelson by Foote's gunboats, 14 February 1862

Attack on Fort Henry by Foote's gunboats, 6 February 1862
Drawing by Thomas Nast

The capture of Fort Henry, 6 February 1862

TENNESSEE RIV.
HENRY

32 POUNDER

FORT HENRY.

Bombardment of Island No. 10
Engraving by W. Ridgway, after a drawing by C. Parsons

Union gunboats bombarding Island No. 10

BOMBARDMENT OF ISLAND NO. 10 AND THE CONFEDERATE

NIGHT ATTACK ON ISLAND NO. 10 BY THE

Union bombardment of Island No. 10 and Confederate fortifications in
Kentucky

'S ON THE KENTUCKY SHORE, OPPOSITE, MARCH 17TH, 1862.

BOATS AND MORTAR FLEET, MARCH 18TH, 1862.

Union gunboat *Carondelet* running past Confederate defenses on Island No. 10, 4 April 1862 *Engraving by Harry Fenn after a sketch by Henry Walke*

~❧12❧~

The Road to Island No. 10

The victories at Forts Henry and Donelson gave the North control of Kentucky and most of middle and western Tennessee and had devastating long-term economic consequences for the Confederacy. In the short run, the Union broke the backbone of the South's western defensive line; a third of Johnston's forces defending Kentucky and Tennessee had been captured and the remainder were now divided between Nashville, Tennessee, and Columbus, Kentucky, two hundred miles apart. On 14 February Johnston evacuated Bowling Green, and on the seventeenth and eighteenth he moved the majority of his troops from Nashville to Murfreesboro, Tennessee. The Confederates evacuated Columbus on 2 March. The Mississippi was now open down to Island No. 10.

It is hard to disagree with Grant's conclusion at the time that only a failure of Union leadership prevented a rapid conquest of the entire West. Halleck's refusal to act, the division of Union forces between himself and Buell, and logistical overreach all denied Union forces an early end to the war in that theater. Immediately after the Battle of Fort Donelson Grant had informed Halleck that the way to Clarksville and Nashville lay open. He proposed to take Clarksville, about sixty miles from Nashville, on the twenty first and Nashville about 1 March.[1]

When the *Carondelet* returned to Cairo on 17 February with news of the victory, Foote, upset at the lack of credit given to the navy, wrote his wife: "We so demoralized the rebels, that it fell an easy prey to the Army the next day as they are afraid to see the black boats arriving into their teeth and belching forth shot and shells."[2] Many Confederates would disagree with this conclusion. Lt. Col. William T. Withers wrote to members of the Confederate Congress: "The fight at Fort Donelson has developed the fact that the boasted invulnerability of the enemy's gunboats is a myth. Every one of the gunboats was disabled in little over one hour, though the armaments of the fort was small and none of the guns were of very large caliber."[3]

Both views were incorrect, of course, but Foote was determined to see that the navy received its due, especially in the forthcoming capture of Nashville. On learning of the fall of Fort Donelson, he left immediately in the *Conestoga*, having already sent ahead the *Cairo* and six mortar boats. He wrote to his wife on 17 February that "the steamer trembles as we are pressing her hard up to fourteen knots for Fort Donelson." Although he was still on crutches as a consequence of his wound, he said that he hoped to be rid of them in a few weeks. Foote was confident the Confederates would not fight for Clarksville, at least.[4]

The next day Foote was at Fort Donelson, and on the nineteenth he made a reconnaissance in force, with the *Conestoga* and *Cairo* carrying some army troops. Fort Defiance, a small fortification near Clarksville, flew a white flag. The fort itself was deserted, and Foote landed troops to take possession. The men also took Fort Clark, a second earthwork farther upriver. When it arrived at Clarksville the Union force found the city abandoned both by Confederate troops and the majority of its citizens; the retreating troops had burned the railroad bridge over the Cumberland. Clarksville officials, including the mayor, called on Foote to ascertain his intentions. In response, Foote issued a proclamation demanding that all military stores be turned over to Union forces but promising that he would protect private property. He also ordered that "no Secession flag, or manifestation of Secession feeling, shall be exhibited." Foote later sent his wife a copy of the proclamation, concluding: "the Clarksville affair will do me credit."[5]

Convinced from what he learned at Clarksville that Nashville was in a state of panic and might be easily taken in a coup de main, Foote returned to Fort Donelson on the twentieth with the intention of returning upriver with an additional gunboat and six to eight mortar boats for a descent on Nashville. Foote and Grant planned a joint assault to begin at four o'clock the next morning and arrive at Nashville before noon. The two men were discussing this when, at midnight on the twentieth, orders arrived from Halleck instructing them not to go beyond Clarksville. Gen. George W. Cullum, Halleck's chief of staff in Cairo, reinforced the order two days later when he telegraphed Foote that he and Grant were not to proceed without Halleck's approval. Foote relayed this message to Grant and at the same time congratulated him on his promotion to major general.

Evidently Halleck was concerned by an erroneous report that Beauregard was reinforcing "the Gibraltar of the West," Columbus, Kentucky, in preparation for an attack against Paducah, Cairo, or Fort Henry. In any case, he and McClellan wanted to use the gunboats and mortar boats against Columbus.[6] Foote and Grant were shocked by Halleck's order. On the twenty-first Foote telegraphed General Cullum from Paducah:

> General Grant and myself consider this a good time to move on Nashville. Six mortar boats and two ironclad steamers can precede the troops and shell the forts. We were about moving for this purpose when General Grant, to my astonishment, received a telegram from General Halleck not to let the gunboats go higher than Clarksville; no telegram sent to me.
>
> The Cumberland is in a good stage of water and General Grant and I believe we can take Nashville.
>
> Please ask General Halleck if we shall do it. We will talk per telegraph.[7]

The cautious Halleck did want to take Nashville, but he first wanted everything to be in place. On the twenty-third he issued detailed instructions concerning the disposition of Union forces in the field, but no reinforcements from Buell reached Grant until 24 February, when General Nelson arrived at Fort Donelson with two brigades.

Foote, meanwhile, had returned to Cairo. On the twenty-third, with five gunboats, two mortar boats, and four transports lifting one thousand troops, he and Cullum undertook a reconnaissance of Columbus during which Polk's batteries there fired several shots in the direction of the Union vessels. The latter were preparing to return fire when a Confederate steamer came out under a flag of truce carrying a message from Polk. The message proposed that the wives of some Confederate officers, who were aboard the vessel, be allowed to visit their husbands, who had been captured at Fort Donelson. Foote dispatched the request to Halleck but dismissed it as a ruse to ascertain Union strength. Halleck granted the request the next day, and the Confederates used the time of truce to prepare the evacuation of Columbus.[8]

Foote still chafed about the missed opportunity to seize Nashville. He wrote to his wife:

> I am disgusted that we were kept from going up and taking Nashville. It was jealousy on the part of McClellan and Halleck. I now am determined to wait till I get the gun and mortar boats ready, and will not obey any orders except the Secretary's and President's.
>
> I shall report McClellan and Halleck to the Department and soon there will be a row. I can well afford to be independent now.

The experience at Donelson had left its mark on Foote:

> I am still on crutches and may be for a week, but my foot is rapidly improving. I have no objection to the wound either in the foot or in the arm, as they are honorable wounds; but I tell you the last was a bad fight, I stood one side of a gun when five out of six were knocked down, and I only escaped serious wounds. I was touching the pilot with my clothes when he was killed, but I won't run into the fire so again, as a burnt child dreads it.[9]

On his return to Cairo from Columbus Foote learned that General McClellan had sent 350 men for the flotilla, but he was far from pleased with them. He reported to Welles that the men seemed to be, "and are represented by their officers, with few exceptions, the offscourings of the Army." Rather than allowing them on his boats, Foote had them disarmed and placed under guard. "They say they have been deceived. I am pained and discouraged to have to take such men into action. We want no more from the Army. I prefer to go into action only half manned than to go with such men."[10] That same day Foote complained in another telegram that he would have been in Nashville on the twenty-second with two gunboats and four mortar boats had not Halleck "directed me to proceed no farther than Clarksville." Meanwhile Foote sent the *Lexington* and the *Tyler* up the Tennessee to patrol the river, gather intelligence, and protect Unionists.[11] Foote's main preoccupation at this time was readying the mortar boats for an assault on Columbus. By early March thirty-five of them had their mortars mounted and were ready for duty. Foote also had added army troops as seamen. And to fill the need for a dispatch boat between the different points of his command, Foote secured approval to outfit the fast prize gunboat *Eastport*.[12]

On the 24 February, Grant, finally unleashed by Halleck, ordered Nelson's two newly arrived brigades aboard transports. Escorted by the *Carondelet,* they proceeded to the Tennessee capital without opposition. With Buell belatedly moving on Nashville from the east, the city fell on the twenty-fifth, the first Confederate state capital to fall into Union hands. But the delay along with energetic efforts by Colonel Forrest enabled the Confederates to save large quantities of cannon, small arms, ammunition, food, uniforms, and vital foundry equipment. Johnston's troops then moved south to Murfreesboro before heading to Alabama and a stand south of the Tennessee River. Ultimately Johnston gathered some forty thousand men at the key rail hub of Corinth, Mississippi, twenty miles inland from the river.[13]

On 1 March the *Tyler* and *Lexington* attacked three Confederate regiments fortifying Pittsburg Landing on the Tennessee River. The gunboats silenced half a dozen Confederate fieldpieces and then landed army troops. The Union side suffered two killed, three missing, and six wounded in the exchange. Confederate losses were estimated at twenty dead and one hundred wounded.[14]

Halleck continued to snipe at Grant, who, in a breakdown in communications, lost contact with his commander. Halleck then misrepresented Grant's actions to McClellan, suggesting that Grant had taken to drink, and proposed replacing him with Gen. Charles F. Smith. McClellan authorized the transfer of authority and Grant's arrest if necessary. Halleck then ordered Grant to Fort Henry and gave command of "the expedition up the Tennessee" to Smith. Grant denied disobeying orders and pointed out to Halleck that he would have to bear responsibility for the troop withdrawals and consequent losses in territory stemming from the transfer of authority. He also asked whether he was to abandon Clarksville. As for the order that he remain at Fort Henry, Grant said that would be difficult as "the water is about six feet deep inside the fort."[15]

Ironically, Smith did not hold his new command for long. After moving his force to Pittsburg Landing he slipped while jumping into a small boat and badly scraped himself. The wound grew septic and he became bedridden and later died from it. But for this, Smith rather than Grant would have commanded at Shiloh. On 11 March Halleck was named to head the Department of the Mississippi, which included all troops west of a north south line through Knoxville, Tennessee, and east of the western borders of Arkansas and Missouri.

Officials back in Washington took note of Grant's dignified and careful response to Halleck's attacks. Although Halleck had McClellan's support, Grant had the more powerful allies in Lincoln and the War Department. Lincoln himself ordered Halleck either to bring charges against Grant or to end the campaign to smear him. When Halleck received overall control of forces in the West, he no longer had to fear Grant, and in late March he restored him to command.

Foote's prediction that the Confederates would fight for Columbus proved incorrect. On 1 March Phelps reported that the rebels were evacuating. Although they were removing guns on the bluffs, the guns in the water battery were still in place. The rebels were also torching huts and stores they could not remove. The next day Foote took the *Cincinnati* and *Louisville* on a reconnaissance to within three to four miles of Columbus. He returned to recommend to Cullum that a land force accompanied by gunboats and mortar boats be sent to take possession, and early on 4 March the expedition, consisting of six gunboats, four mortar boats, and three transports with troops, got under way.

Uncertain whether the Confederates were still at Columbus, a landing party led by Lieutenant Phelps and Brig. Gen. William Tecumseh Sherman stormed ashore, climbed the bluff, and hoisted an American flag. But Columbus had already been taken the evening before by a scouting party of four hundred troopers of the Second Illinois Cavalry Regiment sent by Sherman from Paducah. This did not keep Foote from claiming in a dispatch to Welles that it was his appearance on the second that caused the hasty evacuation. The Confederates managed to move most of their heavy guns via the Mobile & Ohio Railroad. Military stores left behind included shot, shell, and torpedoes. In detailing these to Welles, Foote professed disappointment at not being able to try out his mortars against the Columbus defenses, which Cullum, however, described as "of immense strength."[16]

The next goal of the Union operation down the Mississippi was to secure New Madrid, Missouri, and nearby Island No. 10. Below the mouth of the Ohio, islands in the Mississippi are designated by ascending numbers; Island No. 10 was about sixty miles south of Cairo and forty miles below Columbus. Cullum tried to get Foote to move immediately on the new objectives, but the flag officer insisted on "two to three days" to repair his gunboats.

Foote was now determined not to follow blindly the army's bidding. His own maxim of careful preparation precluded this, and he told Welles that he would move only when he was ready.[17] In a remarkable letter of 9 March from Cairo, a clearly frustrated Foote wrote to an unidentified relative:

> I have to work against a good deal of opposition. Not even a Navy officer at home can conceive of the magnitude of my work—navy-yard and fleet duties; and I would not again pass through the mental agony and bodily effort, certainly for all the credit I do or can receive from the public. It is a bitter cup, and I can hardly drink it. It has added ten years to my age, and it is quite enough to break any man down.

Worn down from his hard work and showing the prickly side of his personality with its stubbornness and thirst for recognition, Foote complained that his accomplishments had been largely ignored. Halleck and McClellan had taken credit for his capture of Fort Henry and for sending Phelps up the Tennessee. Foote had fought at Fort Donelson four days before he was ready, yet his gunboat attack had demoralized the Confederate garrison there and, he believed, led to its surrender. Then he had taken Clarksville, but Halleck's dispatches had mentioned only Smith's occupation of the city four days later, "making no allusion to my command." He was ready then to move on Nashville, which would have netted "a million dollars' worth of rebel arms and a factory for making percussion-caps." Now he had been asked to assault Island No. 10 and New Madrid; "but," he continued in the same letter, "I have refused positively to do it, and will wait till Wednesday, when I will have the mortar-boats and the *Benton,* and can, God willing, who gives the victory, do it easily. I have no fears for this week's work."[18]

Foote wrote much the same thing to Gustavus Fox. After asking for the department's support in his stand, he told his friend:

> It requires some moral courage to decline going into action when urged to do it, but a moral responsibility rests upon me in the matter which cannot be transferred to another. I have been as ready to take the Gun Boats, as General Halleck has to take the field and if personal considerations are imputed to me rather than a higher motive for declining at present to fight the rebels until we are in a condition to do it, I must say that the consciousness of good motive, will never induce me to regret having taken the step, the censure of the unreasoning public to the contrary—notwithstanding.[19]

While the *Benton,* his new flagship, was being made ready, Foote moved his flag from one ironclad to another. Eads had learned from the construction of the earlier ironclads and had improved the *Benton*'s design; undoubtedly the 633-ton stern-wheeler, the converted snagboat *Submarine No. 7*, was the most powerful gunboat on the river. Acquired in November 1861, the *Benton* was commissioned on 24 February 1862. It had a crew of 176 officers and men, and mounted two 9-inch Dahlgren smoothbores, seven 32-pounder smoothbores, and seven 42-pounder rifled guns. Foote gave command of the new gunboat to Lieutenant Phelps.[20]

The man who replaced Foote as commander of the western fleet, Flag Officer Charles Henry Davis, later described the admiral's accommodations on the *Benton*:

> My quarters are well enough in themselves, though small . . . but they are not well situated. They are amidships of the vessel: on one side of them are the pantry and cooking-stove; on the other, the marines; so that I am exposed to all the noises, sights, and smells of the vessel, and am subject to being always overlooked if I let down the blinds and open the doors, and to being suffocated if I don't. Added to these inconveniences, the cabin is dark.

It is thus not surprising that Foote found little rest aboard the *Benton* and that his health failed to improve. The strain of his position also weighed on him. On 12 March he complained to his wife that he could not express the "horrible pressure of [his] responsibility," the "vast responsibility of the river, which, if disaster occur to my boats, the rebels could retake Columbus, capture St. Louis, and command the Mississippi." He continued: "I would this moment give all I am worth could I be on the Atlantic a captain of a good steam-frigate, instead of being out here under a pressure which would crush most men; and how I have stood it thus far I can only account for by the fact that 'God has been my helper.' . . . All is confusion, and I am almost in despair."[21]

Meanwhile the corps under Polk's command that had held Columbus had been divided. Brig. Gen. John P. McCown's division moved south to Island No. 10 to join the fifteen hundred troops already in garrison there. Polk also ordered five gunboats under Cdr. George N. Hollins to Island No. 10. Hollins, who commanded Confederate naval forces on the upper Mississippi, was a former U.S. Navy officer of great longevity who had fought in the War of 1812 and at the outbreak of the Civil War had commanded the *Susquehanna*.[22]

Island No. 10 no longer exists; the ever-changing Mississippi has made it part of the Missouri shore. In 1862, however, it was arguably the strongest natural defensive position on the upper Mississippi. About a mile long and a quarter mile wide, it was situated at the turn of a long, inverted S-bend in the river. Surrounded by cypress-entangled swamps, Reelfoot Lake, and the great river itself, Island No. 10 was not readily accessible to land forces. The Confederates, utilizing many of the heavy guns removed from Columbus, turned it into a formidable position. Its outer defenses consisted of field batteries along the riverbanks that commanded the channel for some ten to twelve miles northward. In the vicinity of the island itself the river channel was swift, which would make it difficult for Union gunboats to maintain position there. And unlike the situation on the Tennessee and Cumberland Rivers, where disabled gunboats merely drifted away from the Confederate batteries, on the Mississippi disabled gunboats would drift south under the Confederate guns.

The natural barrier of swamps inhibited Union land operations, although this would be a liability for the Confederates themselves should they need to escape. The defenders were largely dependent for

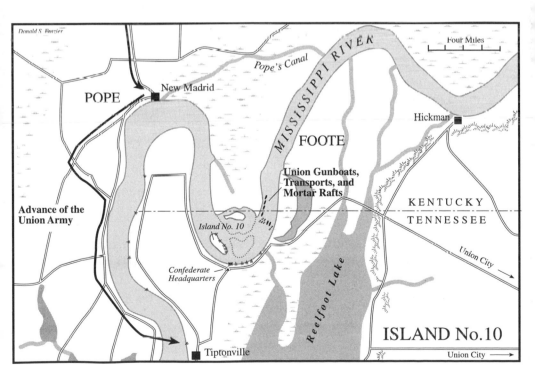

their communications and resupply on a single road on the Tennessee side of the river that passed south from the riverbank opposite Island No. 10 between the Mississippi to the west and Reelfoot Lake to the east through Tiptonville about a dozen miles south. If this road fell to Union troops, the garrison would be trapped.

The Confederates had nineteen guns on the island itself and forty-three more along the land bluffs. Widely separated from one another, the batteries were arranged so that they could deliver concentrated fire on one target. The Confederates also had a floating battery, the *New Orleans,* which Cdr. Henry Walke referred to as the Confederacy's great "war elephant." Fashioned from a floating drydock, the *New Orleans* had been towed up from the Crescent City. Some 60 feet wide by 180 feet long, the battery mounted nine guns—eight 8-inch columbiads and a rifled 32-pounder—and was intended to be moved along the river as required. It remained under Hollins's command throughout the battle.[23]

The Mississippi made a sharp bend at Island No. 10 and then ran to the northwest. The town of New Madrid, which was actually north of the island, was some six miles downriver. At that point the river resumes a southerly direction. In order to prevent the island from being attacked by land forces from the Missouri side, the Confederates also fortified New Madrid, erecting an earthen fort on each side of it: Fort Thompson on the west with fourteen guns and Fort Bankhead at Wilson's Bayou on the east with seven guns. They also fortified the Tennessee side of the river below New Madrid. Clearly New Madrid, the left flank of the Confederate position, was the weak point in the Confederate defenses. Brigadier General McCown, who assumed command of the Madrid Bend area on 26 February, had some seventy-five hundred men. A graduate of West Point, McCown had twenty-one years of army service and had fought in both the Seminole and Mexican Wars. Although he had participated in the Battle of Belmont, this was his first independent command.[24]

In order to take Island No. 10 Union forces would first have to cut it off from resupply downriver by capturing New Madrid. Halleck assigned this task to Brig. Gen. John Pope's new Army of the Mississippi. Pope, another West Point graduate and only thirty-nine years old, had a solid military background that included service in the Mexican War. An Illinois Republican, he also had important political ties to the Lincoln family. Pope arrived at St. Louis to confer with Halleck on 18 February.

Four days later Pope's forces left St. Louis for New Madrid. Union transports put the men ashore at Commerce, Missouri, twenty-five miles north of Cairo, and they marched fifty miles south to New Madrid, which they began besieging on 3 March. Pope and his eighteen thousand or so Union troops were greeted at New Madrid not only by Confederate troops but also by Hollins's six gunboats.

Pope had wanted Foote to stage a demonstration with his ironclads to draw off the Confederate gunboats. He also wanted reinforcements. Since Foote was still at Cairo, however, and Halleck resisted his demands for more troops, Pope sent for siege guns. On 6 March Union troops outflanked the Confederates by taking Point Pleasant, twelve miles farther downriver on the Missouri side. There they positioned artillery to harass Confederate Mississippi River traffic, which, however, they never were able to halt.

McCown had failed to anticipate this obvious Union approach; his attention had been to the north on Island No. 10 rather than to the south. His response was a series of pleas to Beauregard for reinforcements. Unfortunately for him, any possibility of Maj. Gen. Earl Van Dorn's sixteen-thousand-man army in Arkansas reinforcing New Madrid was shattered by its defeat at the hands of eleven thousand Union troops under Maj. Gen. Samuel R. Curtis in the 7–8 March Battle of Pea Ridge. By the time Van Dorn was again ready to move, time had run out for New Madrid.

The Union siege guns arrived at New Madrid on 12 March. Union troops quickly emplaced them and at dawn the next day began a heavy and accurate bombardment. Confederate guns and the river flotilla replied with some hits of their own, but McCown panicked and decided to abandon New Madrid. The Confederates' precipitous evacuation of their forts on the night of the thirteenth was a fiasco, but a violent thunderstorm helped mask their retreat, and Union troops did not realize what had happened until the morning of the fourteenth. The federals then promptly occupied the deserted Confederate positions at New Madrid and secured the supplies and siege guns the Confederates had been unable to remove. The fifteen-day-long campaign had seen surprisingly few casualties—only about fifty killed and wounded on each side—but Island No. 10 was now cut off from most river communication and means of supply.

There is still disagreement over just how Beauregard saw Island No. 10. Was it to be the point for the decisive battle for control of the Mississippi

River, or was it simply the primary defensive position protecting Fort Pillow to the south? After the war he claimed the latter, although he had never indicated this to either Johnston or Polk. Certainly Beauregard hoped that the island's defenders would at least buy sufficient time to allow him to strengthen Fort Pillow and enable Johnston to attack Grant at Pittsburg Landing. He immediately ordered the New Madrid garrison sent on to Pillow and told McCown that he would not be reinforced. Beauregard tried to project optimism: "Even should enemy effect crossing (scarcely probable), you can still defend position of batteries for many days with properly detached field works in their rear." He instructed McCown to "glean the country for provisions. Husband ammunition." Beauregard also made McCown's position perfectly clear: "Your command forms the garrison of that key to Mississippi Valley. Country expects you to defend that post of honor to the last or until we can relieve you with a victory here, then to attack in force your adversary." Beauregard's true appraisal of the situation probably lies in the next sentence: "Meanwhile Pillow is being put in fighting order for another stand, if need be."[25] Actually McCown sent only about half of the Madrid Bend garrison to Pillow, with the result that its garrison was too small and his own was too large.[26]

⁓ 13 ⁓

THE CAPTURE OF
ISLAND NO. 10

*T*he Confederate defenders of Island No. 10 were reasonably confident. Any land movement by Grant to the east would be quickly reported, giving them ample time to evacuate, and Pope's force downriver was not an immediate danger because Hollins's gunboats could prevent them from crossing the river. While Foote's gunboats were much more powerful than their Confederate counterparts and presumably could easily defeat them and allow Pope to cross the river, the Confederates at Island No. 10 were certain that they could beat back any Union gunboat assault from upriver.

Foote was, in fact, taking his time arriving. On 5 March Halleck telegraphed both Cullum and Foote calling for an immediate "demonstration on Island No. 10 & if possible assist Genl. Pope."[1] That same day Foote sent a copy of the message to Fox, telling him that he had not replied. "I shall not again see my brave comrades fall around me," he told the assistant secretary, "when by waiting a few days, I can move with almost a certainty of victory."[2] The next day Cullum again asked Foote to move against the island, but he refused. Foote claimed with some irritation that his gunboats' pilothouses were not safe "and the vessels are not in a condition which would enable them to make any thing of a stand against such a resistance as the rebels have made in every instance."[3]

Halleck vacillated between wishing Foote would move and siding with his naval commander. On 7 March Halleck informed Cullum that he did not want the gunboats to attack Island No. 10. He did not want them put at risk from enemy batteries and saw them merely as protection for the mortar boats from sharpshooters and field batteries. Halleck instructed Cullum: "I repeat, I do not want the gunboats to fight till they are ready."[4] But on the tenth Halleck telegraphed Cullum: "Why can't Commodore Foote move to-morrow? It is all important. By delay he spoils all my plans."[5] Foote reported to Fox on the ninth: " Gen. Halleck has been using every means to force me into this action tomorrow but in truth the vessels will not be ready till Wednesday. . . . I have therefore claimed the right to use my judgment as to the time when we move. Am I not right in this, as I have the responsibility?"[6] One nagging problem, at least, had been solved. Foote now had enough men. The six hundred men detailed from the Army of the Potomac were now aboard the gunboats as seamen. He informed Fox, "We now have men in abundance and want no more."[7]

Part of Foote's preparation involved adding iron plating and chain to protect the gunboats' pilothouses. But he was also apprehensive about approaching his objective from upstream and fighting downstream, especially as the boats could not be held by a stern anchor and disabled boats might be lost.[8] Foote was much more cautious now than he had been at Fort Henry or Fort Donelson, as his 4 March message to Lieutenant Gwin of the *Tyler* indicates. While congratulating him on a successful action ashore, Foote strictly prohibited such activity in the future:

> I must give a general order that no commander will land men to make an attack on shore. Our gunboats are to be used as forts, and as they have no more men than are necessary to man the guns, and as the army must do the shore work, and as the enemy want nothing better than to entice our men on shore and overpower them with superior numbers, the commanders must not operate on shore, but confine themselves to their vessels.
>
> P.S.—Be cautious, as it is an element equally necessary to bravery; and life must not be risked without a prospect of entire success.[9]

This is certainly a contrast to Foote's actions at the Canton barrier forts; but now he had overall command of a squadron and he felt a crushing responsibility for its well-being and probably, as he claimed, the very survival of the Union position in the western theater. He wrote Welles on 12 March that he expected "a hard fight. I shall be very cautious, as I appreciate the vast responsibility of keeping our flotilla from falling into the rebels' hands, as it would turn the whole tide of affairs against us."[10] Halleck now expressed himself as being in complete agreement and wanted Foote to go only as far as he could without engaging the Confederate batteries.[11]

On the twelfth Foote telegraphed Halleck that he was ready to move but that the army troops and transports were not there and he considered it "unsafe to move without troops to occupy Number Ten if we capture it we cannot take prisoners with Gun Boats." If the gunboats got below the island, troops would be necessary to keep the enemy from reoccupying batteries on the Tennessee side of the river and bottling up the gunboats below.[12]

Finally, on 14 March, the same day Pope's land forces occupied New Madrid, Foote set out down the Mississippi from Cairo in the *Benton* accompanied by six other gunboats, ten mortar boats, and an assortment of steamers and tugs. The flotilla reached Columbus the same day, joining twelve hundred Union troops in transports commanded by Col. Napoleon B. Buford and convoying them to Hickman, Kentucky, that evening. The *Louisville*'s boilers were found to be leaking, however, and Foote ordered it back to Columbus for repairs.

The flotilla set out again about 6:00 A.M. on the fifteenth. Just below Island Eight the Confederate steamer *Grampus*, commanded by Capt. Marsh Miller, suddenly appeared out of the fog. The rebel ship stopped its engines and quickly struck its colors; but Miller evidently had second thoughts for he quickly got his boat under way again. With blasts of its whistle, the *Grampus* made its escape downriver in a hail of Union shells.

When they rounded Phillips Point at about 9:00 A.M., the men of the flotilla could see in the distance the Confederate positions on Island No. 10 and transports anchored on the Tennessee side of the river along with the floating battery. The correspondent for the *Chicago Tribune* described the scene: "Looking through a glass, the upper battery seemed to be a simple earthwork 8 to 10 feet in height. . . . The Stars and Bars was flying from the lower corner of the works, and the artillerists could be plainly seen walking along the parapets. . . . In the rear and right [downriver] fortifications are a number of buildings, over which flies a yellow flag, indicating a hospital."[13]

Rain and fog prevented Foote from positioning the flotilla that day apart from two mortar boats used for ranging purposes. The next morning he placed the mortar boats along the shore so that they could reduce the Confederate positions before he ran his gunboats to New Madrid. The 13-inch mortars were formidable weapons. Each weighed 17,250 pounds and rested in a 4,500-pound bed. With a 20-pound charge of powder and an elevation of forty-one degrees a mortar could hurl a 204-pound shell loaded with 7 pounds of powder three miles. At that range the shell took thirty seconds in flight.

Supervised by army ordnance officer Capt. Henry Maynadier, who had charge of the mortar boats, Number 12 at 2:40 P.M. fired the first shell against Island No. 10. At their extreme range the mortars could reach the batteries on the island, the floating battery, and the five batteries on the Tennessee side of the river. Because the mortars were firing diagonally across Phillips Point, however, the crews could not see their targets, and the only immediate effect of the Union shelling was to drive some of the Confederate defenders from their positions. The *Benton* also joined in the firing. The mortars fired nearly three hundred shells, the *Benton*, forty-five.[14]

The mortars seem to have been of little worth, although Foote would never be as forthcoming as the commander of the South Atlantic Blockading Squadron, Flag Officer Samuel Du Pont, was when he assessed their value against Fort Pulaski:

> One item has disappointed me—those great mortars are a dead failure; they did nothing at all, went wild, burst in the air, and caused no apprehension at all to the garrison. I am worried about this because this is the great dependence, those 13-inch mortars, that our friends in the Gulf are looking to, to reduce the forts in the Mississippi.[15]

On the morning of the seventeenth Foote attempted an attack on Island No. 10. Shortly after daybreak he ordered the unwieldy *Benton* lashed between the *Cincinnati* and *St. Louis*. These and the remaining ironclad steamers then moved downriver. Fearful that his vessels could not hold position in the strong current and not wanting to expose them to fire from six Confederate batteries, Foote remained at two thousand yards' range, bows-on. The Union vessels opened fire at noon, concentrating on the upper forts on the Tennessee side of the river, and continued firing until dusk. At the same time ten Union mortar boats along the Missouri shore joined in the shelling, driving some Confederates from their positions, but not those actually manning the batteries. Foote reported that the shelling had "badly cut up" the upper fort, dismounted one of the columbiads, and forced Confederate troops to run for shelter. The steamer *Red Rover* was also hit, but there were no casualties. The net effect of all this for the Confederates was one gun dismounted and one man killed and seven wounded.

The Union side also had losses. In the exchange of fire the *Benton* took four hits, including one 8-inch shell that ripped through the side and scattered splinters about before coming to rest in the drawer of Foote's small desk. A Confederate shell also damaged the *Cincinnati's* engine. But the most costly blow was self-inflicted; one of the old army rifled 42-pounders onboard the *St. Louis* burst, killing and wounding fifteen officers and men. Foote complained about the shells, some of whose fuses dated to before the Mexican War and should have been condemned. A number of them caused premature detonations, forcing his men "to drown them before loading the guns," thus causing them to be fired as solid shot. Foote marveled at the Confederate defenses: "This place is even stronger and better adapted for defense than Columbus has ever been; each fortification commands the one above it."[16]

While the shelling was in progress Foote received a devastating personal blow. Eads had just come onboard the *Benton* along with Illinois congressman Elihu Washburne and was watching the gunboat fire against the Confederate positions when he saw an officer hand Foote a number of letters that had come on the same tug on which they had arrived. Eads later wrote:

> While still conversing with me, his eyes glanced over them as he held them in his hand, and he selected one which he proceeded to open. Before reading probably four lines, he turned to me with great calmness and composure, and said "Mr. Eads, I must ask you to excuse me for a few minutes while I go down to my cabin. This letter brings me the news of the death of my son, about thirteen years old, who I had hoped would live to be the stay and support of his mother."
>
> Without further remark, and without giving the slightest evidence of his feeling to any one, he left me and went to his cabin. . . . [H]e returned after an absence of not more than fifteen minutes, still perfectly composed.[17]

William had died rather suddenly in New Haven on the fourteenth, after only a week's illness. Foote telegraphed his wife: "May God support us. The shock stuns me in the midst of fight. Thy will be done to us and

ours." On 19 March he wrote again to say that they should console themselves in that "our dear boy has escaped great evil, and no doubt he is far
better off than in this life; but Nature mourns." His son's death led to
thoughts of his own mortality, and in a postscript Foote added, "I do not
feel myself in special danger. Still, should I fall, it will be a holy cause,
and I shall die content. So do not mourn on my account."[18]

Foote now settled in for a long siege. Certainly he was disturbed by his
son's death and his nagging foot injury, although it is hard to tell how much
these affected his attitude. On the eighteenth the flotilla again shelled the
upper fort from long range. Their shells reached it only occasionally but
did dismount another Confederate gun. Meanwhile Union mortar fire
on the lower fortifications kept Confederate infantry from their canton-
ments and back out of range. But the small, widely dispersed forts were
difficult targets. Foote ordered harassing fire around the clock to keep
the Confederates from repairing their works.[19]

Meanwhile, on the other side of Island No. 10, on the night of 17–18
March, Union troops used a back road to move a 24-pounder upriver along
the shore to Riddle's Point. The next morning they opened fire across the
river on Confederate steamers unloading supplies at Tiptonville, and shells
from this one Union gun damaged several Confederate vessels. Although
the latter lobbed more than a hundred shells at the federal position, only
one Union soldier was killed. The Confederates attributed their lack of
success to defective fuses; reportedly only about one shell in five exploded.
On the night of the eighteenth Hollins withdrew his vessels below Tiptonville, taking with him much of the garrison's provisions. Hollins was
unwilling to risk his vulnerable wooden vessels to the heavy Union guns;
after that his squadron was not a factor in the battle.[20]

Although Pope held New Madrid, the generally impassable swamps to
the east prevented him from reaching the vicinity of Island No. 10 on the
Missouri side. Without transports he had no means of crossing over to
the Tennessee side and bringing his troops up for an attack against the
rear of the Confederate position. Foote had with him only fifteen hundred Union troops under Buford, hardly sufficient to storm the island's
defenses. Pope was determined, however, to attack the Confederates by
crossing the river. On 18 March his chief engineer, Col. Joshua W. Bissell, carried Pope's request to Foote for some gunboats; Foote refused to
send them, although he did send a few light draft vessels to Pope by
means of a bayou. He told Welles that he hoped soon to be able to send

two gunboats by the same route: "If we can do this, and the two gun-boats coming up and attacking the forts from below with the land attack, I have no doubt but we shall secure a complete victory."[21]

On the twentieth the upper Confederate battery opened fire on the Union gunboats and in the exchange a shot from the *Benton* disabled a Confederate gun. That same day Foote met with his subordinate com-manders in what he himself described as the first "council of war" since he had taken command of the flotilla. The meeting was to consider Pope's request that gunboats run past the batteries of Island No. 10. All save Walke declared themselves opposed, believing it too risky. Any boat passing the island would come within three hundred yards of the Con-federate batteries there. Phelps, Foote's captain on the *Benton,* was also willing to try, and Foote told Welles that he considered it. The *Benton* was better protected than the other gunboats, although "slow and more sluggish." But in the end he decided against an attempt because "her loss would be so great if we failed, and my personal services here consid-ered so important with the fleet and transports."[22]

The siege dragged on and by 24 March was at stalemate with little action except daily shelling by the Union mortars of the Confederate positions, which did little damage and inflicted few casualties. Occa-sionally the gunboats would join in. As Halleck summed up the situa-tion, "Commodore Foote will not attempt to run past the batteries and he can not reduce them." But Halleck also told Pope not to cross the river unless it could be done "with safety."[23]

Foote's brother in Cleveland followed the battle coverage in the newspapers and wrote to complain that Foote "lay off at a distance when attacking any position." He told Foote that the public wanted "dash and close fighting—something sharp and decisive." Hardly impressed with this advice, Foote rebuked his brother:

> Don't you know that my boats are the only protection you have upon your rivers against the rebel gun-boats—that without my flotilla everything on your rivers, your cities and towns would be at the mercy of the enemy? My first duty is to care for my boats, if I am to protect you. Now when I ran up the Tennessee and the Cumberland, and attacked Fort Henry and Fort Donelson, if my boats were rendered unmanageable as my flag-ship was at Donelson, the current took care of me by carrying me away from the enemy's works. But all this is changed when I descend the Mississippi. Then my boats, if they become unmanageable, are carried directly into the hands of the enemy.[24]

Foote was also concerned over reports of some thirteen Confederate gunboats below him on the Mississippi, including the ram *Manassas* at Memphis. Foote informed Welles that while he thought these were not the equal of his flotilla, "still we have no means of ascertaining their character, especially those at New Orleans."[25] Foote continued to keep his ships at long range, occasionally firing rifled shot and mortar shells at Island No. 10 and the Confederate forts on the Tennessee side of the river. On 23 March the *Carondelet* was moored to the Missouri shore when two immense cottonwood trees along the riverbank suddenly fell over on it, apparently from erosion and the shock of the bombardments. One sailor was killed and two were injured, and the ship was damaged. The *Alps* towed the *Carondelet* free and took it upriver, where over the next week carpenters from Cairo put it back in fighting trim.

The monotony of the siege was broken by the ascent of the *Eagle*, a Union observation balloon. McClellan had sent Capt. J. H. Steiner of the Aeronautic Corps and his balloon to the West, but Halleck was not impressed and sent them on to Cairo. Steiner then offered his services to Foote, who placed a large barge at Steiner's disposal for the balloon and its generator. On 23 March hydrogen was pumped into the balloon but high winds prevented an ascent. Two days later, Steiner, Phelps, and Captain Maynadier ascended some five hundred feet in the *Eagle*, which remained tethered to the barge. Haze obscured their vision, but they could see Confederate steamers at the far end of Island No. 10 and no gunboats. An ascent the next day produced information that the mortars were overshooting their target, leading to adjustments in the charges and more satisfactory results. Shortly thereafter, however, Steiner returned to Cairo. It was the only use of balloon observation in the West during the Civil War.[26]

On the twenty-sixth Foote's squadron consisted of six ironclads, the timberclad *Conestoga,* and sixteen mortar boats. He still hoped to find a passage through the bayous in order to get two steamers and several cutters to Pope within the next few days. Although Buford's force had grown to nearly two thousand troops, the water was up and the men were restricted to the transports.[27]

Meanwhile, on 23 March, work had begun on one of the more innovative engineering achievements of the entire war. Over a three-week period hundreds of Union soldiers and sailors, supervised by Colonel Bissell and supported by four shallow-draft steamers and six coal barges, used axes, saws, and tackles and two million feet of lumber to build a canal fifty feet wide and twelve miles long. The canal ran from the bend of the Mississippi near Island Eight across the swampy peninsula to near New Madrid, bypassing, and further isolating, Island No. 10. Although Bissell took advantage of existing streams and bayous, three-fourths of a mile of the canal went through solid earth, and six miles ran through timber that had to be cut off and dragged out from up to four feet under water. Although not deep enough for Foote's gunboats, the canal could take light steamers, tugs, and transports. The Confederate command apparently learned of the canal on 29 March, but McCown did nothing, convinced that it would fail.[28]

The Confederates at Island No. 10 soon got a new commander. Brig. Gen. William W. Mackall, a West Point graduate and veteran of the Mexican War, hailed from Maryland, which fact, he believed, was the reason why President Davis had granted him only a colonel's commission when he enlisted in the Confederate army. Sent to the West, he became a protégé of Davis's enemy Pierre Beauregard, who helped secure his advancement to brigadier general. Beauregard had for some time been disillusioned with McCown, and he now replaced him with Mackall. Both Beauregard and his new commander knew there would be little Mackall could do but surrender, but Beauregard hoped that he could hold out through 8 April to enable Johnston to attack Grant, as he did in what became the Battle of Shiloh. Mackall arrived at Madrid Bend on 31 March in a gunboat up the Mississippi in broad daylight. He asked McCown to stay on for several days and the latter agreed before abruptly changing his mind and departing.[29]

Mackall took command of fifty-one guns, 2,273 infantry (400 without arms), 1,166 heavy artillery troops, a field artillery battery, a sapper company, and two companies of cavalry. He also had the floating battery and seven transports, two of which were used as field hospitals. Mackall reported to Beauregard that his troops were both "disheartened" and "apathetic." He thought one good regiment would be better than the force at his command, which "never had any discipline." Madrid Bend remained flooded, but when the river dropped there would be little he could do to protect the more than twenty miles from Battery No. 1 to Tiptonville. There were simply too many places for Union troops to cross, and too few men to guard them. Mackall concluded, "When the enemy cross the game is practically up."[30]

The frustrated Pope was still determined to cross the Mississippi. He had some steamers available to ferry his troops, but he informed Foote that he would have to have at least one gunboat to control the opposite bank in order to attempt the crossing. The cautious Halleck also urged Foote forward, asking him to give Pope "all the assistance in your power by the use of your gunboats. . . . One or two gunboats are very necessary to protect his crossing. Assist him in this if you can."[31]

When on 29 March Foote asked Walke if he still wanted to try to run the Confederate gauntlet to Pope at New Madrid, the *Carondelet*'s captain replied in the affirmative, and the next day Foote authorized him to proceed. His orders to Walke were as follows: "You will avail yourself of the first fog or rainy night and drift your steamer past the batteries, on the Tennessee shore, and Island No. 10, until you reach New Madrid."[32] Walke remembered it somewhat differently: "Foote accepted my advice, and expressed himself as greatly relieved from a heavy responsibility, as he had determined to send none but volunteers on an expedition which he regarded as perilous and of very doubtful success."[33]

At the same time Walke was preparing to take the *Carondelet* to New Madrid, Pope's men at New Madrid were completing their own floating battery to mount three 32-pounders and an 8-inch columbiad. Clearly disillusioned with his naval counterpart, Pope wrote Halleck: "I have no hope of Commander Foote. He has postponed trying to run any of his gunboats past Island No. 10 until some foggy or rainy night. The moon is beginning to make the nights light, and there is no prospect of fogs during this sort of weather. We must do without him."[34]

Foote was not inactive. Moving at his own deliberate pace, despite pressure from the army and public opinion, he was planning a daring enterprise. On the night of 1 April seamen manning five boats from the flagship and two other gunboats landed an attack party of fifty soldiers of Col. George W. Roberts's Forty-second Illinois Regiment along the shore near the uppermost battery. Although detected by two Confederate sentinels, who fired off their muskets in alarm and fled, the attackers easily overcame a small detachment of defenders and spiked all the battery's six guns; another gun was already dismounted and lying in the water. The raiders then returned to the fleet without loss. Foote was delighted with the operation, which must have reminded him of his own assault on the Canton barrier forts. The next morning Confederate batteries shelled the Union fleet in frustration but without effect.[35]

One of the obstacles barring the passage of Union gunboats had been removed, and on the fourth Foote took out another. For more than an hour the *Benton, Cincinnati,* and *Pittsburg* and three mortar boats concentrated fire on the Confederate floating battery *New Orleans,* finally disabling it. One shot severed its cable, causing the battery to drift downriver two or three miles. The flotilla then concentrated its fire on the remaining forts and the island defenses.[36]

A bad storm on the night of 4–5 April enabled Walke to attempt a run past Island No. 10. Noting the risk of the coming endeavor, Walke asked his men for volunteers. First Master Richard Wade declined, and his place was taken by First Master William Hoel of the *Cincinnati,* who had more than twenty years' experience as a Mississippi River pilot. The *Carondelet's* crew readied the gunboat for the attempt, piling planks from a wreck onto the deck to provide additional protection against plunging shot. They also strung surplus chain around the more vulnerable parts of the vessel and wound an eleven-inch hawser around the pilothouse up to its windows. They stowed hammocks in the netting against small-arms fire and piled cordwood up against the boilers. The men were issued small arms and hand grenades for repelling boarders should the gunboat become disabled. And the *Carondelet* took onboard twenty-three army sharpshooters. Finally, baled hay was piled on a barge that was lashed to the side of the vessel to protect it from shore batteries on the Tennessee side of the river.

Slipping from its anchorage at 10:00 P.M., the *Carondelet* got under way with every light on board extinguished and all gunports closed. It was detected nonetheless, probably as a consequence of bright flames shooting from the stacks as the soot inside them took fire. In order to muffle puffing sounds from the stacks Walke had run pipes aft from the boilers to exhaust excess steam into the paddle-wheel house, and this steam no longer dampened the stacks. Rain, which came down in sheets, prevented accurate observation from the shore batteries. In any case their shot went high, while the "vivid lightning" allowed the Union gunboat to keep in the channel. Only two shots hit home, one of which lodged in the barge. There were no casualties. Three hours after beginning its run, at 1:00 A.M., the *Carondelet* arrived at New Madrid. Walke gave permission for grog to be issued to the crew, a decision that undoubtedly would have appalled Foote.[37]

Pope immediately appealed to Foote for another gunboat, assuring him that it could get through at night without undue risk because the

Union batteries were unable to hit Confederate gunboats running back and forth past his positions on the river at night: "My best artillerists, officers of the Regular Army of many years' service, state positively that it is impossible in the night to fire with any kind of certainty the large guns (32-pounders) of our batteries, especially at a moving object. The guns fired at the *Carondelet* passed 200 feet above her." Pope said he needed a second gunboat and that it was worth the risk of losing a gunboat to reduce the danger to ten thousand men crossing the river: "With the two boats all is safe; with one, it is uncertain."[38]

In his response Foote expressed displeasure, pointing out that Pope had earlier requested only "our smallest gunboat." He could have sent two gunboats the night before "with comparative safety." It was too late, he said, to prepare another gunboat for passage that night. He also disputed Pope's claim about the inability of shore batteries to hit a gunboat at night:

> I can not, neither does a single officer, and I presume not a pilot in the squadron, consider that a gunboat could run the blockade to-night without an almost certainty of being sunk in the attempt. . . .
>
> I cannot consider the running of your blockade, where the river is nearly a mile wide and only exposed to a few light guns, at all comparable to running it here, where a boat has not only to pass seven batteries, but has to be kept "head on" on a battery of eleven heavy guns at the head of Island No. 10, and to pass within 300 yards of thirty strong fortifications.[39]

Nonetheless, Foote agreed to make the attempt:

> In view, however, of rendering you all the aid you request and no doubt require, while I regret that you had not earlier expressed the apprehension of the necessity of two gunboats instead of the smallest gunboat, I will to-morrow endeavor to prepare another boat, and if the night is such that will render her running the blockade without serious disaster at all probable, I will make the attempt.[40]

At 2:00 A.M. on 7 April another heavy thunderstorm provided cover as the *Pittsburg* made its attempt to run the gauntlet to New Madrid. When Lt. Egbert Thompson's gunboat was opposite the Confederate batteries, they opened up. An observer aboard the *Mound City* said that "the flashes of their guns and roaring was almost incessant." Twenty minutes after starting out the *Pittsburg* rounded the bend in the river and was lost to view from the Union ships. At 3:00 A.M. men on the flotilla thought they heard the *Pittsburg*'s signal guns but could not be certain because of the thunder and Confederate batteries. But the *Pittsburg* also had made the passage unscathed.[41]

Pope, certain that the Confederates were well aware of his plans and had been fortifying the Mississippi shore opposite his own position in order to prevent a crossing, sent the *Carondelet* downriver to Tiptonville, where it exchanged fire with Confederate batteries. Then, early on the seventh, the *Carondelet*, soon joined by the *Pittsburg*, shelled and neutralized the principal Confederate batteries opposite Point Pleasant. Gunfire from the *Carondelet* disabled two 64-pound howitzers and a long 64-pounder. A Union shore party took and temporarily spiked two other 64-pound howitzers and found that the Confederates had spiked another.[42] The two Union gunboats then covered Pope's steamers as they ferried troops across the Mississippi to Watson's Landing, beginning at noon. The operation went smoothly, and as the troops worked inland to secure the Tiptonville Road, the two Union gunboats dropped downriver to Tiptonville. Island No. 10 was now completely cut off.

At first Mackall was not aware that Union gunboats had run past Island No. 10, but he soon learned of his perilous situation. Caught in a trap with a combined Union army-navy assault imminent (Foote claimed it would have occurred the next day) and with large numbers of his men deserting, Mackall ordered a withdrawal. On the evening of 7 April Capt. W. Y. C. Hume, commanding Island No. 10, sent two lieutenants to Foote under a flag of truce. Ferried to the flagship by the *De Soto*, they carried an offer to surrender under certain conditions. Foote announced that it was unnecessary for them to name terms because he would accept only unconditional surrender. Phelps accompanied the Confederate officers back to Island No. 10, where he received the formal unconditional surrender of the garrison, which he conveyed to Foote at approximately 2:00 A.M. on 8 April. That morning the entire flotilla dropped down to Island No. 10, which now flew a number of white flags.

The Confederates manning the shore batteries had fled during the night. Only about a thousand men, principally from the upper batteries on the Tennessee side of the river, managed to escape, however, most of them through the swamps. Mackall might have gotten out most of his force had he withdrawn northward rather than to the south toward Tiptonville. Pope's men cut that route off completely.[43] Some Confederates thought the defense had been poorly handled. War correspondent Junius Browne, who interviewed many of the island's more than three hundred defenders, found them angry at their commander and bitter over what they regarded as desertion by those onshore.[44]

The loss of Island No. 10 was a serious setback for the South. Although Pope later cited larger numbers, some forty-five hundred prisoners were taken, including three generals, along with 109 pieces of artillery, five thousand small arms, and a considerable quantity of ammunition and supplies. The Union also secured four steamers, which the Confederates tried and failed to scuttle, and the floating battery, which had sunk. It was a cheap victory in terms of Union casualties: seven killed, fourteen wounded, and four missing, more than half of these to accidental causes.[45]

The surrender of Island No. 10 was hailed throughout the North. Welles told Foote: "Your triumph is not the less appreciated because it was protracted, and finally bloodless."[46] Hundred-gun salutes in Boston and Providence, Rhode Island, heralded the victory. The *New York Times* proclaimed: "Island Number Ten Is Ours!" and an accompanying article concluded that the victory was second only to Fort Donelson, "if indeed, it is second to that achievement."[47]

In early April, Grant prepared to move against Corinth, but Halleck halted him at Savannah, Tennessee, and ordered him to wait until Buell arrived from Nashville. On 6–7 April, in a bloody contest, Johnston struck first in a surprise attack on Grant's inadequately outposted bivouac at Pittsburg Landing. The resulting battle came to be known as Shiloh for a small log church nearby. Historians still debate how close the South really came to victory at Shiloh, but one concluded that five thousand more men would have given the Confederates victory. This puts the loss at Fort Donelson into proper perspective.[48] The Confederates suffered another blow at Shiloh as well when Confederate theater commander Albert Sidney Johnston was hit by a musket ball in the femoral artery and bled to death before help could reach him. He was the highest-ranking general, North or South, killed in the Civil War.

Grant kept his nerve as his troops were driven literally to the banks of the Tennessee, going personally among his men and urging them to hold. With the Confederates poised to win an important victory, two of the timberclads in Foote's flotilla rendered invaluable service. Lt. William Gwin later reported that just as the Confederate advance threatened to drive the Union troops into the river, the *Tyler* and *Lexington* "opened a heavy and well-directed fire on them, and in a short time, in conjunction with our artillery on shore, succeeded in silencing their artillery, driving them back in confusion."[49]

Much of the fire from the two gunboats went long and landed in the rear, where Beauregard was located, helping to bring about his decision at dusk to call off the attack. The arrival of twenty-one thousand fresh troops under Buell that night allowed Grant to win the battle the next day. The Confederates had failed in their bid to drive Union forces back down the Tennessee River.

Not even the reverse of the first day of Shiloh and the enormous bloodshed of that battle—it was the bloodiest battle in the history of North America to that point, with some 10,600 Confederate and 13,000 Union casualties—dimmed Grant's luster. Five days after the battle Halleck arrived to take personal command of the combined Union armies, but his subsequent advance on Corinth covered only about a mile a day. Not until 29 May were Union forces in position before Corinth and ready for battle; that same day Beauregard abandoned Corinth for Tupelo.

The division of the Union resources between Grant and Buell was not the only factor that had inhibited Grant from moving against Johnston earlier; Halleck had begun another attack involving Foote in a move down the Mississippi. Control of the Mississippi River was a vital part of the Union war plan. Securing it would sever the trans-Mississippi theater from the remainder of the Confederacy and cut off the movement of raw materials and food from west to east. Control of the Mississippi was also important to Lincoln politically; it would mean reliable access to foreign markets for many midwestern agricultural products and thus bind that region to the Union cause.

❧14❧

FORT PILLOW

*T*he next Union objective following the capture of Island No. 10 was Fort Pillow, sixty miles to the south. Just north of Fulton, on the Tennessee shore, it guarded the Mississippi approach to the vital Confederate railhead of Memphis forty miles downriver. Originally the Confederates viewed Pillow as a backup position to Columbus and Island No. 10, although the Confederate commander, Capt. Montgomery Lynch, did what he could to make the fort capable of withstanding a siege. After the loss of Forts Henry and Donelson, General Polk had reinforced Pillow by sending a detachment there under Brig. Gen. John B. Villepigue. Following the loss of Island No. 10 and the defeat at Shiloh, the new Confederate commander in the West, General Beauregard, ordered a thousand slaves to Pillow to improve its entrenchments. Fort Pillow was a strong defensive position with batteries located on the high, nearly vertical Chickasaw Bluffs and cut from their face at the water's edge. When completed it mounted some forty heavy guns, including 10-inch columbiads. Most were in the lower batteries. It also had extensive earthworks and was manned by some six thousand men.[1]

Foote hoped to move quickly against Fort Pillow. He told Welles he wanted to take that place "before the rebels recover from their panic; and then we are on to Memphis."[2] On the evening of 11 April 1862 he moved his five gunboats, along with mortar boats, towboats, transports, supply ships, and tugs, south from Island No. 10. They passed two scuttled Confederate steamers on their way to New Madrid, where they joined the *Carondelet* and *Pittsburg*. Foote went ashore to consult with Pope and was miffed to learn that not all his troops were ready to move. Pope assured him that they would all be aboard transports by the thirteenth and would follow then. At New Madrid Foote also learned there were seven Confederate gunboats in the river below.[3]

The Confederate warships introduced a new element in the war on the Mississippi. This had begun on the twelfth when the rebel gunboat *General Sterling Price* pursued a Union transport until it reached the safety of the flotilla. The Confederate River Defense Fleet, as it was officially known, consisted of more than a dozen lightly armed and poorly armored gunboats. They were constructed with double pine bulkheads bolted together and stuffed with compressed cotton. Each boat had only one or two guns, but they were also somewhat faster and more agile than their Union counterparts, and a number had reinforced bows of oak and iron to enable them to act as rams. Former riverboat captains James E. Montgomery and J. H. Townsend commanded the River Defense Fleet, which was manned by civilian steamboat crews who fought on the condition that they would not be subject to the orders of naval officers.[4]

On the thirteenth the Union flotilla traveled some fifty miles to Hale's Point, just below the Arkansas state line, without spotting a single Confederate gunboat. At daybreak on the fourteenth the transports arrived with General Pope and twenty thousand troops. At 8:00 A.M. five Confederate gunboats came out to meet the Union flotilla. Soon the rebels were in retreat, however, with the *Benton* leading the charge after them. About twenty shots were exchanged before the Confederate gunboats reached the protection of Fort Pillow's batteries. The Union gunboats closed to a mile of the fort to undertake a reconnaissance. The fort's guns opened fire but the Confederate shot went high. At about 11:00 A.M. Foote ordered the Union warships to retire. Meanwhile, Union mortar boats were being positioned along the Arkansas side of the river, and at 2:00 P.M. they fired the first Union mortar shell at Fort Pillow. The mortar bombardment would continue for the next seven weeks.[5]

The original Union plan of attack, developed by Foote and Pope in a conference on the thirteenth, called for the mortar boats, protected by the gunboats, to bombard the land batteries while Pope's troops went ashore upriver and outflanked the fort from the rear. But Pope quickly determined that he could not reach the rear of Fort Pillow from any point of the river above it. Instead he decided to repeat his strategy at Island No. 10 by digging a six-mile-long canal on the Arkansas side of the river across Craigshead Point to get federal gunboats below the Confederate position. The Union commanders planned to position four gunboats below Fort Pillow and three above it to halt movement by the six weaker Confederate gunboats in either direction. In the meantime both sides engaged in harassing fire, although the Confederate gunboats remained well out of range. It seemed Fort Pillow would be taken only in a lengthy operation.[6]

By now Foote was increasingly concerned about his health. Although he continued his full work routine, including preaching to the crew of the *Benton* each Sunday, he remained on crutches. Undoubtedly the nervous strain of long hours of work and lack of sleep contributed to the failure of his wound to heal. On 14 April he complained to Welles: "The effect of my wound has quite a dispiriting effect upon me, from the increased inflammation and swelling of my foot and leg, which have induced a febrile action, depriving me of a good deal of sleep and energy. I cannot give the wound that attention and rest it absolutely requires until this place is captured."[7] The next day Foote summoned three surgeons to examine him. They unanimously concluded his wound "would probably soon totally unfit you for the performance of your important duties as flag-officer; and we would therefore respectfully suggest that for the future interest of the flotilla you be permitted to return home to recover your health."[8]

Foote asked Welles to give the command to Capt. Charles H. Davis, a close friend of Foote's since the two had been together as midshipmen in the frigate *United States,* if he should decide to relieve him. Davis, from Boston with a degree from Harvard, was then fifty-five years old. Distinguished in appearance with white whiskers and darker hair and mustaches, his chief attainments had been in scholarly pursuits, namely studies of tides and currents. His one active duty station in the war had been service in Flag Officer Samuel Du Pont's South Atlantic Blockading Squadron in the expedition against Port Royal, South Carolina. At the time Foote wrote, Davis was on detached duty in New Jersey inspecting the always-under-construction Stevens Battery.[9]

Two days later Foote again made reference to his great physical dis-
comfort and his possible replacement when he wrote to Welles:

> I did not foresee all this when I so truthfully stated my case to you, and left it
> with the Department to decide whether to keep me here or relieve me in view
> of the public interest, for I am ready to die for my country; but I do hope that
> if disaster come you will vindicate my memory, as I have been and am doing
> all that a man could do, although now I am suffering so much I can not well
> attend to my duties, and I am unable to move except in case of great neces-
> sity—or, rather, to go on deck on crutches with my foot raised causes
> increased inflammation. . . . I am weak, and have more to do than my
> strength enables me to perform properly.[10]

Welles replied on the twenty-first: "Your life and services are too valuable to be put in jeopardy, even if great events are dependent upon your
continued active duty. . . . You must have a respite." He agreed to send
Davis to take charge while Foote recuperated:

> Unless it is absolutely indispensable, I shall be reluctant to have you leave a
> position where you have earned such renown, and where the whole country
> desires you remain. No other man can inspire the people with equal confi-
> dence in the position you occupy; and it is no disparagement to others to say
> that no one has the experience and right comprehension that you have of the
> required service. I can not express to you how much I have been gratified with
> your labors and efforts. They have given heart to the whole country, and I,
> personally, have been sustained and encouraged by them.[11]

On 24 April Foote reported to Welles that his condition was worse and
that most of the time he was confined to his cabin. An army surgeon had
examined his foot and expressed concern over a possible suppuration
that would "probably permanently injure or destroy it." He wanted to see
"the Expedition reach New Orleans, but still I deemed it my duty to represent my case as it is, to the govt., and let it judge how to dispose of my
case."[12]

Welles assured Foote that wherever he went to recuperate, he would
remain flag officer in command with Davis second to him. Foote, ever
conscious of his public persona, professed himself

> pained to see myself represented in the papers as having applied to be
> detached on account of my wound, implying that I want to leave the com-
> mand on personal grounds. This is doing me a great injustice; and may I beg
> of you to have this impression removed, by its denial. . . for I would far rather

die in harness from sinking or a shot, than to leave my post in face of the
Enemy on personal grounds.[13]

Any possibility of a quick strike at Pillow was dashed when Foote and
Pope learned on 16 April that Halleck was withdrawing Pope's troops for
his snail-like campaign against Corinth. The bulk of the Union land force
departed upriver the next day in twenty transports, taking with them
tools for cutting through the swamps and leaving behind only Col. Graham N. Fitch and twelve hundred infantry to garrison Fort Pillow should
the Confederates decide to evacuate it. Although this seems unlikely,
Foote professed to believe that had Pope's troops not been withdrawn,
Union forces might have taken Fort Pillow in four days, enabling the
flotilla to move on Memphis two days later.[14]

The Union naval bombardment of Fort Pillow continued, but it was
principally harassing fire. One eyewitness, 1st Class Boy George R. Yost
of the *Cairo,* described the Union shelling in his diary:

> I frequently saw as many as a dozen shells in the air at one time, crossing
> each other's fiery tracks; some of them burst in mid air, some landing in the
> water, others in the heavy woods of the Arkansas shore. One shell, a very large
> one passed directly over our upper deck, where I was sitting, missing our
> wheel house about twenty feet, and dropping into the water twenty yards way,
> where it burst, making a tremendous splashing of the water.[15]

On 30 April, somewhat surprisingly in view of his own caution before
Island No. 10, Foote proposed taking advantage of a dark night to run his
seven more powerful gunboats past Fort Pillow to attack and destroy the
Confederate gunboats and rams believed to be located below the fort.
After that the squadron could attack Pillow upstream, take it, and then
steam to Memphis.[16] Meanwhile Union forces were assaulting the Mississippi's mouth. After an unsuccessful effort to silence the Confederate
forts there, Flag Officer David Farragut's ships ran past them, and on 27
April New Orleans fell to the Union.

The Confederates were not quiescent, however. Deserters had for
some time been warning that their gunboats would attempt an attack on
the Union flotilla, and on 8 May Union lookouts sighted smoke downriver, a sure sign that they were coming out. Three rams—the *Sumter,*
General Bragg, and *General Earl Van Dorn*—rounded the point and
made for the area where the Union mortar boats were usually positioned

during firing. These, however, had been moved a short time before and were now protected by the *Cairo, Cincinnati,* and *Mound City.* Soon the Confederate gunboats were in precipitous retreat, pursued by the Union gunboats. The range was too great for the pursuers, however, and Foote soon ordered them to cease firing.[17]

Although Foote remained nominally in command, he was not present for the subsequent Union victories at Fort Pillow and Memphis. Davis arrived on 9 May and found Foote in bed. He reported that Foote "was so overpowered at the sight of me that he was unable for some moments to speak." They both shed tears. Davis found his friend "very reduced in strength, fallen off in flesh and depressed in spirits. His foot is painful and requires rest; his digestive organs are deranged by the disease of the climate; and his mind is exhausted by incessant labor, strain, and responsibility." Davis described Foote as "thin and worn, and his face is marked with the lines of suffering and disease," but he did not believe his health was seriously impaired and thought that with rest he would soon recover.[18]

Foote briefed his successor concerning the squadron, and he insisted that Davis keep his crockery, china, and bed linens, and even a straw hat and mosquito net. The latter was an important gift, for clouds of mosquitoes made life miserable day and night for all those on the flotilla. Having briefed Davis, Foote then informed Secretary Welles: "I shall avail myself of the permission of the Department to visit Cleveland for my health."[19]

Newspaper correspondent Junius Browne observed Foote's departure that same afternoon:

When the hour had come for his going up the river, the deck of the *Benton* was crowded; and as the Flag-officer appeared, supported by Captain Phelps, he was greeted by tremendous huzzas. Old tars swung their hats, and not a few of their eyes moistened when they looked, as they supposed, upon the brave old Commodore for the last time, as indeed they did.

The Flag-officer paused for a few moments, and, removing his cap, gave those near him to understand that he would address them.

The Commodore said that he had asked to be relieved because he could not fill his office in his existing condition of health. He was willing to sacrifice himself for his country, but he knew he would be injuring the cause by retaining his position any longer.

He had been growing feebler and feebler every day, and his physician had often told him he could not improve while exposed to the excitements of the service and confined to the Flag-ship. He complimented the officers and crew of the *Benton* in the highest manner. He had always found them faithful, brave, and true, and had fondly hoped to remain with them until the war was over. That he could not was a cause of a great regret, but wherever he went, he would bear with him the memory of the *Benton* and her gallant crew, and, if his life were spared, he would often revert to the scenes he had passed among them with mingled feelings of sorrow and pride. The interview was impressive and affecting, and at the close the Commodore could hardly speak for emotion, and the tears, answered by many who were present, stole down his thin and pallid cheeks.[20]

Foote was then helped to his cabin. An hour later, at three o'clock, the former Confederate steamer *De Soto* pulled alongside and Phelps and Davis assisted Foote in boarding. Seated on a chair on the transport, Foote, in the words of correspondent Browne, "wept like a child." The men on the *Benton* then gave three cheers. There was hardly a dry eye on the *Benton* as the *De Soto* pulled away for Louisville. Foote would travel from there to his brother John's home in Cleveland.[21]

Shortly after 7:00 A.M. on 10 May, just fifteen hours after Foote left the flotilla, there occurred what Davis characterized as "a smart affair." Known as the Battle of Plum Point Bend, it was the war's first real engagement between naval squadrons.

The sortie on the eighth should have been sufficient warning. Foote had ordered his gunboats to remain headed downstream by securing their sterns to the bank, but no lookouts had been posted downriver. The Union gunboats were in two divisions: three on the Tennessee bank and four on the Arkansas side of the river. Foote claimed the flotilla was prepared for a fight, but this does not seem to have been the case. On 10 May eight Confederate gunboats attacked the squadron and temporarily disabled two of the much more powerful Union gunboats, forcing their withdrawal to Mound City for repairs. The Union side suffered only four casualties; deserters reported up to 108 Confederate dead from the engagement. Captain Montgomery considered the hour-long engagement a great victory, and in his report to General Beauregard he boasted that Union forces would "never penetrate further down the Mississippi" unless they "greatly increase their force."[22]

Davis continued a slow bombardment of the Confederate positions for three weeks. Then, in mid-May, Col. Charles Ellet arrived with several steamers of the army's Mississippi Ram Fleet. These converted Ohio

River steamers carried no ordnance but were designed to counter the Confederate river rams. Ellet was keen for an immediate strike against Fort Pillow, which Davis resisted, but the Confederates took the decision out of Union hands. On 29–30 May, General Beauregard, deciding to save his 50,000 men, evacuated Corinth, leaving it open to General Halleck's 120,000-man army; the Confederates retired to a new line along the Tuscumbia River in Alabama. This left Fort Pillow outflanked and untenable, and on 4 June its defenders abandoned it as well.[23]

On 5 June Davis's flotilla, reinforced by Ellet's rams, moved south to attack the Confederates at Memphis, arriving just above the city that evening. On the next morning, as thousands of Memphis citizens lined the shores to watch, a running battle occurred in which the Union gunboats and rams destroyed all but one of the eight Confederate vessels. Captain Phelps then went ashore and took the surrender of Memphis.

The naval battle of Memphis was perhaps the most lopsided Union victory of the war. At a cost of only four casualties and one badly damaged ram (the *Queen*), it ended Confederate naval power on the Mississippi River and added additional vessels to the Union flotilla. It also gave the Union the fifth largest city in the Confederacy along with important manufacturing resources, including a former Confederate naval yard, which soon became a principal Union base. The Mississippi was now open all the way down to Vicksburg.[24]

Many of his officers, especially Phelps, wrote Foote at his brother's home in Cleveland to pass along reports of the fighting. Foote received these with mixed feelings—delighted with the Union victories yet keenly disappointed not to have shared in the glory. His wife had come out from New Haven, and, despite his poor health, Foote kept up an active correspondence. He wrote Davis on 15 May to congratulate him on the engagement five days earlier, noting: "I . . . must confess to some little envy in not being able to have taken a hand in your dashing affair." Foote concluded his letter by telling Davis: "I am in a great hurry to return and relieve you; my heart is with the flotilla, but I was in a condition wholly unfit to command when I left, and did right in leaving, as the interests of the flotilla required it. . . . I feel rather better, and hope in two weeks to leave for Cairo to join you as soon as possible."[25]

᠃15᠃

FINAL DAYS

On 13 June 1862, still in bed with no great improvement, and with his doctors recommending it as necessary if he were to recover, Foote accepted the inevitable and asked Welles for extended leave "for the purpose of trying the effects of salt air, as recommended, with the hope of an early restoration to health." Then, quite prematurely as it turned out, he added: "I wish further to remark, that when the rebellion is crushed and a squadron is fitted out to enforce the new treaty for the suppression of the African slave-trade, I should be pleased to have command. But so long as the rebellion continues, it will be my highest ambition to be actively employed in aiding its suppression."[1]

On 17 June 1862, the day Davis formally assumed command, Welles wrote Foote to express his appreciation for his hard work with the flotilla. Although the country was grateful to him for his accomplishments, few knew the difficulties he had overcome "in first creating the flotilla and then carrying it into a series of successful actions which have contributed so largely to the suppression of the rebellion throughout the Southwest." Welles admitted that he had been reluctant to give Foote the command because of its difficulties and the army's failure "to estimate the necessity and value of the naval branch of operations on the Western rivers." He had not even shared with him all of his apprehensions. Because the navy had come in for much "censure, or complaint, or denunciation from the thoughtless and the designing," the victories and advances "cheered my heart scarcely less than your own." Welles then told Foote,

> Most sincerely do I regret the necessity which compels you to seek rest, and ask to be detached from the command which you have so much honored; but I am consoled with the belief that you will be able, in a brief period, with vigor and restored health, to again elevate your flag and render additional service.
>
> I shall bear in mind your request, and remembering our association in boyhood, be happy, as a friend and an officer, to exhibit at all times my confidence and abiding friendship.[2]

As Foote left Cleveland for New Haven on 23 June, Welles was pushing through Congress a sweeping reorganization of the navy that included establishing the ranks of rear admiral, commodore, lieutenant commander, and ensign. Four officers immediately became admirals (in order of previous seniority): David G. Farragut, Louis M. Goldsborough, Samuel Du Pont, and Foote. Charles H. Davis and James L. Lardner became commodores. The formal date of the appointments was 30 July, although the promotions were backdated to 16 July.[3]

On 5 July 1862, the bill reorganizing the Navy Department established eight bureaus: Yards and Docks, Equipment and Recruiting, Navigation, Ordnance, Construction and Repair, Steam Engineering, Provisions and Clothing, and Medicine and Surgery.[4] On the fourth, Welles wrote Foote at New Haven asking him to come to Washington and take charge of the Bureau of Equipment and Recruiting, "one of the most important, if not the most important, pillars of the Department and the service."[5]

With the encouragement of his longtime friend Joseph Smith, Foote accepted the post and was formally appointed to it on 22 July. Charles Davis, who had done much to promote science in the navy, headed the Bureau of Navigation. In October, the same month that Congress belatedly gave the Navy Department control over the river operations in the West, David D. Porter took over command of what was now designated the Mississippi Squadron.[6]

Foote's health did not permit him to take up his new duties immediately, and he secured a delay from Welles until 6 August. When he reported for duty on 7 August, Foote was still on crutches and Welles told him to delay again. Meanwhile, on 1 August, President Lincoln wrote Foote to convey a joint resolution of Congress thanking him for his "eminent services and gallantry" that Lincoln himself had requested in early July.[7]

Also during this time Foote had the great satisfaction of seeing temperance become law for the navy. This owed much to Assistant Secretary of the Navy Augustus Fox, who asked his friend Senator James W. Grimes of Iowa, who was on the naval committee, to seek an end to the spirit ration for "the enduring good of the service." Grimes introduced an amendment to the naval appropriations bill that substituted an increase in pay of five cents a day for the grog ration. Congress passed the legislation, Lincoln signed it on 14 July 1862, and it went into effect on 1 September. Welles immediately passed word of this to his commanders.[8]

Despite hopes in Washington of a speedy end to hostilities, the war dragged on. McClellan's prolonged effort to take the Confederate capital of Richmond failed through his own caution; and the effort to open the Mississippi came up against Vicksburg, which the Confederates had turned into a bastion. Union gunboats were largely ineffective against the Confederate forts high on the bluffs and in any case lacked an accompanying substantial land force. In mid-July the ironclad *Arkansas,* which the Confederates had managed to remove from Memphis before that city's capture, caught Union naval forces by surprise in the Yazoo River and ran past the federal fleet to Vicksburg.

Foote was then settling into his new shorebound assignment, and the petulant side of his personality asserted itself. Shortly after taking up his bureau duties Foote wrote to the chief clerk of the Navy Department, William Faxon, threatening to resign if he could not control the appointment of certain clerks. Faxon went to Welles about the matter, and shortly thereafter Foote sent a letter of apology to Faxon.

Foote believed in maintaining a correct distance in his relations with his superiors. Welles noted after Foote's death that

> towards me he exhibited a deference that was to me, who wished a revival and continuance of the friendly and social intimacy of earlier years, often painful. But the discipline of the sailor would not permit him to do differently, and when I once or twice spoke of it, he insisted it was proper, and said it was a sentiment which he felt even in our schoolday intercourse and friendship.[9]

Foote suffered yet another personal tragedy when his two youngest daughters, Emily and Maria, died within ten days of each other. Nonetheless, by early 1863 Foote and his family were settled in Washington and he was busy with the bureau, where he complained of being "overwhelmed with hard work" and short-handed in clerical help. Much of his time was spent securing coal and other supplies for navy, struggling to procure fair shipping costs to get these to the naval stations without undue government expense, and finding men to fill the growing demand generated by the ever-increasing number of Union ships.[10]

Clearly Foote was not happy posted ashore. He wrote a friend: "My duties are laborious in organizing my new Bureau, but I hope in this Department of which I have charge to render the Navy more efficient. I want as soon as possible to be afloat again, and there remain till we, under God, crush this arduous rebellion, which I have the strongest faith God will enable us to do in his good time."[11]

By late spring 1863 the war appeared stalemated. Despite a large Union superiority in manpower, Robert E. Lee defeated Joseph Hooker at Chancellorsville; the Mississippi was still closed to Union shipping between Vicksburg and Port Hudson; and the great southern port of Charleston, the font of the rebellion, remained defiant. The commander of the South Atlantic Blockading Squadron, Admiral Samuel Du Pont, had shown a marked reluctance to attack either Charleston or Fort Sumter. Finally, in April, he had used his monitors to shell Confederate defenses. This was a failure, leading Du Pont to declare that the port could not be taken by naval attack alone. When his words became widely known, Du Pont's defeatism led to calls for his removal.[12]

Meanwhile Foote had already communicated his desire to Welles for a sea command for his "health and public usefulness." Welles recalled after the war: "A few months . . . sufficed to show that Bureau duty was not congenial, and that his health suffered from clerical confinement." Foote's wife did not want him to take another command and met privately with Welles to ask that he not be separated from his family so soon after the deaths of two of their children. But with Foote set on leaving the bureau, she asked Welles that he be given a sea command rather than river duty, "where the risks were great, disease prevalent, and the labors too exacting." Foote was not pleased when he discovered his wife's interference. As Welles put it, "he considered it a duty to obey orders of any and every kind—to go wherever the Department directed or thought he could be most useful, for it could best judge as to the wants of the service."[13]

By May, Welles was convinced that Du Pont would have to go. Foote at first was reluctant to accept a command held by a friend, and not until he learned that Welles was going to relieve Du Pont in any event did he express interest in the post.[14] On 29 May Welles sent for Foote and the two had a frank exchange about the possibility of his taking over for Du Pont. Satisfied that Foote would take the post, Welles then introduced him to Maj. Gen. Quincy Adams Gillmore, who had been named to succeed Maj. Gen. David Hunter as commander of the army's Department of the South to act in conjunction with the squadron. Welles also suggested to Foote that it might be a good idea if John Dahlgren, the navy's leading ordnance expert, went with him to Charleston. Welles considered having the two men together at Charleston to be "the best arrangement I could make." Foote expressed pleasure at the idea of his close friend accompanying him but told Welles that he doubted Dahlgren would accept.[15]

The ambitious Dahlgren had ruthlessly promoted his own advancement to the rank of admiral, which he achieved in February 1863. Many in the navy resented this, believing it to be the result of his ordnance advancements and close friendship with Lincoln rather than a demonstrated ability at sea. Whether to prove his critics wrong, from his own ambition, or both, Dahlgren very much wanted a sea command; but he did not want to accept a post that would make him a mere subordinate to Foote. Welles had serious reservations about Dahlgren as a commander, believing him selfish and self-seeking. These were confirmed when Welles asked Fox to sound out Dahlgren about going to Charleston as second in command. Fox returned with the report that not only would Dahlgren refuse to act as second to Foote, but that he would go to Charleston only if he had command of both naval and land forces. Welles wrote in his diary: "This precludes further thought of him. . . . It is one of the errors of a lifetime." Foote, however, offered to try to persuade Dahlgren.[16]

On 2 June Dahlgren proposed to Fox that the attack on Charleston be made a separate command from that of the blockade. Fox was enthusiastic about the idea and suggested that Dahlgren go to New York and propose it to Foote. The next day, when the two met at the New York City home of publisher David Van Nostrand, Dahlgren proposed dividing the command and Foote agreed to give him command of the ironclads in the attack on Charleston. During the course of the meeting Foote complained of a severe headache.[17]

That same day, Welles wrote Du Pont that Foote would be replacing him, and the next day he formally named Foote to command the South Atlantic Blockading Squadron. In anticipation of his return to sea, Foote had in April sent his family back to New Haven, and he returned there briefly to say good-bye. Reportedly he was in good spirits but not strong. Now subject to fits of nervous prostration, he spoke of his need for rest. But he was determined to succeed in his new command, and those who knew him believed that he would either take Charleston or die in the attempt.[18]

Foote's headache was a symptom of something much worse. On 8 June Welles received a letter from Foote in which he said that he was not ready to relieve Du Point and complained of "bad health and disability." This alarmed Welles, who noted: "It must be real, for . . . Foote promptly obeys orders."[19] On the morning of the ninth Foote made a quick trip to Washington to see Welles and reassure him. He told the secretary how pleased he was with his new command, and Welles noted in his diary with obvious pleasure: "Is ardent and earnest for his new duties. Is fully possessed of my views. Left this evening for New York. Will sail next Monday."[20]

Foote had planned to leave New York on 15 June on the *Tuscarora* for Port Royal. But either through miscommunication or an early departure, the ship left without him. Foote went to the Astor House hotel and telegraphed his family that his departure would be delayed. He then inspected monitors under construction and traveled to Washington that evening and spent the next day there in naval business, returning to New York that night. The next night he fell ill with Bright's disease, a painful condition that affected his kidneys and liver, and had to send for a doctor. Professor Bache of the medical staff at the New York Navy Yard told one of Foote's brothers that he was reluctant to tell Admiral Foote that the disease would be fatal because he was convinced that Foote was determined to take Charleston. But the admiral took the news calmly and told Bache that he was prepared for death and that he had "had enough with guns and war."

Foote lingered for several days in the company of his wife, daughters, brothers Augustus and John, and a number of visitors, including Dahlgren, who made a special trip to see him. He even received visitors when his doctors advised against it. Foote urged several of them to tell Du Pont that he had neither sought nor suggested his removal. Foote also told those who visited him that he was quite prepared for death in these circumstances if it was God's will. On 21 June Welles held a frank discussion with Dahlgren and told him that he would be named to replace Foote in command of the South Atlantic Blockading Squadron, but he made it clear that this was because of pressure from Lincoln, and not his own desire. On 25 June Welles formally detached Foote from command of the squadron.

Foote died on the night of 26 June. New Haven gave him an impressive public funeral on the thirtieth that was attended by the governor and legislature, with Admiral Charles Davis representing the navy. Foote's wife barely survived him; she died that August.[21] Foote's service on the western rivers almost certainly helped bring about his early death because he never really recovered from the effects of his time there. Admiral Davis's son and biographer later asserted that both Davis and Foote were too old for such duty and that river service had killed Foote and hastened his own father's demise.[22]

Admiral Du Pont called Foote's death "a great loss to his country and to his profession. To myself he was a true friend to the last." But Du Pont also expressed a selfish reason for his regret. He believed that "had I been relieved in my command by him as first intended—things could not have gone differently at Charleston even with his skill, pluck, and prestige, and the question would have been more *quickly* settled with a small portion of our public and press. Time however has done this most effectively."[23]

Andrew Hull Foote was a fascinating individual and a man unique in the U.S. Navy of his day. Du Pont called him "earnest, persevering, indomitable, with the best puritan attributes—a sort of Northern Stonewall Jackson, without his intellect and judgment, but altogether a splendid Navy officer."[24] Driven by a sense of duty, first to his God and then to the navy, Foote was nonetheless a very warm and humane person who looked for the best in others. Unlike many staunch Christians, he was open and social; he delighted in and was faithful to his friends. Proof of the latter is that he got along well with, and was respected by, such self-serving individuals as Dahlgren, Du Pont, and Porter. His letters and dispatches reveal a man who was quite ambitious but who never begrudged the success of another, even a potential rival. Hoppin was correct when he wrote, "He did not pull down others to build up his own reputation."[25]

Foote was devoted to his family. He was also generally tolerant for his time. His dominant traits were ability, resolution, zeal, energy, thoroughness in preparation, philanthropy, and ambition. Of his resolution Charles Davis wrote: "When his attention was once turned to a thing, he never relaxed his zeal or his efforts till the object was attained."[26] Foote was a capable tactician, a superb seaman, and an ardent social reformer. His personal courage was undoubted. Although articulate, Foote was not an intellectual; his inspiration came from men rather than books. He was a multifaceted officer known for his high standards, moral integrity, intensity, frankness, strict yet humane discipline, and bulldog tenacity. He was simple in his tastes and habits. He was also popular with his junior officers and men. Welles judged him second only to Farragut in that regard and said that Foote's death affected him more deeply than that of anyone else apart from his own family. In his diary he wrote of Foote: "His judgment in the main good, his intentions pure, and his conduct correct, manly, and firm."[27]

Foote's first biographer, James M. Hoppin, wrote of Foote: "He was a true child of the sea—of a fluent spirit, moved by powerful impulses, loving honor, bold and affectionate."[28] In attaining the position of admiral, "he had risen to the highest rank belonging to his profession, and risen, not by a sudden leap, but by regular steps, by filling every subordinate position, by hard labor and toil, by actual worth and noble deeds."[29] James Eads believed that had fate not intervened, Foote would have won renown comparable to that of Farragut. Eads also wrote of him that, "aside from his martial character, no officer ever surpassed him in those evidences of genuine refinement and delicacy which mark the true gentleman."[30] Foote was certainly driven in his work, and nowhere was that more in evidence than in his command of the Mississippi flotilla during the Civil War. He probably summed up that service and his career best in a letter to Fox when he remarked: "One thing is certain, no one could have worked harder or tried more to do his whole duty here than I have done and will do to the death."[31]

Joint army-navy operations were the key to the Union's success in the West, and Foote helped to cement the cooperation and trust vital in making them work. With the possible exception of Henry Halleck and John Pope, Foote got along well with his army counterparts, an achievement that should not be minimized. Welles summed up: "Foote performed wonders and dissipated many prejudices."[32]

Foote has been criticized for his lack of aggressiveness after the capture of Fort Donelson, especially at Island No. 10 and Fort Pillow. This stemmed from a combination of factors: the heavy strain of his responsibilities, sheer physical and mental exhaustion, the death of his son, and the effects of his wound. But it was also prudence, based on the belief that his gunboats alone prevented a Confederate ascent of the upper Mississippi. Foote passionately loved the sea and seamanship, and he coveted the fame won at sea in ship-to-ship fights by the great captains. Thus it is ironic that his chief accomplishments in battle came in the course of riverine warfare against stationary land forts, first in China and then in the West during the Civil War.

But Foote must not be seen simply as the first truly successful Union naval commander of the Civil War. Davis wrote that "his career in the service . . . would have been long remembered, even without the distinctions of the war."[33] This is true. Foote bridged the important transition period between sail and steam and shot and shell, and during his pre–Civil War service he was one of the most influential figures in the navy advocating reform, while at the same time seeking to elevate the character of naval service. He promoted temperance, fostered education and scientific study, pushed for better conditions for seamen, and fought to reform the navy's promotion system. Foote also sought to bring about an end to the slave trade while at the same time stressing the principle of the inviolability of the American flag. Probably the duty assignment of which he was the most proud during his career was his command of the *Perry* in helping to halt the African slave trade. Foote was also much involved in promoting Christian missionary activity in both Africa and Asia. Any one of these activities, apart from his Civil War achievements, would make Foote deserving of study and recognition. Historian John Milligan encapsulated Foote's life when he wrote that few if any U.S. Navy reformers "exceeded Foote in the catholicity of his concerns or the fervor of his commitment."[34]

~❧ Notes ☙~

Chapter 1. Family and Early Background

1. Unlike his father and grandfather, Andrew added the letter *e* to the family name.
2. William Richard Cutter, ed., *Genealogical and Family History of the State of Connecticut*, 13–14; undated, unsigned letter in Andrew Hull Foote Papers, New Haven Colony Historical Society (henceforth abbreviated NHCHS); John Foote to Hon H. G. Lewis, 30 March and 18 April 1888, ibid.
3. John Foote to Lewis, 30 March 1888, NHCHS; Gerard A. Forlenza Jr., "A Navy Life: The Pre–Civil War Career of Rear Admiral Andrew Hull Foote," 2; Jarvis Means Morse, *A Neglected Period of Connecticut's History, 1818–1850*, 32–34.
4. John Foote, "Notes on the Life of Admiral Foote," 347.
5. John Foote, "Notes on the Life of Admiral Foote," 347; Leonard W. Bacon, "Andrew Hull Foote," 83; Forlenza, "A Navy Life," 4–7.
6. John Foote, "Notes on the Life of Admiral Foote," 347.
7. James M. Hoppin, *The Life of Andrew Hull Foote*, 23; letter from Welles to Hoppin, 8 October 1873, ibid., 391; Foote to Welles, 18 December 1823 and 12 January 1824, Gideon Welles Papers, Library of Congress (henceforth abbreviated LC); Gideon Welles, *Diary of Gideon Welles*, 1:19.
8. Forlenza, "A Navy Life," 7; Foote to Andrew A. Browne, 6 March 1823, quoted in Hoppin, *Foote*, 26.
9. Forlenza, "A Navy Life," 10.
10. Bacon, "Andrew Hull Foote," 84.
11. Ibid.; John Foote, "Remarks made by the Honorable John A. Foote," in "Eulogy on Admiral Foote, by Rev. Professor Hoppin," NHCHS.

Chapter 2. Midshipman Foote: Learning the Profession

1. Gardner W. Allen, *Our Navy and the West Indian Pirates*, 20, 46.
2. *American State Papers, Naval Affairs* (henceforth abbreviated *ASP: Naval*

Affairs), 1:787; also Allen, *Our Navy and the West Indian Pirates*, 26–27, 38; Ira Dye, *The Fatal Cruise of the Argus*, 306–7.

3. Allen, *Our Navy and the West Indian Pirates*, 41–42, 66–70, 81; Edwin M. Hall, "Smith Thompson," 124; Bacon, "Andrew Hull Foote," 84–85; Park Benjamin, *The United States Naval Academy*, 33–34; Forlenza, "A Navy Life," 11–13; letter from Foote to William Browne, 8 March 1823, in Hoppin, *Foote*, 26. Porter was court-martialed for threatening to seize a town in Puerto Rico after two of his officers were jailed on the island. When the court handed out a six-months' suspension, Porter resigned from the navy in protest.

4. Bacon, "Andrew Hull Foote," 84–85; J. T. Headley, *Farragut and Our Naval Commanders*, 154.

5. Christopher McKee, *A Gentlemanly and Honorable Profession*, 131–33, 201; Benjamin, *The United States Naval Academy*, 46–47, 65–70; Henry Burr, "Education in the Early Navy," 114–16.

6. Forlenza, "A Navy Life," 13–14.

7. Foote to William A. Browne, 6 March 1823, in Hoppin, *Foote*, 26.

8. Francis Gregory to David Porter, 3 July 1823; Porter to Gregory, 16, 18 September 1823; Daniel T. Patterson to Gregory, 15 April 1823; all in *ASP: Naval Affairs*, 2:260–61, 291; Charles Lee Lewis, *David Glasgow Farragut*, 158–59; Forlenza, "A Navy Life," 15.

9. Foote to Gideon Welles, 18 December 1823, in Gideon Welles Papers, LC.

10. Robert E. Johnson, *Thence Round Cape Horn*, 33; Forlenza, "A Navy Life," 18.

11. Letter of 29 January 1824, quoted in Hoppin, *Foote*, 28.

12. Foote letter of 15 September 1824, in Hoppin, *Foote*, 28–29.

13. Edward B. Billingsley, *In Defense of Neutral Rights*, 184, 195–97.

14. Hoppin, *Foote*, 29–30.

15. Ibid., 30; Hull to Foot, 8 September 1824, Order Book, November 1823–April 1827, Isaac Hull Papers, New York Historical Society (henceforth abbreviated NYHS).

16. Foote to an unnamed friend, 12 August 1825, in Hoppin, *Foote*, 30–31.

17. Charles H. Davis Jr., *Life of Charles Henry Davis, Rear Admiral*, 44; Gardner W. Allen, *Commodore Hull*, 60; Hoppin, *Foote*, 31.

18. Benjamin, *The United States Naval Academy*, 44, 115; Burr, "Education in the Early Navy," 129, 176–78, 181.

19. Davis, *Charles Henry Davis*, 49–50, 223, 295.

20. Forlenza, "A Navy Life," 38; Davis, *Charles Henry Davis*, 44, 46, 49–52.

21. Lewis, *Farragut*, 170; "Naval Register for 1828," in *ASP: Naval Affairs*, 3:92–122.

22. Hoppin, *Foote*, 31; *ASP: Naval Affairs*, 3:92–122; Davis, *Charles Henry Davis*, 46, 49–52.

23. Bacon, "Andrew Hull Foote," 85–86; Hoppin, *Foote*, 32.

24. John Foote, "Notes on the Life of Admiral Foote," 347; Hoppin, *Foote*, 34.

25. John Foote, "Notes on the Life of Admiral Foote," 347.

26. *ASP: Naval Affairs,* 3:92–122, 107, 242–74, 255.

27. Hoppin, *Foote,* 34.

28. Enoch C. Wines, *Two Years and a Half in the American Navy,* 1:44–45.

29. Forlenza, "A Navy Life," 61–63; John Sloat to Charles B. C. Thompson, 22 April 1831, *ASP: Naval Affairs,* 4:25–26; John Sloat to Edward Livingston, 29 March 1832, ibid., 132–33; Robert Erwin Johnson, "United States Naval Forces on Pacific Station, 1818–1823."

30. Hugh H. Davis, "The American Seamen's Friend Society and the American Sailor," 45–46; *Sailor's Magazine* 3 (1830–31): 63, 78–79, 95, 222, 228, 395.

31. *Sailor's Magazine* 3; Harold D. Langley, *Social Reform in the United States Navy,* 64–65, 243.

32. *Sailor's Magazine* 3:98, 4:64–65; Langley, *Social Reform,* 65, 243.

33. *ASP: Naval Affairs,* 3:409–11, 800, 822–23; Hoppin, *Foote,* 34; Abram W. Foote, *Foote Family, Genealogy and History,* 1:323.

Chapter 3. Lieutenant Foote: Around the World

1. Forlenza, "A Navy Life," 68–69; Hoppin, *Foote,* 35, 414.

2. Forlenza, "A Navy Life," 70; Hoppin, *Foote,* 36.

3. Letter from Mahon of 28 November 1833, in Hoppin, *Foote,* 36.

4. Letter from Bacon to Hoppin, 1 October 1873, in Hoppin, *Foote,* 400, 403–4.

5. Foote letter of 28 November 1833, in Hoppin, *Foote,* 37; Forlenza, "A Navy Life," 74–75; Wines, *Two Years and a Half in the American Navy,* 1:146, 150–51, 154–55, 157, 164, 190, 239–42.

6. Forlenza, "A Navy Life," 75–76; *ASP: Naval Affairs,* 4:958.

7. *ASP: Naval Affairs,* 4:958.

8. *Army and Navy Chronicle* 2 (1836): 128.

9. Forlenza, "A Navy Life," 80–82; Allen Johnson and Dumas Malone, *Dictionary of American Biography,* 3:498.

10. "Annual Report of the Secretary of the Navy for 1834," *ASP: Naval Affairs,* 4:604; "Naval Register for 1836," ibid., 4:800.

11. Langley, *Social Reform,* 22–23; Leonard F. Guttridge and Jay D. Smith, *The Commodores,* 309.

12. Abram Foote, *Foote Family,* 1:323.

13. *Army and Navy Chronicle* 4 (1837): 34, 416; 5 (1837): 61, 72, 126.

14. W. Patrick Strauss, "Mahlon Dickerson," 160–61; Samuel Elliot Morison, "*Old Bruin,*" 127–30.

15. Charles O. Paullin, "Early Voyages of American Naval Vessels in the Orient: The Cruise of Commodore Read," 1074.

16. John Collings Long to Foote, 6 March 1838, Naval Historical Society Collection, NYHS.

17. *Army and Navy Chronicle* 5 (1837): 401, 409; 6 (1838): 30.

18. Long to Foote, 6 March 1838, Naval Historical Society Collection, NYHS.

19. Fitch Waterman Taylor, *The Flag Ship*, 1:7–8, 240; Paullin, "The Cruise of Commodore Read," 1074.

20. Taylor, *The Flag Ship*, 1:31, 107, 130, 138, 146, 161, 165–73; *Army and Navy Chronicle* 9 (1839): 104; Paullin, "The Cruise of Commodore Read," 1074–75.

21. *Army and Navy Chronicle* 9 (1839): 104; Taylor, *The Flag Ship*, 1:198; 2:10, 14, 48–49, 117–20.

22. Hoppin, *Foote*, 403.

23. Taylor, *The Flag Ship*, 1:228, 235, 240, 253–56; *Army and Navy Chronicle* 9 (1839): 104, 329–31; Paullin, "The Cruise of Commodore Read," 1076–77.

24. Taylor, *The Flag Ship*, 1:262–75, 181–85; *Army and Navy Chronicle* 9 (1839): 104, 329–31, 359–60; Read's report, reprinted in Paullin, "The Cruise of Commodore Read," 1076–77.

25. Taylor, *The Flag Ship*, 1:286–87, 290–98; *Army and Navy Chronicle* 8 (1839): 401–3; 9 (1839): 329–31.

26. Taylor, *The Flag Ship*, 1:299–303, 314–15; *Army and Navy Chronicle* 9 (1839): 331; Paullin, "The Cruise of Commodore Read," 1080–81.

27. Hoppin, *Foote*, 100–101.

28. Taylor, *The Flag Ship*, 2:10–14, 48–49; *Army and Navy Chronicle* 8 (1839): 123; Elihu and Clarissa Doty to Foote, 26 February 1840; Alfred North to Foote, 30 November 1839, and 13 October 1840, Foote Papers, NHCHS.

29. *Army and Navy Chronicle* 9 (1839): 310.

30. Taylor, *The Flag Ship*, 2:117–20, 127; William Meacham Murrell, *Cruise of the Frigate* Columbia *around the World*, 374–75.

31. Paullin put the value of the opium imported into China in 1838 at $17 million. Paullin, "The Cruise of Commodore Read," 1081–83; Taylor, *The Flag Ship*, 2:133, 163.

32. Murrell, *Cruise of the Frigate* Columbia, 147–49; Taylor, *The Flag Ship*, 2:117, 133, 146, 157, 163.

33. Alfred North to Foote, 30 November 1839, Foote Papers, NHCHS; Foote journal, 9 June 1840, Foote Papers, LC.

34. Paullin, "The Cruise of Commodore Read," 1083; Taylor, *The Flag Ship*, 2:201–6, 209–10.

35. Taylor, *The Flag Ship*, 2:250–53; Bacon, "Andrew Hull Foote," 87–88; Charles S. Stewart, *A Visit to the South Seas*, 2:79, 125.

36. Joseph Tracy, *History of the American Board of Commissioners for Foreign Missions*, 373–76, 403–6.

37. Ibid., 406–8.

38. Hiram Bingham, *A Residence of Twenty-one Years in the Sandwich Islands*, 311ff., 535–50.

39. Stewart, *A Visit to the South Seas,* 2:79; Taylor, *The Flag Ship,* 2:219–21, 242–46.

40. Andrew H. Foote, "Incidents at Honolulu, Sandwich Islands, 1839. U.S. East India Squadron," 5 November 1839; letter 14, 2 November 1839, Foote Papers, LC.

41. Foote, "Incidents at Honolulu," 5 November 1839.

42. George C. Read to Foote, 19 October 1839, Foote Papers, NYHS.

43. Foote, letter 2, 29 October 1839, Foote Papers, LC.

44. Foote, letter 4, 30 October 1839, Foote Papers, LC.

45. Ibid.; Hoppin, *Foote,* 44–46.

46. Andrew Foote, "Letter in Support of missionaries of these islands," Foote Papers, Huntington Library (henceforth abbreviated HL). This document shows thirteen signatures. In his record of events, however, Foote listed sixteen individuals as having signed and placed his own signature second to that of Magruder. Foote, letter 13, 1 November 1839, Foote Papers, LC.

47. Foote, letter 10, 11 November 1839, Foote Papers, LC.

48. Foote, letter 4, 30 October 1839; 6 November 1839, Foote Papers, LC; Bingham, *Twenty-one Years in the Sandwich Islands,* 551–55.

49. Rev. Hiram Bingham to Foote, 3 November 1839; Mrs. Laura Judd to Foote, 2 November 1839; Foote to missionaries, 2 November 1839, Foote Papers, LC.

50. Murrell, *Cruise of the Frigate* Columbia, 200–202, 204, 209; Foote journal, 18 December 1839, Foote Papers, LC.

51. Foote to Daniel Patterson, to Commander C. K. Stribling, to Rev. Charles Stewart, 11 November 1839, Foote Papers, LC.

52. Foote journal, 18 December 1839, Foote Papers, LC; also in Hoppin, *Foote,* 48–51.

53. Foote journal, 18, 24 December 1839, Foote Papers, LC.

54. Foote letterbook, letter 14, 3 January 1840, but dated 2 November 1839, Foote Papers, LC.

55. Foote journal, 7 February 1840, Foote Papers, LC.

56. Murrell, *Cruise of the Frigate* Columbia, 226; Foote journal, 7 February, 19 March, 2 April, 21 May 1840, Foote Papers, LC.

57. Foote journal, 21 May 1840, Foote Papers, LC.

58. Foote journal, 9 June 1840, Foote Papers, LC; also in Hoppin, *Foote,* 53.

59. Murrell, *Cruise of the Frigate* Columbia, 227, 231; Taylor, *The Flag Ship,* 2:327–31.

Chapter 4. The Campaign for Temperance

1. Foote journal, 12 September 1840, Foote Papers, LC.

2. Bacon, "Andrew Hull Foote," 90; Samuel Castle to Foote, 6 February, 9 May 1840; Alfred North to Foote, 13 October 1840; Clarissa Doty to Foote, 26 February 1840; Elihu Doty to Foote, 26 August 1840, Foote Papers,

NHCHS; Thomas Turner to Foote, 9 July 1840, Naval History Society Collection, NYHS; Thomas Oliver Selfridge to Foote, 5 March 1841, Harbeck Collection, HL.

3. Abram Foote, *Foote Family*, 1:322; Hoppin, *Foote*, 57.

4. Foote to A. P. Upshur, 10 March 1843, Foote Papers, LC.

5. Charles H. Stockton, *Origins, History, Laws, and Regulations of the United States Naval Asylum*, 7–15.

6. Ibid., 18; Charles O. Paullin, "Beginnings of the United States Naval Academy," 190–91.

7. Hoppin, *Foote*, 54–55.

8. Paullin, "Beginnings," 190–91.

9. Ibid., 191–92; Stockton, *Origins*, 19–20.

10. Foote letterbook, 1 January 1842, Foote Papers, LC; Stockton, *Origins*; John D. Milligan, "Andrew Foote," 124; Hoppin, *Foote*, 54.

11. James Barron to Foote, 30 November 1842, Foote Papers, LC; Stockton, *Origins*, 20.

12. Surgeon L. Barrington to Foote, 27 January 1843; Foote to Upshur, 27 January, 4, 8, 18 February 1843; Upshur to Foote, 1 February 1843, Foote Papers, LC.

13. Stockton, *Origins*, 21–23; Foote to Dr. William Barton, 28 December 1842; Foote to Upshur, 4, 6, 9 January, 14, 18 February 1843; Upshur to Foote, 18 February 1843, Foote Papers, LC.

14. Foote to Upshur, 18 February 1843, Foote Papers, LC; Stockton, *Origins*, 21; John Foote, "Notes on the Life of Admiral Foote," 347.

15. Hoppin, *Foote*, 56.

16. Stockton, *Origins*, 18, 21; Bacon, "Andrew Hull Foote," 90; Foote to Upshur, 14 February 1823, Foote Papers, LC.

17. William B. Poole's journal aboard USS *Kearsarge*, quoted in William Marvel, *The* Alabama *and the* Kearsarge, 26, 85; McKee, *A Gentlemanly and Honorable Profession*, 451–53.

18. Langley, *Social Reform*, 209–18, 221–28, 233–38, 242.

19. Foote to Upshur, 19, 23 December 1842, 6 January 1843; Foote to William Murphy, 21 December 1842; Upshur to Foote, 13 January 1842; Upshur to William McKeon, 8 March 1842, Foote Papers, LC.

20. Langley, *Social Reform*, 44; Thomas O. Selfridge to Foote, 5 March 1841, Foote Papers, HL.

21. Foote to Congressman John A. Rockwell, 15 June 1847, in Hoppin, *Foote*, 62–63; Forlenza, "A Navy Life," 142–43.

22. Petition of 4 February 1843, Foote Papers, LC.

23. Stockton, *Origins*, 22–23; Upshur to McKeon, 8 March 1843, Foote Papers, LC.

24. Foote to Upshur, 10 March 1843; Upshur to Foote, 16 March, 8, 10 April 1843; Foote to McKeon, 15 March 1843, Foote Papers, LC.

25. Foote to A. C. Dayton, 15 March 1843; Foote to Upshur, 31 March, 6 April 1843; Dayton to Foote, 22, 29 March 1843; Upshur to Foote, 3, 13 April 1843; Foote Papers, LC; Forlenza, "A Navy Life," 144.

26. Foote to Upshur, 29 June 1843; Samuel Foot to Upshur, 12 May 1843; A. Thomas Smith to Foot, 15 May 1843; Foote to David Henshaw, 27 July, 11 August 1843; A. Thomas Smith to Foote, 22 August 1843, Foote Papers, LC.

27. Foote's journal on the *Cumberland,* 4 December 1843; Henshaw to Foote, 26 August 1843, Foote Papers, LC.

28. Dahlgren letterbook, 29 May 1844, Dahlgren Papers, LC; Madeleine Dahlgren, *Memoir of John A. Dahlgren,* 99, 113–14; Dahlgren letter/journal to Mary B. Dahlgren, 18 December 1843 entry, Dahlgren Papers, LC.

29. Madeleine Dahlgren, *Memoir of John A. Dahlgren,* 86, 90, 114; Langley, *Social Reform,* 236, 243; Dahlgren letterbook, 15, 31 October 1843, 11 February, 14 April 1844, Dahlgren Papers, LC.

30. Dahlgren letterbook, 23 June 1844, Dahlgren Papers, LC; Madeleine Dahlgren, *Memoir of John A. Dahlgren,* 93; *Sailor's Magazine* 8:262; 16:371; 34:218.

31. Dahlgren letterbook, 18 June 1845, Dahlgren Papers, LC.

32. Ibid., 14 December 1844, 22 May, 25 September 1845, Dahlgren Papers, LC; Madeleine Dahlgren, *Memoir of John A. Dahlgren,* 114.

33. Dahlgren letterbook, 6 August 1844, Dahlgren Papers, LC.

34. Dahlgren letterbook, 17 March, 1, 25 December 1844, 2 February, 8 June 1845, Dahlgren Papers, LC; Madeleine Dahlgren, *Memoir of John A. Dahlgren,* 93 109, 112; Caroline Foote to Andrew Foote, 5, 13, 15 November 1844, Foote Papers, NHCHS.

35. Dahlgren letterbook, 3 November 1844, Dahlgren Papers, LC; Madeleine Dahlgren, *Memoir of John A. Dahlgren,* 110; Langley, *Social Reform,* 243.

36. See Andrew Foote, *Farewell Temperance Address. Delivered before the Crew of the U.S. Frigate* Cumberland, *November 1, 1845,* 1–8.

37. Ibid.

38. Langley, *Social Reform,* 245–51; "Spirit Ration in the Navy," 28th Cong., 2d sess., ser. 468, H. Doc. 73.

39. Madeleine Dahlgren, *Memoir of John A. Dahlgren,* 113–19.

40. Ibid., 120, 157–58; Dahlgren letterbook, 22 September 1845, Dahlgren Papers, LC.

41. Bancroft to Foote, 12 November 1845, 17 February, 17 April 1846; Foote to Bancroft, 12 February, 22 April 1846, Foote Papers, LC; Foote's journal on the *Perry,* 1 January 1850, Foote Papers, LC; Madeleine Dahlgren, *Memoir of John A. Dahlgren,* 74–81, 120.

42. Langley, *Social Reform,* 249.

43. John Y. Mason to Foote, 8 October 1845; Foote to Mason, 19 October 1846, with copy of proceedings of court-martial of Seaman David Richards; "Court of Inquiry on Lieutenant Amasa Paine, 14–22 February 1848," Foote Papers, LC.

44. Foote, "Propositions for a Bow Propeller," Foote to Charles Morris, 20 October 1846; Smith to Foote, 30 March 1847, Foote Papers, LC.

45. Abram Foote, *Foote Family,* 1:75, 188, 322–23; Foote to Charles Morris, 20 October 1846, Foote Papers, LC.

46. Hoppin, *Foote,* 60, 64.

47. Abram Foote, *Foote Family,* 323.

48. Secretary of the Navy Preston to Foote, 28 September 1849, Foote Papers NHCHS; Hoppin, *Foote,* 66, 75–76.

CHAPTER 5. AFRICA SERVICE

1. *Statutes at Large of the United States,* 3:532–33, 600–601.

2. The best short treatment of the subject is George M. Brooke Jr., "The Role of the United States Navy in the Suppression of the African Slave Trade," 28–41.

3. Adams quoted in J. Scott Harmon, "The United States Navy and the Suppression of the Illegal Slave Trade," 212.

4. James Tertius de Kay, *Chronicles of the Frigate* Macedonian, 214–15.

5. Hugh Soulsby, *The Right of Search and the Slave Trade in Anglo-American Relations,* 42–49; Brooke, "The Role of the United States Navy," 37–38.

6. Quoted in Hoppin, *Foote,* 73.

7. John R. Spears, *The American Slave-Trade, an Account of Its Origin, Growth, and Suppression,* 38–39.

8. W. Patrick Strauss, "James Kirke Paulding," 169.

9. Brooke, "Role of the United States Navy," 33.

10. Paolo E. Coletta, "Abel Parker Upshur," 189; A. P. Upshur to Cdr. M. C. Perry, 30 March 1843, "Copy of All Instructions to the African Squadron since the Ratification of the Treaty of 1842," 35th Cong., 2d sess., ser. 1008, H. Doc. 104; Morison, *"Old Bruin,"* 164–78; Brooke, "Role of the United States Navy," 33–34.

11. "List of Captures by U.S. Squadron, under Article 8 of August 9, 1842 Treaty," 35th Cong., 2d sess., ser. 1008, H. Doc. 104; Hoppin, *Foote,* 72–74; Brooke, "Role of the United States Navy," 38.

12. Morison, *"Old Bruin,"* 164.

13. Foote to Senator Truman Smith, 15 November 1852, Foote Papers, LC.

14. Howard I. Chapelle, *The History of the American Sailing Navy,* 450, 452, 549; *Perry* station bill, Foote Papers, LC.

15. George A. Magruder to Foote, 29 October 1849, Foote Papers, NHCHS; Foote to Commo. Lewis Warrington, 15 October 1849; Foote to Commo. John Sloat,

31 October 1849; Commo. T. A. Dornin to Foote, 29 November 1849; Smith to Foote, 15 October 1849; Dahlgren to Foote, 30 October 1849, Foote Papers, LC.

16. Foote's journal on the *Perry,* 29 November, 3, 4, 5, 21, 25 December 1849, 1 January 1850; Foote to Preston, 21 December 1849, Foote Papers, LC.

17. Andrew H. Foote, *The African Squadron: Ashburton Treaty,* 9; Andrew H. Foote, *Africa and the American Flag,* 254–57; Foote journal, 31 December 1849, Foote Papers, LC. Secretary Preston's general order concerning "Sanatary [*sic*] Regulations for the U.S. Squadron on the Coast of Africa," 23 January 1850, is in Foote Papers, LC.

18. Foote journal, 12 January 1850, Foote Papers, LC.

19. Foote to Gregory, 23 January, and to Preston, 24 January 1850, Foote Papers, LC; Captain John Marston of the *Yorktown* to Foote, 21 January 1850, Foote Papers, NHCHS; Foote, *Africa and the American Flag,* 257.

20. Foote, *Africa and the American Flag,* 197–99, 205.

21. Foote journal, 7 January 1851, Foote Papers, LC.

22. Foote, *Africa and the American Flag,* 206–9.

23. Foote to Preston, 7 March 1850, Foote Papers, LC; Foote journal, 8 January, 3 April, 29 May 1850, Foote Papers, LC; Foote, *Africa and the American Flag,* 257.

24. Foote journal, 29 January, 2, 9 February 1850, Foote to Preston and Simons to Preston, 12 March 1850, Foote Papers, LC.

25. Foote, *Africa and the American Flag,* 257–60.

26. Ibid., 67–70, 259–64.

27. Foote to Preston, 21 March 1850, Foote Papers, LC; Foote, *Africa and the American Flag,* 258–62.

28. Foote to Preston, 27 March 1850, and to Cdr. Levin M. Powell, 10 April 1850; Foote journal, 29 May 1850, all in Foote Papers, LC; Foote, *Africa and the American Flag,* 258–60.

29. Foote to Gregory, 12 August 1850; G. Hastings to Foote, 24 March 1850; Cdr. John Tudor of the *Firefly* to Foote, 26 March 1850; Foote journal, 27 March, 5 April 1850; *Perry* log, 24 March 1850, all in Foote Papers, LC; Foote, *Africa and the American Flag,* 271, 277, 337; Hoppin, *Foote,* 81.

30. Foote journal, 2 February, 1, 2, 5 April, 29 May 1850, Foote Papers, LC.

31. Foote to Gregory, 27, 29 April 1850, Foote Papers, LC; Foote, *Africa and the American Flag,* 282–84.

32. Gregory to Foote, 2 May 1850, Foote Papers, LC.

33. Foote journal, 29 May 1850, Foote Papers, LC; Foote, *Africa and the American Flag,* 283–84.

34. Gregory to Foote, 6 May 1850, Foote Papers, LC; Foote, *Africa and the American Flag,* 285–86.

35. Foote journal, 21 June 1850, Foote Papers, LC.

36. Foote's order, 1 July 1850, Foote Papers, LC.

37. Foote to Gregory, 7, 12 June 1850; and Foote to Rush and Simmons, both 7 June 1850; Foote journal, 17 June 1850; *Perry* log, 7, 8 June 1850, all in Foote Papers, LC; Foote, *Africa and the American Flag,* 286–92; Forlenza, "A Navy Life," 201; Hoppin, *Foote,* 82–83.

38. Foote journal, 17 June 1850; Foote to Gregory, 5 August 1850, Foote Papers, LC.

39. Foote journal, 17 June 1850; *Perry* log, 3, 9 August 1850, Foote Papers, LC.

40. Foote, *Africa and the American Flag,* 296–300, 339–40.

41. Foote journal, 3 October 1850, Foote Papers, LC; the two-year period is in Foote, *Africa and the American Flag,* 260.

42. Foote to Renshaw, 17 August 1850; Hastings to Foote, 12 August 1850, containing report from Commander Hastings of the *Rattler* concerning the *Chatsworth;* Foote journal, 3 October 1850, Foote Papers, LC.

43. Foote to Acting Lt. Edmund Selden, 5 September 1850, Foote Papers, LC.

44. Foote to Gregory, 11 September 1850, Foote Papers, LC.

45. Foote to Gregory, 14 September 1850; to Allen, 12 September 1850; to Shepherd, 14 September 1850; to Secretary Preston with enclosures, 17 September 1850; Serralunga to Foote, 11, 14 September 1850; Foote journal, 3 October 1850, all in Foote Papers, LC; Foote, *Africa and the American Flag,* 318–23; Theodore Canot, *Adventures of an African Slaver,* xix, 375–76.

46. Foote to Gregory, 17 October 1850; Foote journal, 4, 10 December 1850, 17 November 1851, Foote Papers, LC.

47. Foote to Gregory, 20 October 1850; Foote journal, 10 December 1850, 12 June 1851, Foote Papers, LC.

48. Foote to Preston, 2 November 1850, Foote Papers, LC; Foote, *Africa and the American Flag,* 336.

49. *Perry* log, 8, 22 November 1850, Foote journal, 1 January 1851, Foote Papers, LC.

50. Quoted in Hoppin, *Foote,* 86.

51. Foote to Gregory, 8, 24 January 1851; Foote to Skinner, 22 December 1849, and undated letter; *Perry* log, 8 January 1851, all in Foote Papers, LC.

52. Foote journal, 7 January, 13 March 1851; Foote to Gregory, 24 January 1851; *Perry* log, 8 June 1851, all in Foote Papers, LC.

53. Foote to Gregory, 3, 4, 5 February 1851; Gregory to Foote, 4, 5 February 1851, Foote Papers, LC.

54. Foote to Charles Frost, 15 February 1851; Foote to Joseph Smith, 17 April 1851; Foote to Senator Truman Smith, 15 November 1850, Foote Papers, LC.

55. Foote to Gregory, 17 April 1851; to Joseph Smith, 17 April 1851; to Graham, 17 May 1851; Foote journal, 22 May 1851, Foote Papers, LC.

56. Foote to Graham, 1 June 1851; Foote journal, 23 May, 12 June 1851, Foote Papers, LC.

57. Foote to Graham, 9 July 1851; Foote journal, 14 July 1851; *Perry* log, March–July 1851; all in Foote Papers, LC.

58. Foote journal, 14 July 1851, Foote Papers, LC.

59. Ibid.

60. Foote to La Vallette, 1 October 1851; Foote journal, 23, 26 September 1851, Foote Papers, LC; Lady Newborough to Foote, 2 September 1851; Lord Newborough to Foote, 30 August 1853, Foote Papers, NHCHS; Foote, *Africa and the American Flag*, 369–70.

61. Foote to La Vallette, 1 October 1851; Foote journal, 17 November 1851, Foote Papers, LC.

62. Foote's journal on the *Perry*, 17 November, 12 December 1851, Foote Papers, LC. Foote, *Africa and the American Flag*, 377, incorrectly gives the date of sailing as 15 December; Forlenza, "A Navy Life," 216.

63. *Perry* log, 23 December 1851, Foote Papers, LC.

CHAPTER 6. NAVAL REFORM ASHORE

1. Hoppin, *Foote*, 86–87; Foote, *Africa and the American Flag*, 377–78.

2. Foote's remarks to the American Colonization Society, 18 January 1855, in Hoppin, *Foote*, 88; "African Squadron: Message from the President of the United States Transmitting Information in Reference to the African Squadron," 22 July 1850, 31st Cong., 1st sess., H. Doc. 73, 1–2, ser. 578.

3. Foote, *The African Squadron. Ashburton Treaty*, 7.

4. Foote to William Graham, 7 April 1852, Foote Papers, LC; Hoppin, *Foote*, 88, 96.

5. Foote journal, 11 December 1850, Foote Papers, LC.

6. Langley, *Social Reform*, 144, 246; Foote journal, 11 December 1850, Foote Papers, LC; the Navy Department reported to Congress a total of 5,936 floggings for sixty ships during 1846 and 1847. James E. Valle, *Rocks and Shoals. Order and Discipline in the Old Navy*, 78–79; Andrew H. Foote, "Address by Captain A. H. Foote, U.S.N. Delivered at the Anniversary of the Pennsylvania Seamen's Friend Society, in the Musical Fund Hall, Philadelphia, April 27, 1854," *Sailor's Magazine* 26 (1854): 324–26. See also Jane Litten, "Navy Flogging: Captain Samuel Francis Du Pont and Tradition," 148–65.

7. *Sailor's Magazine* 24 (1852): 587–88, 619–20; 26 (1854): 321–27.

8. *Sailor's Magazine* 24:587–88, 619–20.

9. Foote journal, 29 January 1850, 11 December 1850, 7 January 1851, Foote Papers, LC; Hoppin, *Foote*, 98–99; Foote, *Africa and the American Flag*, 105, 195–99, 205–9, 388.

10. Foote to Dobbin, 29 June 1854, Foote Papers, LC; Elliot Cresson to Foote, 10 June 1851, Foote Papers, NHCHS; Soulsby, *The Right of Search and the Slave Trade*, 135; Warren S. Howard, *American Slavers and the Federal Law*, 48.

11. James L. Lardner to Foote, 9 April 1853, Foote Papers, LC.

12. Foote journal, 11 January 1850, 2 April 1850, 11 January, 14 July 1851, Foote Papers, LC.

13. Court-martial of Lt. Alexander Murray, Foote Papers, LC; Forlenza, "A Navy Life," 237.

14. Abram Foote, *Foote Family,* 1:323; Hoppin, *Foote,* 364.

15. Foote, *Africa and the American Flag,* 15–16.

16. See Foote, *Africa and the American Flag,* especially chap. 24, pp. 379–90.

17. Foote, *Africa and the American Flag,* 15. See also 103–5, 109, 178–79, 196–99.

18. Howard, *American Slavers and the Federal Law,* 48–49; Soulsby, *The Right of Search and the Slave Trade,* 133; "Report of the Secretary of the Navy, 1853," *House Executive Documents,* 33d Cong., 1st sess., vol. 1, pt. 3, p. 299; various letters to Foote acknowledging receipt of his book, Foote Papers, NHCHS.

19. Dobbin to Foote, 9 March 1854, Foote Papers, NHCHS; Hoppin, *Foote,* 104–5; Joseph Smith to Foote, 28 April 1854, Joseph Smith Papers, NYHS.

20. Foote to Mrs. Williams, 22 April 1854, Foote Papers, NYHS.

21. Harold D. Langley, "James Cochrane Dobbin," 279–80, 285–86, 289–90.

22. Valle, *Rocks and Shoals,* 83; Charles O. Paullin, *Paullin's History of Naval Administration, 1775–1911,* 234–36.

23. Langley, "James Cochrane Dobbin," 290.

24. Paullin, *Paullin's History of Naval Administration,* 238–39.

25. Charles O. Paullin, "Naval Administration, 1842–1861," 1469.

26. Senate Bill 574, 32d Cong., 2d sess., 10 January 1853, in Foote Papers, LC; Forlenza, "A Navy Life," 250; Langley, "James Cochrane Dobbin," 290–91.

27. Foote to Edward H. Leffingwell, 19 February 1855, Foote Papers, NYHS; Foote to Senators Seward, Clayton, et al., 17 February 1855, Foote Papers, LC.

28. Foote to Edward Leffingwell, 19 February 1855, Foote Papers, NYHS; Charles H. Davis to Foote, 12 March 1855, Africa and the American Flag File, New York Public Library.

29. Forlenza, "A Navy Life," 254.

30. Ibid.; James M. Merrill, *Du Pont, the Making of an Admiral,* 218–19; James W. McIntosh to Foote, 10 March 1855, Foote Papers, NHCHS.

31. Langley, "James Cochrane Dobbin," 290–91; Henry A. Du Pont, *Rear Admiral Samuel Francis Du Pont,* 76–77; Merrill, *Du Pont,* 220–21.

32. Langley, "James Cochrane Dobbin," 291.

33. Forlenza, "A Navy Life," 257, 260.

34. James C. Palmer to Foote, 9, 22 January 1856; Abraham Bigelow to Foote, 21 December 1855; John Woodruff to Foote, 22 March 1856, Foote Papers, NHCHS; Foote to Mrs. Browne, July 1856, Foote Papers, LC; Forlenza, "A Navy Life," 259–60.

35. Forlenza, "A Navy Life," 161–62.

36. Foote Papers, NHCHS.

37. John S. Missroom to Foote, 8 October 1855; Arthur Sinclair to Foote, 21 November 1855, Foote Papers, NHCHS; Foote to Mrs. Browne, July 1856, Foote Papers, LC; Hoppin, *Foote*, 105–6; Forlenza, "A Navy Life," 262.

Chapter 7. China Service

1. Chapelle, *History of the American Sailing Navy*, 550.
2. Foote to Dobbin, 16 April 1856, Foote Papers, LC.
3. Joseph Smith to Foote, Harbeck Collection, HL; George T. Sinclair to Foote, 21 March 1856; Henry K. Davenport to Foote, 18 April 1856, Foote Papers, NHCHS; Foote to Dobbin, 31 March, 7, 16, 25 April 1856; journal of the USS *Plymouth*, 22 April–3 May 1856, Foote Papers, LC.
4. See Morison, *"Old Bruin."*
5. Dobbin to Foote, 21, 23 April 1856, Foote Papers, LC.
6. George T. Sinclair to Foote, 21 March 1856, Foote Papers, NHCHS; General Orders of the USS *Portsmouth*; Foote to Capt. Duncan Ingraham, 26 July, 5 August 1856, Foote Papers, LC.
7. Foote to John Southall, 26 July 1856; to Duncan N. Ingraham, 5 August 1856; to James Dobbin, 9 August, 4 September 1856; to James Armstrong, 29 August 1856; journal of the USS *Portsmouth*, 3, 19, 27 May, 18 June, 2, 7, 28 August 1856, all in Foote Papers, LC.
8. Charles S. Leavenworth, *The Arrow War with China*, 23–33; David F. Long, "A Case for Intervention: Armstrong, Foote, and the Destruction of the Barrier Forts, Canton, China, 1856," 222–24, 226.
9. Armstrong to Foote, 6 October 1856; Foote to Armstrong, 4 November 1856, Foote Papers, LC.
10. Journal of the USS *Portsmouth*, 22 October 1856; Foote to Dobbin, 14 October 1856; Foote to Armstrong, 4 November 1856, all in Foote Papers, LC; Perry to Foote, 21 October 1856, Foote Papers, NHCHS.
11. Te-Kong Tong, *United States Diplomacy in China*, 185; William Maxwell Wood, *Fankwei; or The San Jacinto in the Seas of India, China and Japan*, 276, 283, 415–16. Wood was the squadron's surgeon and Armstrong's confidante.
12. Armstrong to Foote, 17 October 1856; Foote to Armstrong, 4 November 1856, Foote Papers, LC; Wood, *Fankwei*, 276, 283, 415–16.
13. Foote circular of 29 October 1856; Foote to Armstrong, 4 November 1856, Foote Papers, LC.
14. Foote to Armstrong, 4 November 1856; draft letter, Foote to Keenan, November 1856, Foote Papers, LC.
15. Journal of the USS *Portsmouth*, 29 October 1856; Foote to Armstrong, 4, 8 November 1856, Foote Papers, LC.
16. Foote to Armstrong, 4 November 1856; Foote order, 6 November 1856, Foote Papers, LC.

17. Foote to Armstrong, 8 November 1856, Foote Papers, LC.

18. Ibid.; Foote to Sir Michael Seymour, 25 October 1856; Foote to J. O. Bradford, 27 January 1858, Foote Papers, LC.

19. Armstrong to Dobbin, 12 November 1856, Foote Papers, LC; Long, "A Case for Intervention," 226.

20. Armstrong to Dobbin, 10 December 1856; Foote to Armstrong, 13 November 1856, Foote Papers, LC.

21. Foote to Armstrong, 26 November 1856, in Hoppin, *Foote,* 113–14.

22. Long, "A Case for Intervention," 227.

23. Journal of the USS *Portsmouth,* 16 November 1856; Armstrong to Dobbin, 10 December 1856, Foote Papers, LC; Wood, *Fankwei,* 426–27; Charles O. Paullin, "Early Voyages of American Naval Vessels to the Orient: The East India Squadron in the Waters of China and Japan," 395.

24. Armstrong to Dobbin, 10 December 1856, Foote Papers, LC; journal of the USS *Portsmouth,* 16 November 1856, Foote Papers, LC; Wood, *Fankwei,* 428–32.

25. Armstrong to Foote, 18 November 1856; Armstrong to Dobbin, 10 December 1856, journal of the USS *Portsmouth,* 17 November 1856, all in Foote Papers, LC.

26. Armstrong to Foote, 18 November 1856; Foote to Armstrong, 26 November 1856, Foote Papers, LC; Wood, *Fankwei,* 440–41.

27. Armstrong to Foote, 18 November 1856; Foote to Armstrong, 19 November 1856, Foote Papers, LC.

28. Foote to Armstrong, second letter of 19 November 1856, Foote Papers, LC.

29. Armstrong to Foote, 19 November 1856, Foote Papers, LC [date incorrectly given as 18 November 1856].

30. Foote to Armstrong, 19 November 1856; Armstrong to Foote, 19 November 1856, Foote Papers, LC.

31. Foote to Armstrong, 26 November 1856, Foote Papers, LC; Rev. George B. Bacon to Hoppin, 1 October 1873, reprinted in Hoppin, *Foote,* 401; Captain Simms's report, 7 December 1856, in E. N. McClellan, "The Capture of the Barrier Forts in the Canton River," 268.

32. Foote to Armstrong, 26 November 1856, Foote Papers, LC; also Hoppin, *Foote,* 113–19; Paullin, "The East India Squadron in the Waters of China and Japan," 394–96; Julius W. Pratt, "Our First 'War' in China: The Diary of Wm. Henry Rowell," 782–84; Captain Simms's report of 7 December 1856, in McClellan, "The Capture of the Barrier Forts," 269–72.

33. Journal of Lt. George Colvocoresses aboard the *Levant,* 3 December 1856, in Harold Colvocoresses, "The Capture and Destruction of the Barrier Forts," 682–83; Foote to Armstrong, 30 November, 6 December 1856; journal of the USS *Portsmouth,* 23 November–6 December 1856, Foote Papers, LC.

34. Armstrong to Foote, 24 November 1856, Foote Papers, LC; Wood, *Fankwei,* 448–53, 461–62.

35. Foote to Armstrong, 26 November, 12 December 1856, Foote Papers, LC; also Colvocoresses journal, 24 November 1856, in Colvocoresses, "The Capture and Destruction of the Barrier Forts," 682.

36. Armstrong to Dobbin, 12 December 1856, Foote Papers, LC.

37. Ibid.

38. Journal of the USS Portsmouth, 13 December 1856, Foote Papers, LC; Hoppin, Foote, 122–23; Forlenza, "A Navy Life," 299.

39. Foote to Peter Parker, 30 December 1856; Rev. Beecher to Foote, 16 November 1857, Foote Papers, LC; Long, "A Case for Intervention," 231–32.

40. Hoppin, Foote, 124.

41. Dobbin to Armstrong, 27 February 1857, Foote Papers, LC. Marcy at first misunderstood developments, believing that the Americans had fired first. Curtis T. Henson, "The United States Navy and China," 261–63.

42. H. H. Bell to Foote, 18 December 1856; Foote to Armstrong, 16 December 1856, Foote Papers, LC.

43. Long, "A Case for Intervention," 233; Forlenza, "A Navy Life," 303.

44. Armstrong to Foote, 24 December 1856; journal of the USS Portsmouth, 28, 30 November, 1, 8, 9, 10, 14 December 1856, Foote Papers, LC; Hoppin, Foote, 402–8.

45. Foote to Armstrong, 6, 16 February 1857; to Edward Cunningham, 25 January 1857; journal of the USS Portsmouth, 1, 5, 23, 30 January, 1 February 1857, Foote Papers, LC.

46. Foote to Armstrong, 6, 11 March 1857; journal of the USS Portsmouth, 8, 9, 10 March 1857, Foote Papers, LC; Elihu Doty to Foote, 12 January 1857, Foote Papers, NHCHS.

47. Foote to Armstrong, 11 March 1857; journal of the USS Portsmouth, 14 March 1857, Foote Papers, LC; Wood, Fankwei, 290–91.

48. Foote to Edward A. Blundell, 5, 8, 20 May 1857, Foote Papers, LC; the complete correspondence between Blundell and Foote is in "Report of the Secretary of the Navy . . . ," 5 March 1859, 35th Cong, special sess., Sen. Ex. Doc. 1, no. 12; Edward Cunningham to Foote, 22 May 1857, Foote Papers, NHCHS.

49. Foote to Armstrong, 15 May, 15 June 1857, journal of the USS Portsmouth, 27 May, 2 June 1857, Foote Papers, LC.

50. Foote to Armstrong, 15 June 1857; Stephen Mattoon to Foote, 15 June 1857, Foote Papers, LC.

51. Armstrong to Foote, 15 June 1857, Foote Papers, LC; Forlenza, "A Navy Life," 314.

52. Foote to Armstrong, 21 April, 15 June, 8 August 1857; journal of the USS Portsmouth, 1, 4, 13, 23 July, 9, 11, 15, 18, 19 August 1857, Foote Papers, LC.

53. Armstrong to Foote, 20 August 1857; journal of the USS Portsmouth, 23 August, 6, 7, 8 September 1857, Foote Papers, LC; Andrew H. Foote, "Visit

to Simoda and Hakodadi in Japan," 129–33; Foote letter of 15 September 1857, Foote Papers, LC.

54. Foote to Armstrong, 10 October 1857; Foote letter of 15 September 1857; inventory of boxes sent by Foote to Mrs. Foote from Hong Kong, 14 November 1857, Foote Papers, LC; Foote, "Visit to Simoda and Hakodadi," 131–32.

55. Journal of the USS *Portsmouth*, 12, 18 September 1857; Foote letters of 25 January and 5 October 1857, Foote Papers, LC.

56. Journal of the USS *Portsmouth*, 18 September 1857; Foote to Armstrong, 10 October 1857, Foote Papers, LC.

57. Foote letter dated 5 October 1857, and postscript of 7 October 1857; Foote to Japanese governor at Hakodate, 7 October 1857, Foote Papers, LC; Foote, "Visit to Simoda and Hakodadi," 133–34.

58. Journal of the USS *Portsmouth*, 26, 28 September, 10, 26 October 1857, Foote to Elisha Rice, 21 September 1857; Foote letter and postscript, 5, 7 October 1857, all in Foote Papers, LC; Foote, "Visit to Simoda and Hakodadi," 134–37.

59. Armstrong to Foote, 20 August 1857; Foote to Isaac Toucey, 28 October 1857, Foote Papers, LC; Foote to Second King of Siam, 1 November 1857, 11 January 1858; Foote to First King of Siam, December 1857, Foote Papers, LC; Foote, "Visit to Simoda and Hakodadi," 129–37.

60. Armstrong to Foote, 12 November, 21 December 1857; journal of the USS *Portsmouth*, 10, 16, 20 November, 2 December 1857, Foote Papers, LC.

61. Journal of the USS *Portsmouth*, 15, 29 January 1858, Foote Papers, LC.

62. Journal of the USS *Portsmouth*, 21 December 1857, 9, 12, 17 February, 5, 7 March 1858, Foote Papers, LC; Jos. Tatnall to Foote, 4, 5 March 1858, Foote Papers, NYHS.

63. Tatnall to Foote, 4 March 1858; journal of the USS *Portsmouth*, 5, 8, 31 May, 13, 14 June 1858; Foote to Toucey, 23 April, 13 June 1858, Foote Papers, LC.

Chapter 8. The Brooklyn Naval Yard

1. Journal of the USS *Portsmouth*, 14, 15, 16 June 1858; Foote to Toucey, 14 June 1858; Foote to Lenthall, 14 June 1858, Foote Papers, LC.

2. Forlenza, "A Navy Life," 340–41, 348–51.

3. Abram Foote, *Foote Family*, 1:323.

4. Henry H. Lewis to Foote, 12 February 1859, Foote Papers, NHCHS; H. P. Blanchard to Foote, 29 August 1859, Foote Papers, LC; Foote to D. Kendal, 27 October 1859, Foote Papers, NYHS; Hoppin, *Foote*, 139; Forlenza, "A Navy Life," 356.

5. "Interview of Commander A. H. Foote before the Board of Inspection of Navy Yards," 8, 11, 12, 19 April 1859, Foote Papers, LC; Forlenza, "A Navy Life," 344–45.

6. John A. Dahlgren, *Shells and Shell Guns*.

7. "Rear-Admiral Andrew H. Foote," *Sailor's Magazine* 35 (1862): 365–66, 36 (1863): 170.

8. Hoppin, *Foote,* 142–43.

9. Foote to Toucey, 22 January 1859, Foote Papers, LC.

10. *Sailor's Magazine* 34:364.

11. Foote to Toucey, 14 July 1859, Foote Papers, LC.

12. Hoppin, *Foote,* 143–44.

13. Simpson to Foote, 12 March 1860, Foote Papers, NHCHS; Hoppin, *Foote,* 143–44; Du Pont to Foote, 25 January 1861, in Samuel F. Du Pont, *Samuel F. Du Pont: A Selection from His Civil War Letters,* 1:27.

14. Langley, "Issac Toucey," 325; William S. Dudley, *Going South: U.S. Navy Officer Resignations and Dismissals on the Eve of the Civil War,* 13.

15. Hoppin, *Foote,* 146–48, 150–51.

16. Du Pont to Foote, 25 January 1861, in Du Pont, *Civil War Letters,* 1:27–28.

17. "Remarks made by the Honorable John A. Foote," in *Eulogy on Admiral Foote,* by James M. Hoppin, NHCHS, 41.

18. Welles, *Diary,* 1:346.

19. Ibid., 1:19; John Niven, *Gideon Welles, Lincoln's Secretary of the Navy,* 324–25.

20. Welles, *Diary,* 1:346, 2:353.

21. Ibid., 2:135.

22. Ibid., 1:3–21; Niven, *Gideon Welles,* 325–32; also David D. Porter, *Incidents and Anecdotes of the Civil War,* 13–16.

23. Porter, *Incidents and Anecdotes of the Civil War,* 16–20; Niven, *Gideon Welles,* 332–33.

24. Porter, *Incidents and Anecdotes of the Civil War,* 17–20.

25. Lt. T. A. Roe to Foote, 5.00 P.M., 6 April 1861, Foote Papers, NHCHS; Niven, *Gideon Welles,* 335–36; Welles, *Diary,* 1:24–25; Porter, *Incidents and Anecdotes of the Civil War,* 20–22.

26. Porter, *Incidents and Anecdotes of the Civil War,* 22; Welles, *Diary,* 1:25, 31, 35–36, 346; Niven, *Gideon Welles,* 336; Foote to Welles, 9 April 1961, Foote Papers, LC and HL.

27. Letter from Samuel Mercer to Foote, 7 August 1861, in Hoppin, *Foote,* 149; Mercer to Foote, 14 June 1861, Foote Papers, NHCHS; Niven, *Gideon Welles,* 356–57, 359–64.

28. Abram Foote, *Foote Family,* 1:323, 892.

29. Langley, *Social Reform,* 263–64.

30. Mercer to Foote, 7 August 1861, in Hoppin, *Foote,* 149; Mercer to Foote, 14 June 1861, Foote Papers, NHCHS; Langley, *Social Reform,* 262–63.

31. Eads to Welles, 29 April 1861, in U.S. Navy Department, *Official Records of the Union and Confederate Navies in the War of the Rebellion* (henceforth abbreviated *ORN*), ser. 1, 22:278–79; Welles to Cameron and Cameron to McClellan,

both 14 May 1861, ibid., 277, 279; John D. Milligan, *Gunboats down the Mississippi*, 3–4.

32. Welles to Rodgers, 16 May 1861, John Rodgers Family Papers, LC; also in *ORN*, ser. 1, 22:280.

33. Robert E. Johnson, *Rear Admiral John Rodgers*, 156–57; Jay Slagle, *Ironclad Captain. Seth Ledyard Phelps and the U.S. Navy*, 113.

34. Phelps to Rodgers, 16 August 1861, *ORN*, ser. 1, 22:299.

35. U.S. Department of War, *The War of the Rebellion. A Compilation of the Official Records of the Union and Confederate Armies* (henceforth abbreviated *ORA*), ser. 1, 3:390; Johnson, *Rodgers*, 165–66; Niven, *Gideon Welles*, 378; Milligan, *Gunboats down the Mississippi*, 19.

36. In Hoppin, *Foote*, 152–53.

37. William Howard Russell, *My Diary North and South*, 516–17.

CHAPTER 9. THE WESTERN FLOTILLA

1. Private letter, Foote to Fox, 8 September 1861, *ORN*, ser. 1, 22:321; Welles to Hoppin, 8 October 1873, in Hoppin, *Foote*, 392–93; Rodgers to Welles, 7 September 1861, *ORN*, ser. 1, 22:320.

2. Description by unidentified visitor to Foote in June 1862, in Hoppin, *Foote*, 351–52.

3. Henry Walke, "The Gun-Boats at Belmont and Fort Henry," 360.

4. Hoppin, *Foote*, 404.

5. Foote to Welles, 13 November 1862, HL; Clarence E. Macartney, *Mr. Lincoln's Admirals*, 88–89.

6. Edwin C. Bearss, *Hardluck Ironclad*, 27; David D. Porter, *Naval History of the Civil War*, 134–35; Milligan, *Gunboats down the Mississippi*, 20.

7. General Order No. 6, 17 December 1861, *ORN*, ser. 1, 22:466–67.

8. Frémont to Foote, 16 September 1861, *ORN*, ser. 1, 22:335.

9. Foote to Fox, 2 November 1861, *ORN*, ser. 1, 22:390–91; Captain A. A. Harwood to Foote, 9 December 1861; and A. Constable to Foote, 24 December 1861, Foote Papers, NHCHS; Dahlgren to Harwood, 20 January 1862, in Hoppin, *Foote*, 160–61, 183.

10. Foote to Fox, 11 January 1862, *ORN*, ser. 1, 22:492.

11. Foote to Fox, 4, 27 January 1862, in Gustavas Fox, *Confidential Correspondence of Gustavus Vasa Fox, Assistant Secretary of the Navy*, 2:24–27, 33.

12. Foote to Fox, 19 October 1861, 22:373–74; Fox to Foote, 28 October 1861, 22:385; Foote to Col. William A. Howard, 29 November 1861, 22:446; Foote to Welles, 10 December 1861, 22:59; Halleck to Foote, 17 December 1861, 22:465; Meigs to Foote, 23 December 1861, 22:468; Foote to Halleck, 25 December 1861, 22:470; Foote to Halleck, 28 December 1861, 22:475; Foote to Meigs, 2 January 1862, 22:483; Foote to Welles, 22 January 1862, 22:515; A.

H. Kilty to Navy Dept., 4 February 1862, 22:532, all in *ORN*, ser. 1; Fox to Foote, 17 November 1861, 1 March 1862, in Hoppin, *Foote*, 180, 239; Fox to Paulding, 17 September 1861, *ORN*, ser. 1, 22:337; Foote to Fox, 2 November 1861, 11 January 1862, in Fox, *Correspondence of Fox*, 2:9, 30.

13. Milligan, *Gunboats down the Mississippi*, 28.
14. Ibid., 21.
15. Ibid., 22–23.
16. Foote to Welles, 16 January 1862, 22:502; Foote to Cdr. Joseph Smith, 18 January 1862, *ORN*, ser. 1, 22:506; Bearss, *Hardluck Ironclad*, 33–34.
17. Foote to Fox, 2 November 1861, *ORN*, ser. 1, 22:391.
18. Frémont to Foote, 11 October 1861, *ORN*, ser. 1, 22:366.
19. Hoppin, *Foote*, 184; the first noted published reference in which Foote used his new title is on 24 November 1861. See *ORN*, ser. 1, 22:442.
20. Foote to Fox, 30 December 1861, *ORN*, ser. 1, 22:477–78; Bern Anderson, *By Sea and by River*, 86–87.
21. Welles, *Diary*, 1:120; Hoppin, *Foote*, 185; Foote to Fox, 5 March 1862, Fox, *Correspondence of Fox*, 2:39.
22. Dave Page, *Ships versus Shore. Civil War Engagements along Southern Shores and Rivers*, 253; Rowena Reed, *Combined Operations in the Civil War*, 65.
23. Reed, *Combined Operations*, 65–67; Milligan, *Gunboats down the Mississippi*, xxiv–xxv.
24. Reed, *Combined Operations*, 67–68.
25. Stephen E. Ambrose, "The Union Command System and the Donelson Campaign," 78–86.
26. T. Harry Williams, *P. G. T. Beauregard, Napoleon in Gray*, 116; Shelby Foote, *The Civil War. A Narrative*, 208–9.
27. James M. McPherson, *Battle Cry of Freedom. The Civil War Era*, 395.
28. Ibid., 394.
29. Charles P. Roland, *Albert Sidney Johnston, Soldier of Three Republics*, 348.
30. Milligan, *Gunboats down the Mississippi*, 32.
31. Walke, "The Gun-Boats at Belmont and Fort Henry," 367.
32. Rodgers to Welles, 4 September 1861, *ORN*, ser. 1, 22:309.
33. Phelps to Foote, 10 September 1861, 22:324–25; Stembel to Foote, 13 September 1861, 22:326–27; Grant to Frémont, 10 September 1861, 22:328, all in *ORN*, ser. 1; Slagle, *Ironclad Captain*, 124–25.
34. Phelps to Foote, 18 October 1861, *ORN*, ser. 1, 22:371; Slagle, *Ironclad Captain*, 135–38.
35. Phelps to Foote, 28 October 1861, 370–80; Brigadier General Smith to headquarters, 31 October 1861, *ORN*, ser. 1, 22:380.
36. Phelps to Foote, 10 December 1861, *ORN*, ser. 1, 22:457–58.
37. William S. McFeely, *Grant, a Biography*, 92.

38. On the battle, see various reports, U.S. and Confederate, in *ORN*, ser. 1, 22:402–28. For a short account of the battle, see William M. Polk, "General Polk and the Battle of Belmont," 1:348–57. The definitive account of the battle is Nathaniel Cheairs Hughes Jr., *The Battle of Belmont. Grant Strikes South*. Walke's quote is from his report of 9 November 1861 to Foote, *ORN*, ser. 1, 22:400–402; also in Foote Papers, LC.

39. The casualty figures here are Grant's. Polk gave his as 641 but claimed enemy losses of at least 1,500. Polk to CSA War Dept., 10 November 1861, *ORN*, ser. 1, 22:410.

40. Ulysses S. Grant, *Memoirs and Selected Letters*, 178–86.

41. Phelps to Foote, 19 November 1861, *ORN*, ser. 1, 22:435–37; Slagle, *Ironclad Captain*, 145.

42. M. F. Force, *From Fort Henry to Corinth*, 26–27; Foote to Welles, 12 January 1862, 22:498; W. D. Porter to Foote, 13 January 1862, 22:499–500; Phelps to Foote, 18 January 1862, 22:507–8, all in *ORN*, ser. 1.

43. Reed, *Combined Operations*, 78–80.

44. Ibid., 78.

45. Lieutenant Shirk to Foote, 24 January 1862, *ORN*, ser. 1, 22:520–21.

46. Grant, *Memoirs*, 189.

47. McFeely, *Grant*, 96.

48. Grant, *Memoirs*, 190; McFeely, *Grant*, 97.

49. Phelps to Foote, 7, 18 January 1862, *ORN*, ser. 1, 22:485–86, 507; Herman Hattaway and Archer Jones, *How the North Won. A Military History of the Civil War*, 61–62.

50. Foote to Welles, 13 November 1862, *ORN*, ser. 1, 22:314; also HL.

51. John Foote, "Notes on the Life of Admiral Foote," 347.

52. Force, *From Fort Henry to Corinth*, 27.

53. Foote to Halleck, 28 January 1862, *ORN*, ser. 1, 22:524.

54. Halleck to Grant, 30 January 1862, *ORA*, ser. 1, 7:122.

55. Ibid., 121.

56. Force, *From Fort Henry to Corinth*, 27; Anderson, *By Sea and by River*, 93; McFeely, *Grant*, 97.

CHAPTER 10. FORT HENRY

1. Force, *From Fort Henry to Corinth*, 28. Force gives twelve guns, but most other sources give only eleven. See Walke, "The Gun-Boats at Belmont and Fort Henry," 366.

2. Tilghman's addendum to report of the Battle of Fort Henry, 9 August 1862, *ORA*, ser. 1, 7:144.

3. Report of 12 February 1862, *ORA*, ser. 1, 7:139.

4. Heiman, Taylor, and Tilghman reported sixteen guns but the Union side reported seventeen captured; Gilmer also reported seventeen. Types also differ. See *ORA*, ser. 1, 7:120, 132, 140, 148. Taylor, "The Defense of Fort Henry," 369; report of Lt. Col. Jeremy F. Gilmer, 17 March 1862, *ORA*, ser. 1, 7:131–32.

5. Taylor, "The Defense of Fort Henry," 370.

6. Phelps to Foote, 31 January 1862, *ORN*, ser. 1, 22:528; Slagle, *Ironclad Captain*, 153–55.

7. Foote to Welles, 3 February 1862, *ORN*, ser. 1, 22:534–35.

8. Slagle, *Ironclad Captain*, 155.

9. Foote to Halleck, 22 January 1862, 22:514; Foote to Henry Wise and to Welles, 27 January 1862, 22:522–23; Fox to Foote, 27 January 1862, 22:522; Wise to Foote, 31 January 1862, 22:527, all in *ORN*, ser. 1. In any event Ripley remained at his post until September 1863.

10. Phelps expected to receive command of one of the new ironclads; when a more senior lieutenant arrived and he did not get the command, he asked for a transfer. Foote, unwilling to lose an experienced and aggressive commander, promised Phelps command of the *Benton*, which would be the flagship when ready. Slagle, *Ironclad Captain*, 149–50; Grant, *Memoirs*, 119–120; Macartney, *Mr. Lincoln's Admirals*, 91. Walke said the squadron anchored six miles from Henry. Walke, "The Gun-Boats at Belmont and Fort Henry," 361–62.

11. Walke, "The Gun-Boats at Belmont and Fort Henry," 362.

12. Taylor, "The Defense of Fort Henry," 369; Tilghman to S. Cooper, 9 August 1862, *ORN*, ser. 1, 22:554.

13. Tilghman to Pope, 4 February 1862; Tilghman to Colonel Mackall, 5 February 1862; *ORA*, ser. 1, 7:858.

14. Grant, *Memoirs*, 119–20; Force, *From Fort Henry to Corinth*, 28; Macartney, *Mr. Lincoln's Admirals*, 91.

15. Porter, *Naval History of the Civil War*, 144.

16. Grant, *Memoirs*, 119–20; Porter, *Naval History of the Civil War*, 141.

17. Taylor, "The Defense of Fort Henry," 370; Walke, "The Gun-Boats at Belmont and Fort Henry," 364.

18. Grant, *Memoirs*, 191–92; see also Grant's Field Orders, no. 1, 5 February 1862, *ORA*, ser. 1, 7:125–26.

19. Slagle, *Ironclad Captain*, 158.

20. Porter, *Naval History of the Civil War*, 145.

21. See Foote's Special Orders Nos. 1 and 2, of 2 February 1862, *ORN*, ser. 1, 22:535–36; Slagle, *Ironclad Captain*, 159.

22. Foote to Welles, 7 February 1862, *ORN*, ser. 1, 22:537–39; Force, *From Fort Henry to Corinth*, 29–30; Porter, *Naval History of the Civil War*, 146; Walke,

"The Gun-Boats at Belmont and Fort Henry," 362–63; Slagle, *Ironclad Captain*, 159.

23. Taylor, "The Defense of Fort Henry," 370; Foote to Welles, 7 February 1862, *ORN*, ser. 1, 22:539; Slagle, *Ironclad Captain*, 160–61. Figures of killed and wounded aboard the *Essex* vary. I have used those in an account by 2d Master James Laning, quoted by Porter in *Naval History of the Civil War*, 145–46.

24. Taylor, "The Defense of Fort Henry," 370–71.

25. Foote to his wife, 9, 12 March 1862, National Archives, Record Group 45 (henceforth abbreviated NA, RG 45), in Slagle, *Ironclad Captain*, 161.

26. Taylor, "The Defense of Fort Henry," 371; Tilghman to S. Cooper, 12 February 1862, *ORN*, ser. 1, 22:559.

27. Hoppin, *Foote*, 204.

28. Force, *From Fort Henry to Corinth*, 32; see also McClernand's report in *ORA*, ser. 1, 7:126–30; McClernand to Foote, 7 February 1862, *ORN*, ser. 1, 22:544.

29. McFeely, *Grant*, 98; Halleck to Foote, 9 February 1862, *ORN*, ser. 1, 22:547.

30. Foote to Welles, 6 February 1862, *ORN*, ser. 1, 22:537.

31. Tilghman to S. Cooper, 9 August 1862, *ORN*, ser. 1, 22:560. The full report is on pp. 553–62.

32. McFeely, *Grant*, 98–99.

33. James B. Eads, "Recollections of Foote and the Gun-Boats," 343; Acting Ensign Symmes E. Brown to his fiancée, 9 [10] February 1862, in John D. Milligan, comp., *From the Fresh-Water Navy, 1861–64: The Letters of Acting Master's Mate Henry R. Browne and Acting Ensign Symmes E. Browne*, 24.

CHAPTER 11. FORT DONELSON

1. Force, *From Fort Henry to Corinth*, 34, 46; Porter, *Naval History of the Civil War*, 150.

2. Johnston to J. B. Benjamin, 8 February 1862, *ORA*, ser. 1, 7:130–31.

3. Williams, *P. G. T. Beauregard*, 118, 120; Larry J. Daniel and Lynn N. Bock, *Island No. 10: Struggle for the Mississippi Valley*, 21–22.

4. Maj. Gen. Lew Wallace, "The Capture of Fort Donelson," 1:401.

5. Williams, *P. G. T. Beauregard*, 118–19.

6. Macartney, *Mr. Lincoln's Admirals*, 93–94.

7. Roland, *Albert Sidney Johnston*, 271; Williams, *P. G. T. Beauregard*, 119.

8. Reed, *Combined Operations*, 87.

9. Shelby Foote, *The Civil War*, 1:194.

10. Anderson, *By Sea and by River*, 92; R. M. Kelly, "Holding Kentucky for the Union," 385.

11. Edwin C. Bearss, *Unconditional Surrender: The Fall of Fort Donelson*, 37.

12. Grant, *Memoirs*, 206.

13. Wallace, "The Capture of Fort Donelson," 403–10; see also *ORA*, ser. 1, 7:328.

14. Special Order No. 3, 2 February 1862, *ORN*, ser. 1, 22:537; Foote's claim that this order was his is in Foote to Fox, 9 March 1862, Fox, *Correspondence of Fox*, 2:49.

15. Paul H. Silverstone, *Warships of the Civil War Navies*, 156; Porter, *Naval History of the Civil War*, 149–50; Phelps to Foote, 10 February 1862, *ORN*, ser. 1, 22:571–74; Slagle, *Ironclad Captain*, 162–73.

16. Grant, *Memoirs*, 197.

17. Halleck to Foote, 11, 12 February 1862, in Hoppin, *Foote*, 232; Halleck to Brig. Gen. John Pope, 11 February 1862, *ORA*, ser. 1, 7:553; Grant, *Memoirs*, 197.

18. Grant, *Memoirs*, 197.

19. Henry Walke, "The Western Flotilla at Fort Donelson, Island Number Ten, Fort Pillow and Memphis," 431–32.

20. Foote to his wife, 6 February 1862, NA, RG 45, in Slagle, *Ironclad Captain*, 176.

21. Foote to Welles, 11 February 1862, *ORN*, ser. 1, 22:550.

22. Slagle, *Ironclad Captain*, 176–77; Porter, *Naval History of the Civil War*, 150.

23. Grant, *Memoirs*, 197–98.

24. Grant, *Memoirs*, 198; Force, *From Fort Henry to Corinth*, 43; McFeely, *Grant*, 99; Wallace, "The Capture of Fort Donelson," 410.

25. Wallace, "The Capture of Fort Donelson," 407.

26. Ibid.

27. Grant, *Memoirs*, 199–201.

28. Walke, "The Western Flotilla," 431–32; Grant, *Memoirs*, 201.

29. McClernand's report to Grant, 28 February 1862, in *ORA*, ser. 1, 7:172–73; Grant, *Memoirs*, 198, 201.

30. McFeely, *Grant*, 99.

31. Wallace, "The Capture of Fort Donelson," 409.

32. Ibid., 415.

33. Grant, *Memoirs*, 202.

34. Ibid.; Egbert Thompson to Foote, 17 February 1862, *ORN*, ser. 1, 22:592.

35. Walke, "The Western Flotilla," 433.

36. Ibid., 434–45; Slagle, *Ironclad Captain*, 179–80.

37. Walke, "The Western Flotilla," 433–34; Foote to Welles, 17 February 1862, *ORN*, ser. 1, 22:587.

38. Foote to Welles, 15 February 1862, *ORN*, ser. 1, 22:585–86.

39. Ibid., 586.

40. Foote to Welles, 16 February 1862, 22:584–85; Foote to Welles, 15 February 1862, 22:585–86; Walke to Foote, 15 February 1862, 22:590–91; Thompson to Foote, 17 February 1862, 22:592, all in *ORN*, ser. 1.

41. Hoppin, *Foote*, 223; Walke, "The Western Flotilla," 436n.

42. Porter, *Naval History of the Civil War*, 162.

43. Ibid., 151.

44. Grant, *Memoirs*, 203.

45. Ibid., 199–200.

46. McPherson, *Battle Cry of Freedom*, 400.

47. Grant, *Memoirs*, 201.

48. Wallace, "The Capture of Fort Donelson," 415.

49. See McClernand's report in *ORA*, ser. 1, 7:175–79; report of Col. William H. L. Wallace, 17 February 1862, in ibid., 197.

50. Wallace, "The Capture of Fort Donelson," 418–19, 420–21; Wallace's report to Grant, 20 February 1862, *ORA*, ser. 1, 7:236–40; Force, *From Fort Henry to Corinth*, 53–54; Grant, *Memoirs*, 206; report of Gilmer, 2 December 1862, 7:265–66; report of Pillow, 18 February 1862, 7:283; report of Buckner, 11 August 1862, 7:328–29, 332–33, all in *ORA*, ser. 1. On Pillow's attempt to shift the blame, see his letter to Secretary of War George W. Randolph of 10 October 1862 and Randolph's reply of 21 October 1862, in *ORA*, ser. 1, 7:316–21.

51. Grant, *Memoirs*, 205; McFeely, *Grant*, 99–100, 205–6, 295; Wallace, "The Capture of Fort Donelson," 421–22.

52. Grant, *Memoirs*, 206; Wallace, "The Capture of Fort Donelson," 422–23.

53. Wallace, "The Capture of Fort Donelson," 422–25; Bearss, *Unconditional Surrender*, 4.

54. Foote to Welles, 15 February 1862, 22:586; Dove to Foote, 16 February 1862, 22:588–89; Thompson to Foote, 17 February 1862, 22:593, all in *ORN*, ser. 1.

55. Buckner's report, 11 August 1862, *ORA*, ser. 1, 7:334.

56. Wallace, "The Capture of Fort Donelson," 401, 426; Grant, *Memoirs*, 206; report of Pillow, 14 March 1862, 7:288; report of Forrest, 15 March 1862, 7:295; statement of Maj. Gus. A. Henry, 13 March 1862, 7:296–97; statement of Major W. H. Haynes, 13 March 1862, 7:297–98, all in *ORA*, ser. 1.

57. Grant, *Memoirs*, 207–8; Shelby Foote, *The Civil War*, 1:211.

58. McFeely, *Grant*, 101.

59. Grant to General G. W. Cullum, 16 February 1862, *ORA*, ser. 1, 7:15.

60. Halleck to Grant, 18 February 1862, *ORN*, ser. 1, 22:616; Grant, *Memoirs*, 214.

61. Hoppin, *Foote*, 270.

CHAPTER 12. THE ROAD TO ISLAND NO. 10

1. Grant, *Memoirs*, 215–16.

2. Foote to his wife, 18 February 1862, NA, RG 45, in Slagle, *Ironclad Captain*, 185.

3. Withers to various individuals, 28 February 1862, *ORN*, ser. 1, 22:829.

4. Foote report, 19 or 20 February 1862, *ORN*, ser. 1, 22:617; Foote to Mrs. Foote, 17 February 1862, in Hoppin, *Foote*, 229–30.

5. Foote to Mrs. Foote, 18 February 1862, in Hoppin, *Foote,* 230. Foote's report of 19 or 20 February 1862, *ORN,* ser. 1, 22:617–19; Foote to Mrs. Foote, 19 February 1862?, in Hoppin, *Foote,* 235; Bearss, *Hardluck Ironclad,* 40.

6. Foote to Welles, 20 February 1862, 22:618–19; various telegrams from McClellan, Halleck, and Cullum, 20–21 February 1862, 22:621–22; Halleck to Phelps, 22 February 1862, 22:624; Foote to Grant, 22 February 1862, 22:624, all in *ORN,* ser. 1; Halleck to Grant, 20 February 1862, in Hoppin, *Foote,* 235.

7. Foote to Cullum, 21 February 1862, *ORN,* ser. 1, 22:622–23.

8. Halleck to Sherman, 23 February 1862, 22:625; Foote to Welles, 22 February 1862, 22:624; Foote to Mrs. Foote, 23 February 1862, 22:626; Foote to Welles, 23 February 1862, 22:627–31, all in *ORN,* ser. 1; Grant, *Memoirs,* 215–16; Milligan, *From the Fresh-Water Navy,* 32.

9. Foote to Mrs. Foote, 23 February 1862, *ORN,* ser. 1, 22:626.

10. Foote to Welles, 21 February 1862, *ORN,* ser. 1, 22:632.

11. Ibid., 633.

12. Foote to Chief of Bureau of Ordnance, 1 March 1862 (2), 22:642, 650; Foote to Meigs, 28 February 1862, 22:642; Foote to Welles, 3 March 1862, 22:643, all in *ORN,* ser. 1.

13. David Nevin, *The Road to Shiloh: Early Battles in the West,* 98; Forrest's report of 22 March 1863 in *ORA,* ser. 1, 7:427–29.

14. Gwin to Foote, 1, 5 March 1862, *ORN,* ser. 1, 22:643–45, 646–47.

15. McFeely, *Grant,* 105, 107.

16. Foote to Chief of Bureau of Ordnance, 28 February 1862, 22:642; Foote to Welles, 1, 4 March 1862, 22:650–52; Cullum to Halleck, 4 March 1862, 22:653, all in *ORN,* ser. 1; Slagle, *Ironclad Captain,* 194–95.

17. Cullum to McClellan, 4 March 1862, 653; Foote to Welles, 4 March 1862, *ORN,* ser. 1, 22:652.

18. Foote letter of 9 March 1862, in Hoppin, *Foote,* 259–60.

19. Foote to Fox, 5 March 1862, Fox, *Correspondence of Fox,* 1:40.

20. Foote to Welles, 28 April 1862, HL; Silverstone, *Warships of the Civil War Navies,* 155.

21. Foote to Mrs. Foote, 12 March 1862, in Hoppin, *Foote,* 261–62.

22. Daniel and Bock, *Island No. 10,* 25.

23. Numbers of guns vary according to sources. See Daniel and Bock, *Island No. 10,* 35; also *ORA,* ser. 1, 8:809, 811; and Walke, "The Western Flotilla," 445.

24. Walke, "The Western Flotilla," 445; Daniel and Bock, *Island No. 10,* 4–6, 13–14, 27–28.

25. Daniel and Bock, *Island No. 10,* 21–22, 24; Beauregard to McCown, 21, 22 March 1862, *ORA,* ser. 1, 8:794, 797.

26. Daniel and Bock, *Island No. 10*, 94–95.

CHAPTER 13. THE CAPTURE OF ISLAND NO. 10

1. Halleck to Foote, 5 March 1862, Fox, *Correspondence of Fox*, 2:50.
2. Foote to Fox, 5 March 1862, Fox, *Correspondence of Fox*, 2:50.
3. Cullum to Foote, 6 March 1862, 22:658; Foote to Cullum, 8 March 1862, *ORN*, ser. 1, 22:662.
4. Halleck to Cullum, 7 March 1862, *ORN*, ser. 1, 22:658–59.
5. Halleck to Cullum, 10 March 1862, *ORN*, ser. 1, 22:663–64.
6. Foote to Fox, 9 March 1862, Fox, *Correspondence of Fox*, 1:44–45.
7. Fox, *Correspondence of Fox*, 2:41.
8. Foote to Chief of Bureau of Ordnance Henry A. Wise, 7, 13 March 1862, *ORN*, ser. 1, 22:659–60, 665.
9. Foote to Gwin, 4 March 1862, *ORN*, ser. 1, 22:655–56.
10. Foote to Welles, 12 March 1862, in Hoppin, *Foote*, 266.
11. Halleck to Assistant Secretary of War Thomas A. Scott, 10 March 1862, *ORN*, ser. 1, 22:664.
12. Foote to Halleck, 12 March 1862, Foote Papers, Tennessee State Library and Archives.
13. Foote to Welles, 17 March 1862, *ORN*, ser. 1, 22:693; Slagle, *Ironclad Captain*, 196–97; *Chicago Tribune*, 21 March 1862, quoted in Daniel and Bock, *Island No. 10*, 73.
14. A. H. Kelty, etc., to Foote, 9 February 1862, Foote Papers, LC; Foote to Welles, 17 March 1862, 22:693; A. M. Pennock to Chief of Bureau of Ordnance Wise, Navy Dept., 20 February 1862, *ORN*, ser. 1, 22:620–21.
15. Du Pont to his wife, 12 April 1862, Du Pont, *Civil War Letters*, 1:423.
16. Foote to Welles, 17 March 1862, *ORN*, ser. 1, 22:693–94.
17. Eads, "Recollections of Foote and the Gun-Boats," 345.
18. Foote to Welles, 27 March 1862, *ORN*, ser. 1, 22:703; the telegram and letter from Foote to his wife are in Hoppin, *Foote*, 269.
19. Foote to Welles, 19 March 1862, *ORN*, ser. 1, 22:696.
20. Daniel and Bock, *Island No. 10*, 98–99, 101.
21. Ibid., 84–85; Foote to Welles, 19 March 1862, *ORN*, ser. 1, 22:696.
22. Walke, "The Western Flotilla," 441; Foote to Welles, 20 March 1862, *ORN*, ser. 1, 22:697; Slagle, *Ironclad Captain*, 202, 205.
23. Daniel and Bock, *Island No. 10*, 86–87; Halleck to Pope, 24 March 1862, *ORN*, ser. 1, 22:698.
24. John Foote, "Notes on the Life of Admiral Foote," 347.
25. Foote to Welles, 26 March 1862, *ORN*, ser. 1, 22:700.
26. Slagle, *Ironclad Captain*, 204; Daniel and Bock, *Island No. 10*, 91.
27. Foote to Welles, 26 March 1862, *ORN*, ser. 1, 22:699–700.

28. Daniel and Bock, *Island No. 10*, 104–8.

29. Ibid., 115–16; William W. Mackall, *A Son's Recollections of His Father*, 169–71.

30. *ORA*, ser. 1, 8:809, 811–14.

31. Pope to Foote, 26 March 1862, 22:701; Halleck to Foote, 28 March 1862, *ORN*, ser. 1, 22:703.

32. Foote to Walke, 30 March 1862, *ORN*, ser. 1, 22:704.

33. Walke, "The Western Flotilla," 442.

34. Pope to Halleck, 2 April 1862, *ORN*, ser. 1, 22:708.

35. Foote to Welles, 2 April 1862, 22:706–7; Roberts to Foote, 2 April 1862, *ORN*, ser. 1, 22:707–8.

36. Foote to Welles, 4 April 1862, 22:709; Thomas A. Scott to E. M. Stanton, 4 April 1862, *ORN*, ser. 1, vol. 22.

37. Walke to Foote, 4 April 1862, 22:710; Foote to Pope, 4 April 1862, *ORN*, ser. 1, 22:713. For a vivid description of the *Carondelet*'s run to New Madrid, see Charles B. Boynton, *History of the Navy during the Rebellion*, 1:549–53.

38. Pope to Foote, 5 April 1862, *ORN*, ser. 1, 22:713–14.

39. Foote to Pope, 6 April 1862, *ORN*, ser. 1, 22:714–15.

40. Ibid.

41. Foote to Welles, 7 April 1862, *ORN*, ser. 1, 22:719; Acting Ens. Symmes E. Browne, in Milligan, *From the Fresh-Water Navy*, 55; Junius Henri Browne, *Four Years in Secessia*, 123–27.

42. Walke to Pope, 7 April 1862, *ORN*, ser. 1, 22:718.

43. Foote to Welles, 7, 8 April 1862, 22:720–21; *Benton* log, 8 April 1862, *ORN*, ser. 1, 22:777; Browne, *Four Years in Secessia*, 128–30; Milligan, *Gunboats down the Mississippi*, 59; Milligan, *From the Fresh-Water Navy*, 59; Slagle, *Ironclad Captain*, 209; Daniel and Bock, *Island No. 10*, 133–36.

44. Browne, *Four Years in Secessia*, 130–31.

45. Daniel and Bock, *Island No. 10*, 144–45; Milligan, *From the Fresh-Water Navy*, 57–60.

46. Welles to Foote, 9 April 1862, *ORN*, ser. 1, 22:724.

47. Daniel and Bock, *Island No. 10*, 142.

48. Roland, *Albert Sidney Johnston*, 342.

49. Gwin to Foote, 8 April 1862, *ORN*, ser. 1, 22:763.

Chapter 14. Fort Pillow

1. Report of 4th Master S. Kellogg to Capt. W. D. Porter, 8 April 1862, *ORN*, ser. 1, 22:767–78; Foote to Welles, 19 April 1862, *ORN*, ser. 1, 23:9.

2. Foote to Welles, 9 April 1862, *ORN*, ser. 1, 22:722–23.

3. Foote to Welles, 12 April 1862, *ORN*, ser. 1, 23:3–4.

4. Slagle, *Ironclad Captain*, 211.

5. Foote to Welles, 14 April 1862, in Hoppin, *Foote*, 297–98.

6. Ibid.

7. Foote to Welles, 14 April 1862, *ORN,* ser. 1, 23:5; Browne, *Four Years in Secessia,* 152–53.

8. John Ludlow, J. S. McNeeley, and George E. Jones to Foote, 15 April 1862, *ORN,* ser. 1, 23:63.

9. Foote to Welles, 15 April 1862, *ORN,* ser. 1, 23:63.

10. Foote to Welles, 17 April 1862, in Hoppin, *Foote,* 299.

11. Welles to Foote, 21 April 1862, in Hoppin, *Foote,* 315.

12. Foote to Welles, 24 April 1862, HL.

13. Welles to Foote, 23 April 1862, *ORN,* ser. 1, 23:70; Foote to Welles, 29 April 1862, HL.

14. Foote to Welles, 19, 23 April 1862, *ORN,* ser. 1, 23:9–11.

15. In Bearss, *Hardluck Ironclad,* 53.

16. Foote to Welles, 30 April 1862, *ORN,* ser. 1, 23:12.

17. Foote to Welles, 29 April 1862, HL; *Benton* log, 8 May 1862, *ORN,* ser. 1, 23:669; Slagle, *Ironclad Captain,* 216; Bearss, *Hardluck Ironclad,* 55–56.

18. Davis, *Charles Henry Davis,* 222–23.

19. Ibid., 223; Davis to Welles, Foote to Welles, Foote to Davis, all 9 May 1862, 23:85–86; Commander Pennock to Davis, 10 May 1862, 23:89; *Benton* log, 9 May 1862, 23:669, all in *ORN,* ser. 1; Browne, *Four Years in Secessia,* 147–49.

20. Browne, *Four Years in Secessia,* 165.

21. Ibid., 166, 168.

22. Davis letter, quoted in Davis, *Charles Henry Davis,* 223–25; also see pp. 226–27; Davis to Welles, 11, 12 May 1862 (2), 23:14, 16–17; Walke to Davis, 10 May 1862, 23:15; Gregory to Capt. Henry Maynadier, 10 May 1862, 23:15–16; Montgomery to Beauregard, 12 May 1862, 23:55–57, all in *ORN,* ser. 1; report of Phelps to Foote, 11 May 1862, in Hoppin, *Foote,* 310, 317–18; Walke, "The Western Flotilla," 447–49; Ivan Musicant, *Divided Waters,* 212–15; Milligan, *Gunboats down the Mississippi,* 64–67; Acting Ensign Browne of the *Mound City* to his fiancée, 12 May 1862, in Milligan, *From the Fresh-Water Navy,* 74–77; Browne, *Four Years in Secessia,* 169–78; Slagle, *Ironclad Captain,* 219–25.

23. Slagle, *Ironclad Captain,* 225, 230, 232.

24. Davis to Welles, two letters of 6 June 1862, 23:119–21; Ellet to Stanton, 11 June 1862, 23:132–34; Phelps to Foote, 9 June 1862, 23:135–36, all in *ORN,* ser. 1; Browne, *Four Years in Secessia,* 179–91; Musicant, *Divided Waters,* 215–16; Milligan, *Gunboats down the Mississippi,* 68–77.

25. Foote to Davis, 15 May 1862, in Davis, *Charles Henry Davis,* 229.

CHAPTER 15. FINAL DAYS

1. Foote to Fox, 10 June 1862, in Fox, *Correspondence of Fox,* 2:54; Foote to Welles, 13 June 1862, in Hoppin, *Foote,* 328–29.

2. Welles to Davis, and Welles to Foote, both 17 June 1862, *ORN*, ser. 1, 23:213–14.

3. Hoppin, *Foote*, 331; Musicant, *Divided Waters*, 246. Davis and Dahlgren became rear admirals in February 1863. Davis, *Charles Henry Davis*, 286; Robert J. Schneller Jr., *A Quest for Glory*, 234.

4. "An Act to Reorganize the Navy Department of the United States," 5 July 1862, 37th Cong. 1st sess., Exec. Doc. 1, 96; *Statutes at Large of the United States*, 12:510–12; on the bureaus, see Paullin, *Paullin's History of Naval Administration*, 260–62.

5. Hoppin, *Foote*, 339–40.

6. Ibid., 340, 344; Charles G. Hearn, *Admiral David Dixon Porter*, 144; Welles, *Diary*, 1:167.

7. Edward W. Callahan, ed., *List of Officers of the Navy of the United States*, 199; Lincoln to Foote, 1 August 1862, *ORN*, ser. 1, 22:735; Hoppin, *Foote*, 343–44; Welles, *Diary*, 1:74.

8. Langley, *Social Reform*, 264–65; *Statutes at Large of the United States*, 12:565; Welles to Davis and Farragut, 15 July 1862, *ORN*, ser. 1, 23:584.

9. Welles, *Diary*, 1:92–93, 346.

10. Foote to his brother Augustus, 6, 18 November 1862; 6 January 1863, Foote Papers, NHCHS; Hoppin, *Foote*, 364, 366–67.

11. Foote to Benjamin Hoppin, in Hoppin, *Foote*, 367–68.

12. Welles to Hoppin, 8 October 1873, in Hoppin, *Foote*, 395; Du Pont to his wife; 26 May 1863, in Du Pont, *Civil War Letters*, 3:137.

13. Welles to Hoppin, 8 October 1873, in Hoppin, *Foote*, 394–95; Welles, *Diary*, 1:346.

14. Welles, *Diary*, 1:311 15, 317, 346; 2:135; Hoppin, *Foote*, 388.

15. Welles, *Diary*, 1:315, 317; Welles to Hoppin, 8 October 1873, in Hoppin, *Foote*, 395–96.

16. Welles, *Diary*, 1:317. Du Pont related in October 1862 that Foote and Wise had approached him about giving up his command to Dahlgren, an idea Du Pont rejected immediately, as well as with the suggestion that Dahlgren become his ordnance officer, replacing Rodgers. Du Pont said he would give him command of an ironclad and that was all. Du Pont told Fox: "Dahlgren is a diseased man on the subject of preferment and position. As I told Foote, he chose one line in the walks of his profession while Foote and I chose another; he was licking cream while we were eating dirt and living on the *pay* of our *rank*. Now he wants all the honors belonging to the other but without having encountered its joltings—it is a disease and nothing else" (Du Pont to Fox, 8 October 1862, Du Pont, *Civil War Letters*, 2:243).

17. Schneller, *A Quest for Glory*, 233–34.

18. Hoppin, *Foote*, 372–73.

19. Welles, *Diary,* 1:325.

20. Ibid., 1:326.

21. Augustus Foote to his wife, 19 June 1863; John Foote, "Notes on the Life of Admiral Foote," 347; Hoppin, *Foote,* 375–81; letter from Welles to Hoppin, 8 October 1873, in ibid., 396; letter from James Wilson Grimes to Du Pont, 1 July 1863, in Du Pont, *Civil War Letters,* 3:191; Schneller, *A Quest for Glory,* 243–44; Welles, *Diary,* 1:326–27.

22. Davis, *Charles Henry Davis,* 314.

23. Du Pont to William King Hall, in Du Pont, *Civil War Letters,* 3:401–2.

24. Du Pont to his wife, 24 June 1863, in Du Pont, *Civil War Letters,* 3:180.

25. Hoppin, *Foote,* 388.

26. In Davis, *Charles Henry Davis,* 294.

27. Welles, *Diary,* 2:335, 346.

28. Hoppin, *Foote,* vi; Welles to Hoppin, 8 October 1873, in ibid., 397.

29. Hoppin, *Foote,* 354.

30. Eads, "Recollections of Foote and the Gun-Boats," 346.

31. Foote to Fox, 9 March 1862, in Fox, *Correspondence of Fox,* 2:47.

32. Welles, *Diary,* 1:167.

33. Quoted in Davis, *Charles Henry Davis,* 294.

34. Milligan, "Andrew Foote," 122.

~✷ *Bibliography* ✷~

Unpublished Material

Henry E. Huntington Library (HL), San Marino, California
  Andrew Hull Foote Papers
  Gideon Welles Papers
  Harbeck Naval Collection
Library of Congress (LC), Washington, D.C.
  Andrew Hull Foote Papers
  Gideon Welles Papers
  John Adolphus Bernard Dahlgren Papers
  John Rodgers Family Papers
National Archives (NA), Washington, D.C.
  Record Group 45, Area 5 File, 1861–65
  Record Group 45, Letters Received by the Secretary of the Navy from Commanding Officers of Squadrons, Mississippi, 1861–65
  Record Group 92, Letter Books, Office of the Quartermaster General (October 1861–July 1862)
Naval Historical Center, Washington Navy Yard, Washington, D.C.
New Haven (Connecticut) Colony Historical Society (NHCHS), Whitney Library
  Andrew Hull Foote Papers, 1824–65
New York Historical Society (NYHS), New York City, New York
  Andrew H. Foote Papers
  Isaac Hull Papers
  Joseph Smith Papers
  Naval Historical Society Collection
New York Public Library, New York City, New York
Tennessee State Library and Archives, Nashville, Tennessee
  Rear Admiral Andrew Hull Foote Papers

PUBLISHED MATERIAL

Allen, Gardner W., ed. *Commodore Hull: Papers of Isaac Hull, Commodore, United States Navy.* Boston: Atheneum, 1929.

———. *Our Navy and the West Indian Pirates.* Salem, Mass.: Essex Institute, 1929.

Ambrose, Stephen E. "The Union Command System and the Donelson Campaign." *Military Affairs* 24 (Summer 1960): 78–86.

American State Papers: Naval Affairs. 4 vols. Washington, D.C.: Gales and Seaton, 1835–61.

Anderson, Bern. *By Sea and by River: The Naval History of the Civil War.* New York: Alfred Knopf, 1962.

Bacon, Leonard W. "Andrew Hull Foote." *Hours at Home* 1 (May–October 1865): 83–92.

Bauer, K. Jack, comp. *New American State Papers: Naval Affairs.* 10 vols. Wilmington, Del.: Scholarly Resources, 1981.

Bearss, Edwin C. "The Fall of Fort Henry, Tennessee." *West Tennessee Historical Society Journal* (1963): 85–107.

———. *Hardluck Ironclad. The Sinking and Salvage of the Cairo.* Baton Rouge: Louisiana State University Press, 1966.

———. *Unconditional Surrender: The Fall of Fort Donelson.* Dover, Tenn.: Eastern National Park and Monument Association, 1962.

———. "Unconditional Surrender: The Fall of Fort Donelson." *Tennessee Historical Quarterly* (March–June 1962): 47–65, 140–61.

Benjamin, Park. *The United States Naval Academy.* New York: G. P. Putnam's Sons, 1900.

Billingsley, Edward B. *In Defense of Neutral Rights. The United States Navy and the Wars of Independence in Chile and Peru.* Chapel Hill: University of North Carolina Press, 1967.

Bingham, Hiram. *A Residence of Twenty-one Years in the Sandwich Islands, or, The Civil, Religious, and Political History of Those Islands . . .* 3d ed., rev. Hartford, Conn.: H. Huntington, 1849. Reprint edition.

Blue, George Verne. "The Project for a French Settlement in the Hawaiian Islands, 1824–1842." *Pacific Historical Review* 2 (1933): 85–99.

Bonner-Smith, David, and E. W. R. Lumby, eds. *The Second China War, 1856–1860.* London: Navy Records Society, 1954.

Boynton, Charles B. *History of the Navy during the Rebellion.* 2 vols. New York: D. Appleton, 1867–68.

Bradford, James C., ed. *Captains of the Old Steam Navy. Makers of the American Naval Tradition, 1840–1880.* Annapolis: Naval Institute Press, 1986.

Brooke, George M. Jr. "The Role of the United States Navy in the Suppression of the African Slave Trade." *American Neptune* 21 (1961): 28–41.

Brookes, John Ingram. *International Rivalry in the Pacific Islands: 1800–1875.* Berkeley: University of California Press, 1941.

Browne, Junius Henri. *Four Years in Secessia.* Hartford: O. D. Case, 1865. Reprint. Arno Press, 1970.

Burr, Henry. "Education in the Early Navy." Ph.D. diss., Temple University, 1939.

Callahan, Edward W., ed. *List of Officers of the Navy of the United States and of the Marine Corps from 1775 to 1900.* 1901. Reprint. New York: Haskell House, 1969.

Canot, Theodore. *Adventures of an African Slaver.* Edited by Malcolm Cowley. New York: Albert and Charles Boni, 1928.

Chapelle, Howard I. *The History of the American Sailing Navy. The Ships and Their Development.* New York: W. W. Norton, 1949.

Coletta, Paolo E. "Abel Parker Upshur." In *American Secretaries of the Navy,* vol. 1, ed. Coletta. Annapolis: Naval Institute Press, 1980.

———, ed. *American Secretaries of the Navy.* 2 vols. Annapolis: Naval Institute Press, 1980.

Colvocoresses, Harold. "The Capture and Destruction of the Barrier Forts." *United States Naval Institute Proceeedings* 44 (May 1938): 680–84.

Cooling, Benjamin Franklin. *Forts Henry and Donelson: The Key to the Confederate Heartland.* Knoxville: University of Tennessee Press, 1987.

Coombe, Jack D. *Thunder along the Mississippi. The River Battles that Split the Confederacy.* New York: Sarpedon, 1996.

Cutter, William Richard, ed. *Genealogical and Family History of the State of Connecticut.* New York: Lewis Historical Publishing, 1911.

Dahlgren, John A. *Shells and Shell Guns.* Philadelphia: King and Baird, 1856.

Dahlgren, Madeleine Vinton. *Memoir of John A. Dahlgren.* New York: Charles L. Webster, 1891.

Daniel, Larry J., and Lynn N. Bock. *Island No. 10: Struggle for the Mississippi Valley.* Tuscaloosa: University of Alabama Press, 1996.

Davis, Charles H. Jr. *Life of Charles Henry Davis, Rear Admiral, 1807–77.* Boston: Houghton Mifflin, 1899.

Davis, Hugh H. "The American Seamen's Friend Society and the American Sailor, 1828–1838." *American Neptune* 29 (January 1979): 45–57.

de Kay, James Tertius. *Chronicles of the Frigate* Macedonian, *1809–1922.* New York: W. W. Norton, 1995.

DuBois, William E. B. *The Suppression of the African Slave Trade to the United States of America, 1638–1870.* 1888. Reprint. New York: Russell and Russell, 1965.

Dudley, William S. *Going South: U.S. Navy Officer Resignations and Dismissals on the Eve of the Civil War.* Washington: Naval Historical Foundation, 1981.

Du Pont, Henry A. *Rear Admiral Samuel Francis Du Pont, United States Navy: A Biography.* New York: National Americana Society, 1926.

Du Pont, Samuel F. *Official Despatches and Letters . . . 1846, 1848, 1861, 1863.* Wilmington, Del.: Ferris Brothers, 1883.

———. *Samuel F. Du Pont: A Selection from His Civil War Letters.* 3 vols. Ithaca: Cornell University Press, 1969.

Dye, Ira. *The Fatal Cruise of the* Argus. *Two Captains in the War of 1812.* Annapolis: Naval Institute Press, 1994.

Eads, James B. "Recollections of Foote and the Gun-Boats." In *Battles and Leaders of the Civil War: Being for the Most Part Contributions by Union and Confederate Officers,* vol. 1, ed. Robert U. Johnson and Clarence C. Buel. 1883. Reprint. Secaucus, N.J.: Castle, n.d.

Foote, Abram W. *Foote Family, Geneology and History.* Vol. 1. Rutland, Vt.: Marble City Press, 1907.

Foote, Andrew H. "Address by Captain A. H. Foote, U.S.N. Delivered at the Anniversary of the Pennsylvania Seamen's Friend Society in the Musical Fund Hall, Philadelphia, April 27, 1854." *Sailor's Magazine* 26 (1854): 321–27.

———. *Africa and the American Flag.* New York: D. Appleton, 1854.

———. *The African Squadron: Ashburton Treaty: Consular Sea Letters. Reviewed, in an Address by Commander A. H. Foote, U.S.N.* Philadelphia: William F. Geddes, 1855.

———. *Farewell Temperance Address. Delivered before the Crew of the U.S. Frigate* Cumberland, *November 1, 1845.* Boston: Samuel N. Dickinson and Company, 1845. 8 pp.

———. "Visit to Simoda and Hakodadi in Japan." *Journal of the Shanghai Literary and Scientific Society* 1 (June 1858): 129–37.

Foote, John A. "Notes on the Life of Admiral Foote." In *Battles and Leaders of the Civil War: Being for the Most Part Contributions by Union and Confederate Officers,* vol. 1, ed. Robert U. Johnson and Clarence C. Buel. 1883. Reprint. Secaucus, N.J.: Castle, n.d.

Foote, Shelby. *The Civil War. A Narrative.* Vol. 1: *Fort Sumter to Perryville.* New York: Random House, 1958.

Force, M. F. *From Fort Henry to Corinth.* 1881. Reprint. Wilmington, N.C.: Broadfoot Publishing, 1989.

Forlenza, Gerard A. Jr. "A Navy Life: The Pre–Civil War Career of Rear Admiral Andrew Hull Foote." Ph.D. diss., Claremont Graduate School, 1991.

Fox, Gustavus. *Confidential Correspondence of Gustavus Vasa Fox, Assistant Secretary of the Navy, 1861–1865.* Edited by Robert Means Thompson and Richard Wainwright. New York: De Vinne Press, 1918.

Gosnell, Harper Allen. *Guns on the Western Waters.* Baton Rouge: Louisiana State University Press, 1949.

Grant, Ulysses S. *Memoirs and Selected Letters.* New York: Library of America, 1990.

Guttridge, Leonard F., and Jay D. Smith. *The Commodores. The U.S. Navy in the Age of Sail.* New York: Harper and Row, 1969.

Hall, Edwin M. "Smith Thompson." In *American Secretaries of the Navy,* vol. 1, ed. Paolo E. Coletta. Annapolis: Naval Institute Press, 1980.

Harmon, J. Scott, "The United States Navy and the Suppression of the Illegal Slave Trade, 1830–1850." In *New Aspects of Naval History. Selected Papers Presented at the Fourth Naval History Symposium,* ed. Craig L. Symonds, 211–19. Annapolis: Naval Institute Press, 1981.

Hattaway, Herman, and Archer Jones. *How the North Won: A Military History of the Civil War.* Urbana: University of Illinois Press, 1983.

Headley, J. T. *Farragut and Our Naval Commanders.* New York: E. B. Treat, 1867.

Hearn, Charles G. *Admiral David Dixon Porter.* Annapolis: Naval Institute Press, 1996.

Henson, Curtis T. "The United States Navy and China, 1839–1861." Ph.D. diss., Tulane University, 1965.

Hibbert, Christopher. *The Dragon Wakes. China and the West 1793–1911.* New York: Harper and Row, 1970.

Hoppin, James M. *The Life of Andrew Hull Foote, Rear Admiral, United States Navy.* New York: Harper and Brothers, 1874.

Howard, Warren S. *American Slavers and the Federal Law, 1837–1862.* Los Angeles: University of California Press, 1963.

Hughes, Nathaniel Cheairs Jr. *The Battle of Belmont. Grant Strikes South.* Chapel Hill: University of North Carolina Press, 1991.

Johnson, Allen, and Dumas Malone. *Dictionary of American Biography.* Vol. 3. New York: Charles Scribner's Sons, 1931.

Johnson, Robert Erwin. *Far China Station: The U.S. Navy in Asian Waters, 1800–1898.* Annapolis: Naval Institute Press, 1979.

———. *Rear Admiral John Rodgers, 1812–1882.* Annapolis: Naval Institute Press, 1967.

———. *Thence Round Cape Horn. The Story of United States Naval Forces on Pacific Station, 1812–1923.* Annapolis: Naval Institute Press, 1963.

———. "United States Naval Forces on Pacific Station, 1818–1923." Ph.D. diss., Claremont Graduate School, 1956.

Johnson, Robert Underwood, and Clarence Clough Buel, eds. *Battles and Leaders of the Civil War: Being for the Most Part Contributions by Union and Confederate Officers.* 4 vols. 1883. Reprint. Secaucus, N.J.: Castle, n.d.

Jones, George. *Sketches of Naval Life.* 2 vols. New Haven: Hezekiah Howe, 1829.

Kelly, R. M. "Holding Kentucky for the Union." In *Battles and Leaders of the Civil War: Being for the Most Part Contributions by Union and Confederate Officers,* vol. 1, ed. Robert U. Johnson and Clarence C. Buel. 1883. Reprint. Secaucus, N.J.: Castle, n.d.

Langley, Harold D. "James Cochrane Dobbin." In *American Secretaries of the Navy,* vol. 1, ed. Paolo E. Coletta. Annapolis: Naval Institute Press, 1980.

———. "Issac Toucey." In *American Secretaries of the Navy,* vol. 1, ed. Paolo E. Coletta. Annapolis: Naval Institute Press, 1980.

———. *Social Reform in the United States Navy, 1798–1862.* Urbana: University of Illinois Press, 1967.

Leavenworth, Charles S. *The Arrow War with China.* London: S. Low, Marston, 1901.

Lewis, Charles Lee. *Admiral Franklin Buchanan.* Baltimore: Norman, Remington, 1929.

———. *David Glasgow Farragut: Admiral in the Making.* Annapolis: Naval Institute Press, 1941.

Litten, Jane. "Navy Flogging: Captain Samuel Francis Du Pont and Tradition." *American Neptune* 58, no. 2 (1998): 148–165.

Long, David F. "A Case for Intervention: Armstrong, Foote, and the Destruction of the Barrier Forts, Canton, China, 1856." In *New Aspects of Naval History. Selected Papers Presented at the Fourth Naval History Symposium,* ed. Craig L. Symonds, 220–37. Annapolis: Naval Institute Press, 1981.

———. *Sailor-Diplomat: A Biography of Commodore James Biddle, 1783–1848.* Boston: Northeastern University Press, 1983.

Lovette, Leland P. *Naval Customs, Traditions and Usage.* Annapolis: Naval Institute Press, 1939.

Macartney, Clarence Edward. *Mr. Lincoln's Admirals.* New York: Funk and Wagnalls, 1956.

McClellan, E. N. "The Capture of the Barrier Forts in the Canton River, China." *Marine Corps Gazette* 5 (September 1920): 262–76.

McFeely, William S. *Grant, a Biography.* New York: W. W. Norton, 1981.

Mackall, William W. *A Son's Recollections of His Father.* New York: E. P. Dutton, 1960.

McKee, Christopher. *A Gentlemanly and Honorable Profession. The Creation of the U.S. Naval Officer Corps, 1794–1815.* Annapolis: Naval Institute Press, 1991.

Maclay, Edgar Stanton. *A History of the U.S. Navy: From 1775 to 1902.* Enl. ed. 3 vols. New York: D. Appleton, 1906.

McPherson, James M. *Battle Cry of Freedom. The Civil War Era.* New York: Oxford University Press, 1988.

Marvel, William. *The* Alabama *and the* Kearsarge. Chapel Hill: University of North Carolina Press, 1996.

Merrill, James M. *Battle Flags South: The Story of the Civil War Navies on the Western Waters.* Rutherford, N.J.: Fairleigh Dickinson University Press, 1970.

———. *Du Pont, the Making of an Admiral.* New York: Dodd, Mead, 1986.

Miles, Jim. *Piercing the Heartland. A History and Tour Guide of the Fort Donelson, Shiloh, and Perryville Campaigns.* Nashville: Rutledge Hill Press, 1991.

Milligan, John D. "Andrew Foote: Zealous Reformer, Administrator, Warrior." In *Captains of the Old Steam Navy. Makers of the American Naval Tradition, 1840–1880,* ed. James C. Bradford. Annapolis: Naval Institute Press, 1986.

―――, comp. *From the Fresh-Water Navy, 1861–64: The Letters of Acting Master's Mate Henry R. Browne and Acting Ensign Symmes E. Browne.* Annapolis: U.S. Naval Institute, 1970.

―――. "From Theory to Application: The Emergence of the American Ironclad War Vessel." *Military Affairs* 48 (1984): 126–32.

―――. *Gunboats down the Mississippi.* Annapolis: Naval Institute Press, 1965.

Morison, Samuel Elliot. *"Old Bruin." Commodore Matthew Calbraith Perry.* Boston: Little, Brown, 1967.

Morse, Hosea B. *The International Relations of the Chinese Empire.* 3 vols. London: Longmans, Green, 1910–18.

Morse, Jarvis Means. *A Neglected Period of Connecticut's History, 1815–1850.* New Haven: Yale University Press, 1930.

Murrell, William Meacham. *Cruise of the Frigate Columbia around the World, under the Command of Commodore George C. Read in 1838, 1839, 1840.* Boston: Benjamin B. Mussey, 1840.

Musicant, Ivan. *Divided Waters. The Naval History of the Civil War.* New York: HarperCollins, 1995.

Nevin, David. *The Road to Shiloh: Early Battles in the West.* Alexandria, Va.: Time-Life Books, 1983.

Niven, John. "Gideon Welles." In *American Secretaries of the Navy,* vol. 1, ed. Paolo E. Coletta. Annapolis: Naval Institute Press, 1980.

―――. *Gideon Welles, Lincoln's Secretary of the Navy.* New York: Oxford University Press, 1973.

Page, Dave. *Ships versus Shore. Civil War Engagements along Southern Shores and Rivers.* Nashville: Rutledge Hill Press, 1994.

Paullin, Charles O. "Beginnings of the United States Naval Academy." *U.S. Naval Institute Proceedings* 50 (1924): 173–94.

―――. "Early Voyages of American Naval Vessels to the Orient. The Cruise of Commodore Read, 1838–1840." *U.S. Naval Institute Proceedings* 36 (December 1910): 1073–99.

―――. "Early Voyages of American Naval Vessels to the Orient. The East India Squadron in the Waters of China and Japan: 1854–1865." *United States Naval Institute Proceedings* 37 (1911): 387–417.

―――. "Naval Administration, 1842–1861." *U.S. Naval Institute Proceedings* 33 (1907): 1435–77.

―――. *Paullin's History of Naval Administration, 1775–1911.* Annapolis: Naval Institute Press, 1968.

Polk, William M. "General Polk and the Battle of Belmont." In *Battles and Leaders of the Civil War: Being for the Most Part Contributions by Union and Confederate Officers*, vol. 1., ed. Robert U. Johnson and Clarence C. Buel. 1883. Reprint. Secaucus, N.J.: Castle, n.d.

Porter, David Dixon. *Incidents and Anecdotes of the Civil War*. New York: D. Appleton, 1985.

———. *Naval History of the Civil War*. New York: Sherman, 1886.

Pratt, Julius W. "Our First 'War' in China: The Diary of Wm. Henry Rowell." *American Historical Review* 50 (July 1944): 782–84.

Reed, Rowena. *Combined Operations in the Civil War*. Annapolis: Naval Institute Press, 1978.

Roland, Charles P. *Albert Sidney Johnston: Soldier of Three Republics*. Austin: University of Texas Press, 1964.

Russell, William Howard. *My Diary North and South*. Boston: T. O. H. P. Burham, 1863.

Schneller, Robert J. Jr. *A Quest for Glory. A Biography of Rear Admiral John A. Dahlgren*. Annapolis: Naval Institute Press, 1996.

Shippen, Edward. "Some Account of the Origin of the Naval Asylum at Philadelphia." *Pennsylvania Magazine of History and Biography* 7 (1883): 117–42.

Shoemaker, Raymond L. *Diplomacy from the Quarterdeck: The U.S. Navy in the Caribbean, 1815–1830*. Bloomington: Indiana University Press, 1976.

Silverstone, Paul H. *Warships of the Civil War Navies*. Annapolis: Naval Institute Press, 1989.

Slagle, Jay. *Ironclad Captain. Seth Ledyard Phelps and the U.S. Navy, 1841–1864*. Kent, Ohio: Kent State University Press, 1996.

Smith, Bradford. *Yankees in Paradise: The New England Impact on Hawaii*. Philadelphia: Lippincott, 1900.

Soulsby, Hugh G. *The Right of Search and the Slave Trade in Anglo-American Relations, 1814–1862*. Baltimore: Johns Hopkins University Press, 1933.

Spears, John R. *The American Slave-Trade, an Account of Its Origin, Growth, and Suppression*. New York: Charles Scribner's Sons, 1900.

Statutes at Large of the United States. Vol. 12, pp. 329 and 510–12.

Stewart, Charles S. *A Visit to the South Seas in the U.S. Ship* Vincennes *during the Years 1829 and 1830*. 2 vols. New York: J. P. Haven, 1831.

Stockton, Charles H. *Origins, History, Laws, and Regulations of the United States Naval Asylum, Philadelphia, Pennsylvania*. Washington, D.C.: Government Printing Office, 1886.

Strauss, W. Patrick. "James Kirke Paulding." In *American Secretaries of the Navy*, vol. 1, ed. Paolo E. Coletta. Annapolis: Naval Institute Press, 1980.

———. "Mahlon Dickerson." In *American Secretaries of the Navy*, vol. 1, ed. Paolo E. Coletta. Annapolis: Naval Institute Press, 1980.

Sturdy, Henry Francis. "The Establishment of the Naval School at Annapolis." *U.S. Naval Institute Proceedings* 71 (1945): 1–17.

Taylor, Fitch Waterman. *The Flag Ship; or, a Voyage around the World in the United States Frigate* Columbia. 2 vols. New York: Appleton, 1846.

Taylor, Jesse. "The Defense of Fort Henry." In *Battles and Leaders of the Civil War: Being for the Most Part Contributions by Union and Confederate Officers*, vol. 1, ed. Robert U. Johnson and Clarence C. Buel. 1883. Reprint: Secaucus, N.J. : Castle, n.d.

Tong, Te-Kong. *United States Diplomacy in China, 1844–60.* Seattle: University of Washington Press, 1964.

Tracy, Joseph. *History of the American Board of Commissioners for Foreign Missions.* New York: M. W. Dodd, 1842.

Tucker, Spencer C. *Arming the Fleet. U.S. Navy Ordnance in the Muzzle-Loading Era.* Annapolis: Naval Institute Press, 1989.

U.S. Congress. House. "Spirit Ration in the Navy." 28th Cong., 2d sess., H. Doc. 73, ser. 468.

———. "African Squadron: Message from the President of the United States Transmitting Information in Reference to the African Squadron." 31st Cong., 1st sess., H. Doc. 73, pp. 1–2, ser. 578.

———. "Copy of All Instructions to the African Squadron since the Ratification of the Treaty of 1842." 35th Cong., 2d sess., H. Doc. 104, ser. 1008.

U.S. Congress. Senate. *Mr. Reed's Diplomatic Correspondence with China Communicated to the Senate of the United States, March 12, 1860.* 36th Cong., 1st sess., Exec. Doc. 7, ser. 1027.

U.S. Department of the Navy. *Official Records of the Union and Confederate Navies in the War of the Rebellion.* Series 1, vols. 22 and 23. Washington, D.C.: Government Printing Office, 1908 and 1910.

U.S. Department of War. *The War of the Rebellion. A Compilation of the Official Records of the Union and Confederate Armies.* Series 1, vols. 4, 7, and 8. Washington, D.C.: Government Printing Office, 1882, 1883.

Valle, James E. *Rocks and Shoals. Order and Discipline in the Old Navy, 1800–1861.* Annapolis: Naval Institute Press, 1980.

Walke, Henry. "The Gun-Boats at Belmont and Fort Henry." In *Battles and Leaders of the Civil War: Being for the Most Part Contributions by Union and Confederate Officers*, vol. 1., ed. Robert U. Johnson and Clarence C. Buel. 1883. Reprint. Secaucus, N.J.: Castle, n.d.

———. *Naval Scenes and Reminiscences of the Civil War in the United States . . .* New York: F. R. Reed, 1877.

———. "The Western Flotilla at Fort Donelson, Island Number Ten, Fort Pillow and Memphis." In *Battles and Leaders of the Civil War: Being for the Most Part Contributions by Union and Confederate Officers*, vol. 1., ed.

Robert U. Johnson and Clarence C. Buel. 1883. Reprint. Secaucus, N.J.: Castle, n.d.

Wallace, Lew. "The Capture of Fort Donelson." In *Battles and Leaders of the Civil War: Being for the Most Part Contributions by Union and Confederate Officers*, vol. 1., ed. Robert U. Johnson and Clarence C. Buel. 1883. Reprint. Secaucus, N.J.: Castle, n.d.

Welles, Gideon. *Diary of Gideon Welles, Secretary of the Navy under Lincoln and Johnson*. 3 vols. Boston: Houghton Mifflin, 1911.

Wilkes, Charles. *Autobiography of Rear Admiral Charles Wilkes, U.S. Navy 1798–1877*. Edited by William James Morgan et al. Washington, D.C.: Department of the Navy, 1978.

Williams, T. Harry. *P. G. T. Beauregard, Napoleon in Gray*. Baton Rouge: Louisiana State University Press, 1955.

Wines, Enoch Cobb. *Two Years and a Half in the American Navy, or, Journal of a Cruise in the Mediterranean and Levant on Board the U.S. Frigate* Constitution *in the Years, 1829, 1830 and 1831*. 2 vols. London: Richard Bentley, 1833.

Wood, William Maxwell. *Fankwei; or The* San Jacinto *in the Seas of India, China and Japan*. New York: Harper and Brothers, 1859.

———. *The Naval Institutions of a Republic*. Buffalo: George H. Derby, 1852.

~ ❧ Further Reading ☙ ~

Andrew Foote has been the subject of only one full-length biography. Written by Foote's friend and admirer, Yale professor James M. Hoppin, *The Life of Admiral Andrew Hull Foote* is dated in language and approach, but it is nonetheless mostly factual and quite valuable; it is also largely uncritical of the admiral. Gerard A. Forlenza Jr.'s doctoral dissertation, "A Navy Life: The Pre–Civil War Career of Rear Admiral Andrew Hull Foote" is a font of information and a useful guide to sources on Foote's career up to the time he assumed command of the western flotilla. Also worthy of mention is John D. Milligan's excellent short essay, "Andrew Foote: Zealous Reformer, Administrator, Warrior," in James C. Bradford's *Captains of the Old Steam Navy.*

The limited number of biographies is not the product of a shortage of source materials. During his naval career Foote wrote many letters, and these provide considerable insight into Foote the man. The Library of Congress has a large collection of Foote's letters and record books, and there are others in the collections of the Henry E. Huntington Library and the New Haven (Connecticut) Colony Historical Society. A good bit of Foote's Civil War correspondence appears in the U.S. Navy Department's *Official Records of the Union and Confederate Navies in the War of the Rebellion.*

For general information on the period, there are a variety of sources. On administration and individual secretaries of the navy, see Paolo E. Coletta, ed., *American Secretaries of the Navy,* and Charles Oscar Paullin, *Paullin's History of Naval Administration, 1775–1911.* On U.S. Navy sailing ships of the period, see Howard I. Chapelle, *The History of the American Sailing Navy. The Ships and Their Development;* and Paul H. Silverstone, *Warships of the Civil War Navies.* On naval ordnance, see Spencer C. Tucker, *Arming the Fleet. U.S. Navy Ordnance in the Muzzle-Loading Era.*

On temperance and discipline in the navy, see Harold D. Langley, *Social Reform in the United States Navy, 1798–1862.*

For Foote's family background and youth, see Abram W. Foote, *Foote Family, Genealogy and History;* William R. Cutter, ed., *Genealogical and Family History of the State of Connecticut;* and Leonard W. Bacon, "Andrew Hull Foote," in *Hours at Home.* Introductions to the navy during Foote's early career include Gardner W. Allen, *Our Navy and the West Indian Pirates;* Edward B. Billingsley, *In Defense of Neutral Rights. The United States Navy and the Wars of Independence in Chile and Peru;* and Charles H. Davis Jr., *Life of Charles Henry Davis, Rear Admiral, 1807–77.* A contemporary publication, the *Sailor's Magazine,* is another useful source. For key Foote associates, see Davis, *Life of Charles Henry Davis;* Jay Slagle, *Ironclad Captain. Seth Ledyard Phelps and the U.S. Navy, 1841–1864;* and Robert J. Schneller Jr., *A Quest for Glory. A Biography of Rear Admiral John A. Dahlgren.*

On Foote's around-the-world cruise, see William M. Murrell, *Cruise of the Frigate* Columbia *around the World, under the Command of Commodore George C. Read in 1838, 1839, 1840;* and Fitch Waterman Taylor, *The Flag Ship; or, A Voyage around the World in the United States Frigate* Columbia. Also useful are several articles by Charles O. Paullin under the general heading of "Early Voyages of American Naval Vessels to the Orient" that appeared in 1910 and 1911 issues of *Naval Institute Proceedings.* Regarding the controversy over the missionaries in the Hawaiian Islands, see John Ingram Brookes, *International Rivalry in the Pacific Islands: 1800–1875;* and Bradford Smith, *Yankees in Paradise: The New England Impact on Hawaii.*

The best short essay of U.S. Navy efforts to suppress the African slave trade is George M. Brooke Jr., "The Role of the United States Navy in the Suppression of the African Slave Trade." Foote's own book *Africa and the American Flag* is invaluable, as is his pamphlet *The African Squadron: Ashburton Treaty: Consular Sea Letters Reviewed, in an Address by Commander A. H. Foote, U.S.N.*

On China and the reduction of the barrier forts, see Robert E. Johnson, *Far China Station: The U.S. Navy in Asian Waters, 1800–1898;* and William M. Wood, *Fankwei; or The* San Jacinto *in the Seas of India, China and Japan.*

On the Civil War in the West, apart from the *Official Records of the Union and Confederate Navies in the War of the Rebellion,* for insight into policy, see Gideon Welles, *Diary of Gideon Welles, Secretary of the*

Navy under Lincoln and Johnson; and Gustavus Fox, *Confidential Correspondence of Gustavus Vasa Fox, Assistant Secretary of the Navy, 1861–1865.* See also Ulysses S. Grant, *Memoirs and Selected Letters;* M. F. Force, *From Fort Henry to Corinth;* and two articles by Henry Walke: "The Gun-Boats at Belmont and Fort Henry" and "The Western Flotilla at Fort Donelson, Island Number Ten, Fort Pillow and Memphis."

Useful secondary accounts on warfare in the West include Slagle's work cited above; Benjamin F. Cooling, *Forts Henry and Donelson: The Key to the Confederate Heartland;* and Larry J. Daniel and Lynn N. Bock, *Island No. 10: Struggle for the Mississippi Valley.* Other more general accounts are John D. Milligan, *Gunboats down the Mississippi;* Jack D. Coombe, *Thunder along the Mississippi. The River Battles that Split the Confederacy;* and James M. Merrill, *Battle Flags South: The Story of the Civil War Navies on the Western Waters.*

This by no means exhausts the sources consulted in writing this book, but, combined with the endnotes, it will guide readers to the best studies on Foote and the U.S. Navy of the mid-nineteenth century.

⤜ Index ⤜

About the Author

Spencer C. Tucker holds the John Biggs Chair in Military History at the Virginia Military Institute, where he also earned his B.A. degree. Subsequent to earning his B.A. he studied in France on a Fulbright scholarship, then received M.A. and Ph.D. degrees from the University of North Carolina at Chapel Hill in 1962 and 1966, respectively. He served as a captain in army intelligence from 1965 to 1967 and was professor of history at Texas Christian University from 1967 to 1997.

Tucker is the author or editor of ten books, treating a variety of military and naval history subjects.

The Naval Institute Press is the book-publishing arm of the U.S. Naval Institute, a private, nonprofit, membership society for sea service professionals and others who share an interest in naval and maritime affairs. Established in 1873 at the U.S. Naval Academy in Annapolis, Maryland, where its offices remain today, the Naval Institute has members worldwide.

Members of the Naval Institute support the education programs of the society and receive the influential monthly magazine *Proceedings* and discounts on fine nautical prints and on ship and aircraft photos. They also have access to the transcripts of the Institute's Oral History Program and get discounted admission to any of the Institute-sponsored seminars offered around the country.

The Naval Institute also publishes *Naval History* magazine. This colorful bimonthly is filled with entertaining and thought-provoking articles, first-person reminiscences, and dramatic art and photography. Members receive a discount on *Naval History* subscriptions.

The Naval Institute's book-publishing program, begun in 1898 with basic guides to naval practices, has broadened its scope in recent years to include books of more general interest. Now the Naval Institute Press publishes about one hundred titles each year, ranging from how-to books on boating and navigation to battle histories, biographies, ship and aircraft guides, and novels. Institute members receive discounts of 20 to 50 percent on the Press's more than eight hundred books in print.

Full-time students are eligible for special half-price membership rates. Life memberships are also available.

For a free catalog describing Naval Institute Press books currently available, and for further information about subscribing to *Naval History* magazine or about joining the U.S. Naval Institute, please write to:

Membership Department
U.S. Naval Institute
291 Wood Road
Annapolis, MD 21402-5034
Telephone: (800) 233-8764
Fax: (410) 269-7940
Web address: www.usni.org